OXFORD POLITICAL THEORY

Series Editors: Will Kymlicka, David Miller, and Alan Ryan

LINGUISTIC JUSTICE
FOR EUROPE AND FOR THE WORLD

OXFORD POLITICAL THEORY

Oxford Political Theory presents the best new work in contemporary political theory. It is intended to be broad in scope, including original contributions to political philosophy, and also work in applied political theory. The series contains works of outstanding quality with no restriction as to approach or subject matter.

LINGUISTIC JUSTICE
FOR EUROPE AND
FOR THE WORLD

PHILIPPE VAN PARIJS

OXFORD
UNIVERSITY PRESS

OXFORD

UNIVERSITY PRESS

Great Clarendon Street, Oxford OX2 6DP

Oxford University Press is a department of the University of Oxford.
It furthers the University's objective of excellence in research, scholarship,
and education by publishing worldwide in

Oxford New York

Auckland Cape Town Dar es Salaam Hong Kong Karachi
Kuala Lumpur Madrid Melbourne Mexico City Nairobi
New Delhi Shanghai Taipei Toronto

With offices in

Argentina Austria Brazil Chile Czech Republic France Greece
Guatemala Hungary Italy Japan Poland Portugal Singapore
South Korea Switzerland Thailand Turkey Ukraine Vietnam

Oxford is a registered trade mark of Oxford University Press
in the UK and in certain other countries

Published in the United States
by Oxford University Press Inc., New York

British Library Cataloguing in Publication Data
Data available
Library of Congress Cataloging in Publication Data
Data available

Typeset by SPI Publisher Services, Pondicherry, India
Printed in Great Britain
on acid-free paper by
MPG Books Group, Bodmin and King's Lynn

ISBN 978-0-19-920887-6

1 3 5 7 9 10 8 6 4 2

To the memory of G. A. Cohen (1941–2009)

ACKNOWLEDGEMENTS

Some of the central claims of this book were presented, from 1998 onwards, to a wide linguistic variety of audiences in Aix-en-Provence, Antwerp, Barcelona, Berlin, Brussels, Cambridge (MA), Canberra, Florence, Fukuoka, Helsinki, Kinshasa, L'Escurial, Kyoto, Louvain-la-Neuve, Leuven, London, Ljubljana, Oñati, Madison, Madrid, Manchester, Medellin, Mexico City, Milan, Montevideo, Montreal, New Delhi, New Haven, New Orleans, New York, Oxford, Paris, Princeton, Québec, Salerno, San Diego, Siena, Stanford, Vilnius and Zurich.

I am particularly grateful to Bruce Ackerman, Arthur Applbaum, Xabier Arzoz, Miriam Aziz, Jean-Claude Barbier, Rajeev Bhargava, Idil Boran, Sam Bowles, Andreas Cassee, the late Jerry Cohen, Josh Cohen, Laurent de Briey, Helder De Schutter, Abram de Swaan, Bruno De Witte, Paulin Djite, Frédéric Docquier, Ina Druviete, Paul Dumouchel, Ronald Dworkin, John Edwards, Marc Fleurbaey, Hannah Forbes-Black, Barbara Fried, Anselmo García Cantú, Anca Gheaus, Victor Ginsburgh, François Grin, Jostein Gripsrud, Michael Ignatieff, Jane Jensen, the late Kande Mutsaku Kamilamba, Zdenko Kodelja, Peter Kraus, David Laitin, Jean Laponce, Alain Leroux, Sebastiano Maffetone, Branko Milanovic, Darrell Moellendorf, Timothée Mukash Kalel, Thomas Nagel, Ruwen Ogier, Michael Otsuka, Alan Patten, Robert Phillipson, John Pitseys, Johanne Poirier, Aurélien Portuese, Eric Rakowski, Rob Reich, Mathias Risse, David Robichaud, Maria de Lourdes Ros Torres, Emma Rothschild, Stefan Rummens, Tim Scanlon, Samuel Scheffler, Harold Schiffman, Amartya Sen, Niamh Shuibhne, Nenad Stojanovic, Humphrey Tonkin, Neus Torbisco, Michel Van den Abeele, Toon Vandevelde, Jonathan Van Parys, Andrew Williams, Marc Wilmet, Erik Olin Wright, my students at Aix-en-Provence ('Diversité linguistique et justice sociale', 2004), Harvard ('Social Justice and Cultural Diversity', 2005) and Louvain ('Questions approfondies de philosophie politique', 2009), all members of the September Group and of Louvain's Chaire Hoover, and not least my series editors Will Kymlicka and David Miller, for providing me with insightful oral or written comments and, in the case of several of them, for organizing meetings at which I could receive useful feedback from others.

This book is dedicated to the memory of G. A. (Jerry) Cohen. My first sketchy attempt to deal with 'linguistic justice' was presented at a seminar on 'Justice and Responsibility' I taught with him at All Souls College, Oxford, in the Spring of 1998. It was developed into a paper presented under the title 'If you are an egalitarian, how come you speak English?' at the conference organized at Yale University in May 2001 to celebrate his 60th birthday. I discussed linguistic matters further with him in the course of some of our subsequent September Group meetings and on several other occasions. On these matters as on any other, Jerry was a permanent invitation to fight lazy thinking and sloppy writing, to think rigorously and honestly, without dodging intellectual difficulties or shelving the ambition of contributing in this way to making our world a better world. I am most grateful to him for all I learned from him, not only as a scholar. His sudden death, in August 2009, was a great loss to me.

Finally, I want to thank my wonderfully multilingual family, to which my confidence in speaking languages and in writing about languages owes far more than to all the lessons I followed and all the books I read.

Earlier versions of some of the material included in this book were previously published as:

'The Ground Floor of the World', *International Political Science Review* 21, 2000; reprinted in P. James (ed.), *Globalization and Culture*, London: Sage.

'Must Europe Be Belgian ?', in C. McKinnon and I. Hampsher-Monk (eds), *The Demands of Citizenship*, London and New York: Continuum, 2000; reprinted in K. Hinrichs, H. Kitschelt, and H. Wiesenthal (eds), *Contingency and Crisis*, Frankfurt: Campus, 2000.

'Linguistic Justice', *Politics, Philosophy and Economics* 1, 2002; reprinted in W. Kymlicka and A. Patten (eds), *Language Rights and Political Theory*, Oxford: Oxford University Press, 2003; translated and expanded (with L. de Briey) in *Revue de philosophie économique* 5, 2002.

'Language Legislation for XXIst century Europe' (with M. Aziz), UCLouvain: Chaire Hoover, DOCH 87, 2002, http://www.uclou vain.be/Publications/dochs.htm.

'Europe's Linguistic Challenge', *Archives européennes de sociologie* 45(1), 2004; reprinted in D. Castiglione and C. Longman (eds), *The Language Question in Europe and Diverse Societies*, Oxford: Hart, 2007.

'Tackling the Anglophone's Free Ride', in *Towards More Linguistic Equality in Scientific Communication*, special issue of *AILA Review* 20, 2007.

'Linguistic Diversity as a Curse and as a By-Product', in X. Arzoz (ed.), *Respecting Linguistic Diversity in the European Union*, Amsterdam: John Benjamins, 2007.

'Grab a Territory!', in J. Poirier, J. E. Fossum, and P. Magnette (eds), *Ties that Bind. Accommodating Diversity in Canada and the European Union*, Bern: Peter Lang, 2009.

'Linguistic Justice and the Territorial Imperative', *Critical Review of International Social and Political Philosophy* 12(4), 2009; reprinted in M. Mattravers (ed.), *Democracy, Justice and Equality*, London: Routledge.

CONTENTS

Introduction

Language issues I have long found puzzling. And disturbing. And intellectually fascinating. No wonder, you might say. I carry a linguistic border between my first name and my surname. My mother tongue is not my best language—nor the language I now speak with my mother. When all my children are home for dinner, four languages are being spoken around the dinner table. Moreover, I teach at both of the institutions that were born as a result of a 550-year old university splitting up along a language divide at the time I joined it as a student. Most significantly, I was born, grew up and am now living again in Brussels: the city in which Pieter Breughel happened to settle the very year in which he painted his two Babel Towers; a city that became much later, as one of the outcomes of a long struggle, the officially bilingual capital city of an officially trilingual country; a city that has now also become, by chance far more than by design, the capital of the European Union, a weird political entity of an unprecedented kind committed to granting equal status to the official languages of all its national components and hence forced to develop the bulkiest interpreting and translating services in the history of mankind.

This is plenty to account for my sensitivity to language issues, though not enough to explain why I bothered to spend years of my life concocting a book about them. More was needed. And more was provided as I gradually realized that the language issues in question, though exceptionally salient in Brussels, were by no means the parochial preserve of the tiny hybrid of a country of which I happen to be a citizen and of the Euro-bureaucracy scattered in a hundred buildings or so within a mile of my Brussels home. These issues are nearly universal, and increasingly so, for three main reasons. First, all over the world more multilingual countries are entering, albeit quite chaotically, the democratic era, and are therefore facing the challenge of getting a democracy to work in the presence of separate public opinions, that is precisely the central challenge Belgium faced once it ceased to be ruled by a country-wide Francophone elite. Secondly, all over the world we increasingly need to function on a scale that brings together people with different native languages—no longer only merchants and diplomats, immigrants and tourists, but a great variety of participants in economic and intellectual life, in political institutions and civil society organizations—and therefore have to face ever more intensively the challenge perceived with great acuity inside and around the core institutions of the European Union. Thirdly, more and more countries all over the world face the immigration of large numbers of native speakers of a wide variety of languages that are being maintained and transmitted to the next generation more than was ever the case before. As a result, permanent linguistic diversity has become a common experience in many places essentially devoid of it so far.

The importance I came to attach to language issues derives in part from the realization of their increasing salience and universality, along the three paths just mentioned. But it derives even more from the realization of their crucial relevance to the prospects of social justice, whether on the national, European or global scale. This relevance first caught my attention as I discovered, in the early 1990s, how Belgium's language quarrels risked tipping into a precipitous decline the country's national welfare state that had served until then as a powerful instrument for the alleviation of poverty and the reduction of inequality. Language quarrels often seem trivial to those incensed by social injustice. But failing to handle them adequately can seriously impair the pursuit of social justice. For closely analogous reasons, Karl Renner and Otto Bauer, the leading social-democratic thinkers of the Austrian Empire and first theorists of multilingual democracy, reluctantly came to the conclusion that they had to devote whatever time and energy was necessary to addressing properly the *Nationalitätenfrage*, lest the *Sozialfrage*, of prior importance to them, could never be tackled effectively. Too late, no doubt, as the Austrian empire dislocated along linguistic lines before their solutions could even be tried. Our present situation in the European Union, however, is not fundamentally different. As will be argued below, the persistent 'Euro-malaise', the EU's 'democratic deficit', the stagnation of 'social Europe' admit of no structural solution in the absence of a fair and efficient solution to Europe's central language problem.

This last claim alone, if true, makes the issue of linguistic justice well worth the effort of a book. It also justifies the choice of my central illustration. At a stunning pace, competence in English is spreading throughout Europe and throughout the world. This massive, irreversible phenomenon, I shall argue, must be welcomed. Yet, it generates injustices, which the core of the book will consist in exploring. Much of what I shall have to say claims to apply far more widely than the current EU-wide and worldwide expansion of the learning and use of English. There have been, are, and will be many other cases of language competition that lead to more acute, more spectacular, more violent conflict. But none of them is of a magnitude that approaches that of the establishment of the first worldwide lingua franca. None of them has anything like the same importance for the future of Europe and the fate of the world. Whether as part of this central illustration or beyond, I shall use many examples throughout the book. Some will be drawn from the scholarly literature. But many will be drawn from situations I am familiar with, especially in the Belgian and European context. In the light of the countless occasions I have had to benefit from perceptive first-hand accounts of language matters elsewhere, I am confident that there is nothing exceptional about these examples, as regards the basic patterns they are meant to highlight, and that analogous illustrations could easily be adduced from many other places. Given the specific ambition of this book—by no means encyclopaedic—the conscious strong geographical bias of the illustrative sample should not be a problem.

What is then the ambition of a philosophical book on language issues? It has two logically distinct but intimately interconnected components. One consists in helping all those interested in such issues—whether as scholars, activists, policy makers, or ordinary citizens—to look up, by sketching a simplified 'big picture' of where we are and where we are going. This part of the job involves factual claims, especially about mechanisms and trends. Some of them are unavoidably speculative. But I hope that guidance and feedback by many colleagues from various disciplines will have saved most of those I shall be making from being too naïve. Though they may occasionally sound like dogmatic assertions, they are of course nothing but conjectures open to empirical challenge, as are those of my conclusions that hinge on them.

The other component of the philosopher's job consists in spelling out a normative framework robust enough to withstand philosophical objections, plausible enough to accommodate our well-considered ethical judgements, and precise enough to be able to inspire and justify, when combined with factual claims, a set of specific policy proposals. Both components of the job are intimately connected not only because a factual analysis and normative guidelines are both needed to generate policy conclusions, but also because a meaningful discussion of the plausibility of normative principles requires a well-informed reflection on their implications in the real world. By putting particular conflicts into perspective, by highlighting the generality of some basic mechanisms, by helping those used to one position in the language game to look at the situation from the opposite side, this twofold job, if successful, should help instil critical distance where emotion often rules unbridled, and substitute reason and fairness for passion and partiality.

In the attempt to perform this twofold job, this book will be structured as follows. Chapter 1 will propose a stylized picture of the mechanism that underpins many linguistic phenomena, including the spreading of the lingua franca, and present an argument in support of the presumption that this spreading should not be halted but accelerated. Chapters 2 to 5 will characterize the various senses in which injustice can arise as a result of one language being given a privileged status. They will specify the principles that should guide us when attempting to remove or minimize injustice in each of these senses. And they will spell out policy implications for today's Europe and today's world. Chapter 6 will focus on linguistic diversity, ask whether there is any good reason to advocate its preservation or promotion, and discuss its relationship with justice concerns.

In a nutshell, the core of what will end up being proposed in this book consists in combining an accelerated worldwide democratization of competence in English with the territorial protection of a large number of languages. The bulk of the book will consist in a normative argument for this position on the basis of a conception of global justice that articulates fair distribution and equal respect, against the background of an analysis of contemporary language trends that gives a key role to what I shall call the 'maxi-min dynamics'. Cynics will find such a normative approach pointless. Sheer power, they believe, has always settled linguistic issues like any other, and will always do so. They are wrong. An articulate conception of what linguistic justice means and of what it requires supplies resources for undermining the arrogance of the powerful, for empowering the indignation of the powerless, and for guiding the judgement of anyone who might happen to be in a position to arbitrate. So at least I hope, for reasons that reach far beyond linguistic justice. And so I believe.

CHAPTER 1

Lingua franca

1.1. Europe's lingua franca

Never since the European subcontinent was first inhabited by speaking beings has its linguistic landscape changed so deeply in such a short time as in the last few decennia. This phenomenon is all the more remarkable as it has been happening without conquest, without war, without much by way of top-down imposition. I shall focus shortly on the underlying mechanism, and I shall argue that this phenomenon is to be welcomed. But let us first have a closer look at its nature and magnitude, by using the European Union's Eurobarometer dataset on self-reported linguistic competence, broken down into age groups.[1]

Consider the proportion of Europeans who say they know well or very well the most widely spoken EU languages, whether as their native language or as a learned language, as estimated on the basis of a December 2005 survey in the twenty-five member states the EU then had (Figure 1.1). The dynamics at work can be read by moving from the oldest to the youngest cohort. What can we see? As we move to the younger generation, German, the most widespread native language in all age groups (Figure 1.2) and still the top language for the older generation, is in the process of being overtaken by French, while Spanish and Polish are catching up with Italian. However, overshadowing all the rest, English leaps far above all other languages in terms of (self-declared) speakers, with over double the score of German in the youngest generation.

Why such a leap? Obviously not—judging by the figures about native Anglophones (Figure 1.2)—because of an intensification of procreative activity in the United Kingdom or anything else

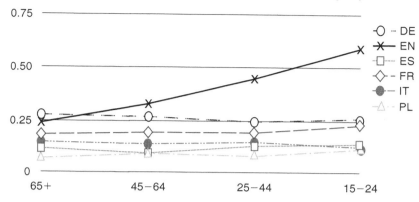

Fig. 1.1. Proportion of people (whether or not native speakers) who say they know well or very well the various languages (EU25, December 2005)

Source: Eurobarometer 2006. Data processing: Jonathan Van Parys.

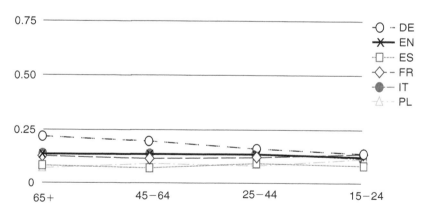

Fig. 1.2. Proportion of native speakers of the various languages (EU25, December 2005)

Source: Eurobarometer 2006. Data processing: Jonathan Van Parys.

happening in the British Isles. The cause is rather to be found in the ever swelling rush towards learning English as a second or third language throughout continental Europe. This can be documented by looking at the proportion of non-native speakers of the same languages in the various cohorts (see Figure 1.3). For the younger generation, German is now ahead of French as a learned language, not because it is more popular as a foreign language, but essentially because German residents of Turkish descent tend to retain Turkish as their home language, whereas French residents of North African origin tend to switch entirely to French. The fourth position is secured by Spanish, now decisively above Russian among the young. However, these shifts are of little significance compared to what is happening with English. The small margin by which English was ahead of German and French as a learned language in the generation born before World War II has been turned into a huge gap in the younger generation, with secondary competence in English now five times more common than secondary competence in German or French, and with over double as many secondary speakers of English as secondary speakers of all other languages

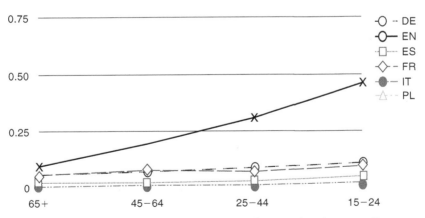

Fig. 1.3. Proportion of non-native speakers who say they know well or very well the various languages (EU25, December 2005)

Source: Eurobarometer 2006. Data processing: Jonathan Van Parys.

taken together. This powerful trend affects all member states of the EU, especially those with a more modest point of departure.[2]

I shall refer to this trend as the emergence of English as Europe's lingua franca. A *lingua franca* will here be defined as any language widely used for communication between people with different mother tongues, whether or not it enjoys an exclusive or privileged official status, and whether or not it has been from the start, or has gradually become, the native language of some of the linguistic communities it links together.[3] A lingua franca, so defined, does not need to be known by all members of the communities it links. Nor does there need to be only one lingua franca at a time. Spanish, for example, can operate as a lingua franca in this sense within Spain, while English operates as a lingua franca within Europe, Spain included. Crucial is that a significant proportion of the native speakers of different languages should all learn the same language and use it to communicate with each other. In this sense, more than Latin, French, or any other language has ever been, English has become— and, judging by the age pattern of linguistic competence documented above is becoming every day even more—Europe's lingua franca.

1.2. A global lingua franca?

Is English also becoming the world's lingua franca? Anecdotes abound in favour of this assertion, but there is no dataset that could document it with anything like the same precision as the Eurobarometer, using random samples and identical questions. It is therefore impossible to seriously estimate worldwide, using some common standard, the number of secondary speakers of the main languages, let alone to capture the dynamics at work by estimating the proportion of speakers in successive cohorts. The most authoritative yet extremely rough assessment is provided by the *Ethnologue* Website. Table 1.1 summarizes the *Ethnologue* data for those twelve languages that seem to be spoken, as native or as learned languages, by over 100 million people.[4]

If these figures are to be trusted,[5] if only in broad outline, the picture is far less univocal at the global than at the European level. True, among mankind as a whole just as among EU citizens, English

Table 1.1. Number of native and secondary speakers of the world's most widely used languages (millions of speakers)

	Natives (N)	All	Secondary (S)	Ratio S/N
Mandarin	873 (845)	1051	178	20.4
Spanish	322 (329)	382	60	18.6
English	309 (328)	508	199	64.4
Arabic	206 (221)	246	40	19.4
Hindi	181 (182)	301	120	66.3
Portuguese	176 (178)	191	15	8.5
Bengali	171 (181)	211	40	23.4
Russian	145 (144)	255	110	75.9
Japanese	122 (122)	123	1	0.8
German	95 (90)	113	18	18.9
French	65 (68)	115	50	76.9
Urdu	61 (61)	104	43	70.5

Source: http://www.ethnologue.com/language, July 2006 for all figures without brackets, February 2010 for those in brackets.

has the largest absolute number of non-native speakers, but Mandarin Chinese comes quite close, and dwarfs English altogether when native speakers are added to non-native speakers. Moreover, the ratio of non-native speakers to native speakers—a good proxy, it seems, for the spreading power of a language beyond its native population—is lower for English than it is for French, Russian, Urdu and Hindi. But there is of course a major difference. Urdu and Hindi operate as lingua francas for tens of millions of people, but are confined to the borders of the two nation states of which they are the (main) official language, while the bulk of secondary speakers of Russian and French are to be found in a small number of countries that used to be part of Russia's and France's respective empires. Moreover, the number of Russian speakers is bound to decrease quite fast, both because of Russia's low birth rate and because of the sharp fall in the learning of Russian in Eastern Europe, while the maintenance of French in Africa is threatened by the collapse of the educational system in several countries.

Spanish looks like a more serious competitor. According to these figures, it boasts somewhat more native speakers than English, but far less secondary speakers. However, Spanish is now challenging the unquestioned dominance of English on some significant portions of the most powerful Anglophone country. Is this not a major threat to the march of the English language towards a global lingua franca status? Quite the opposite. It would constitute such a threat if the USA were turning bilingual as a result of Anglophones becoming Hispanophones. But its becoming bilingual is due instead to massive and concentrated migration by millions of people who will end up knowing far more English and less Spanish than if they had stayed in their linguistic homes, albeit at a lower rate than was and still is the case with other waves of migrants. The residential language course is less effective than it used to be, but it is still overwhelmingly a one-way learning process that further boosts the spreading of English.

Finally, what about language number 1, Chinese? No doubt the bulk of the estimated 178 million secondary speakers of Mandarin are within China itself. But 40 million people are reputed to be currently learning Mandarin outside China, and the exceptionally fast growth of the Chinese economy since the 1980s might be expected to boost this number, starting with Korea and Japan. However, this trend is over-shadowed by the learning of English by the Chinese. Since 2001, English lessons are compulsory from primary school onwards, and in 2005, an estimated 177 million Chinese were studying English in China, more than in any other country in the world.[6]

Hence, although the phenomenon may be less advanced than in Europe and although it is far less comprehensively documented, it is English and English alone that can reasonably claim to have become a global lingua franca. Before asking ourselves whether this is something we should cheer or lament, slow down or accelerate, it is crucial to reflect on the micro-mechanisms that underlie the spectacular progress we can observe with some accuracy in Europe and can reasonably conjecture to be happening throughout the world. Observed trends cannot confidently be extrapolated and used to anticipate the future without an understanding of what drives them. As we shall see, such understanding will also prove crucial to the normative assessment of the trends, and to the evaluation of policies proposed to address their consequences.

1.3. Probability-driven language learning

The mechanism through which linguistic competence spreads in a population can be given, I submit, the following stylized description.

First of all, there is what I shall call *probability-driven learning*: how well and how fast one improves one's competence in a language, how fully, and for how long one retains it is strongly affected by the probability with which one can expect to have to operate in that language, whether actively or passively.

This is partly a matter of expected benefit, and hence of *motivation*: the more likely it is that competence in a particular language will be useful to understanding and being understood in contexts in which one expects to have to operate, the greater the effort one will decide to invest in the learning of it, whether at the individual level by allocating time, energy, and money to studying and practising it, or at the institutional level by organizing and funding the teaching of that language. This expected communicative benefit will tend to have a material dimension—if the learning of a language enables us to better understand and be better understood in many circumstances likely to arise, it is likely to boost our potential earnings—but it need not have one, and certainly does not reduce to it. Our interest in communicating with other human beings is not fully captured by the money we can make as a result.

Probability-driven learning is also, secondly, a matter of *opportunity*: the more often one finds oneself in a context in which a particular language is actually being used, the smaller the effort required to learn it or to retain it. Put more loosely: the bulk of the language competence we possess we do not owe to the professionals who were paid to teach it to us, but to the countless speech partners who were patient enough to listen and talk to us in a language we mastered only poorly. The opportunity dimension is at least as important as the motivation dimension, and each feeds into the other. The motivation to learn a language triggers the search for opportunities to practise it over and above those that offer themselves spontaneously. Conversely, experiencing these opportunities tends to make people realize what a difference it makes to be able to understand what is being said and to take an active part in the conversation, and thereby strengthens their motivation to gain greater proficiency in the language concerned.

Other factors may affect significantly either the motivation to learn a language or the ease with which one learns it or both. The aesthetic attractiveness of the languages one considers learning can play a role, for example, as can the proximity of its lexicon or grammar to those of one's own native tongue, or the size and prestige of the literary corpus it gives access to. However, bearing in mind that it operates through the two channels of motivation and opportunity to learn (and to retain), the probability of interaction in a particular language can be regarded as the central determinant of the extent to which average competence in a particular non-native language tends to expand or shrink in a particular population. A greater probability means both a larger expected benefit from any given level of linguistic proficiency in the language concerned and a lower cost of acquiring or maintaining it.[7]

This probability is not a simple reflection of the proportion of the world's population consisting of speakers of that language, let alone of native speakers of it. The per capita wealth of a linguistic group, for example, may be a further strong determinant of that probability, because of its impact on both the mobility of members of that group—for example as tourists or as businessmen—and the keenness of other people to interact with them—for example as sellers or as employees. But even the proportion of people competent in a language weighted by the probability of meeting them would still be, in many circumstances, a very poor predictor of the probability of interacting in that language because of the crucial role played by a second micro-mechanism, to which we now turn.[8]

1.4. Maxi-min language use

What I shall call the *maxi-min-guided choice of the language used in communication between multilingual speakers*—or, for short, *maxi-min use*—captures a distinct, somewhat less obvious but no less general mechanism, which can be presented as follows. Suppose you have to address simultaneously a set of people who each know to various extents a number of languages and by all of whom you wish to be understood. When deciding which language among those you know you should pick, what is the question you will spontaneously tend to ask yourself? Will you ask yourself in which language you express yourself most comfortably or most elegantly? In other words, will you tend to opt for the *egocentric* criterion? Certainly not. Will you tend to ask yourself which language is the native language or the best language of a majority among the members of your audience? In other words, will you tend to opt for the *democratic* criterion? Certainly not. Will you rather tend to ask yourself which language is best known on average by your audience? In other words, will you tend to opt for the *maxi-mean* criterion? Certainly not. Is the problem with all these criteria that they are all of the winners-take-all type, that is that they favour the choice of a single language for the whole conversation? Will you not tend to opt instead for some criterion *of fair division*, which would require each language to be spoken, as far as possible, in proportion to the number of its native speakers or in proportion to average competence in that language among the audience? Even more certainly not.

When reflecting on your own experience in multilingual contexts, you will soon realize that when efficient and inclusive communication is the sole concern a different criterion, of the winners-take-all type, is at work. What you and your conversation partners will systematically tend to ask yourselves is which language is best known by the member of your audience who knows it least well.[9] This language I shall call the *maxi-min* language—the language of maximal minimal competence.[10] I have no doubt that each of my multilingual readers has experienced this mechanism thousands of times, most strikingly perhaps in situations in which the arrival of a new speech partner, by modifying the ranking of languages in terms of minimal competence, leads to a switch of language regime.[11]

This maxi-min criterion can be spelled out more fully as follows. When having to address a multilingual audience—from a single person to a crowd—you will spontaneously ask yourself whether there is any language that is known to some extent by yourself and everyone else involved. If, to the best of your knowledge, there is one and only one such language, you will choose it as the single medium of communication. If there is none, you will tend to choose the language known to some extent by the greatest number. And if there is more than one, you will make a guess for each of them about the level of competence achieved by the person least competent in it, and you will choose the language for which this level of competence is highest.[12] Choosing the maxi-min language amounts to minimizing exclusion, in the sense of achieving, as far as possible, effective communication with all addressees. It can also be viewed as minimizing effort, not in the sense that it allows speakers to express themselves in the language in which it is most comfortable for them to communicate—which will tend to be their native language—but in the sense that it makes communication between the people involved least laborious. One important direct corollary of the prevalence of this criterion is the systematic victory, in bilateral communication, of the language of the 'worst linguist', that is of the partner who knows least well the language of the other and systematically tends to be—owing to probability-driven learning—the speaker of the more widely spread of the two languages.

1.5. The maxi-min dynamics

The two micro-mechanisms thus identified—probability-driven learning and maxi-min use—powerfully interact to generate an explosive process, which I shall call the *maxi-min dynamics*. First, the more a specific language is being learned by members of some linguistic community with a different mother tongue, the more likely that language is to turn out to be the maxi-min language in contexts of communication between people who belong to that community and people who do not. Secondly, the more often a particular language, being the maxi-min language, is picked as the language of communication, the stronger the motivation for learning it and the more frequent the opportunity to learn it. This positive feedback loop would also exist if the choice of the language of communication were guided by any other criterion positively related to the speech partners' overall linguistic competence—as opposed to criteria referring to nothing but their native languages. But compared to other such criteria—for example, the maxi-mean, that would require the maximization of average competence—the maxi-min criterion makes the feedback loop particularly quick. For it is obviously far easier for a single newcomer to upset the prevailing choice of a language under maxi-min than under maxi-mean: it suffices for her to be about totally ignorant of the language that prevailed before her arrival, while all others know to some extent at least one of the languages she knows to some extent.

To illustrate the differential impact, consider what happened as a result of the 1995 enlargement of the European Union. Until then, both the maxi-mean and the maxi-min language in contexts of informal communication between multilinguals within and around the European institutions tended to be English and French in varying proportions, with German quite often the maxi-mean but very seldom the maxi-min. Given that they accounted together for only about 5 per cent of the EU population at the time, the arrival of the Austrians, Swedes and Fins was unlikely to change much in terms of average competence in the various languages at most gatherings of Eurocrats, Euro-lobbyists, etc., and hence in the probability of one language rather than another turning out to be the maxi-mean. But it made a huge difference in terms of which language was likely to be the maxi-min. For while the second best language for most of the British was and is French, the new entrants' average competence in French was far poorer, and therefore tended to make English, rather than French, a clear winner in terms of minimal knowledge—though only slightly better than before in terms of average knowledge—at most of the meetings they attended. As a result, there was then an oft reported leap in the informal use of English in European institutions—as there was, for analogous reasons, as a result of the subsequent 2004 enlargement. Probability-sensitive language learning was accordingly redirected for both incentive and opportunity reasons, leading further contexts to switch, and so on. The unprecedented expansion of competence in English throughout the European population documented earlier is nothing but a reflection of this sort of explosive interaction between maxi-min use and probability-driven learning, that is of the maxi-min dynamics.

The process thus sketched can be viewed as a particular instance of a quite general pattern of convergence towards a single standard, as illustrated further by bolt sizes or computer softwares. Whether or not Word had any intrinsic advantage over Word Perfect, it was in your interest to adopt the most widespread of the two if you expected to interact a lot with a fairly representative sample of text editor users. The fact that the utility expected from the choice of some item grows with the number of people who make the same choice—the opposite of the phenomenon of congestion—has two important implications. First, the fact that one more person opts for the item creates a *positive network externality*, that is a (probabilistic) benefit for those who have previously opted for that item. Secondly, the dissemination already achieved by some item endows those who possess some property rights over it, or who have easy access to it, with *network power*, that is power they owe to the fact that those who fail to opt for this item incur a cost, irrespective of the item's intrinsic qualities.[13] For a language as for software, any additional user creates a positive externality for those already competent in it, and its diffusion confers more power to those with comparatively easy access to it.[14] Both these implications will prove important in subsequent chapters.

1.6. Deviation from maxi-min: didactic and symbolic

Before proceeding, let us briefly pause to question the central role ascribed above to maxi-min use. Are there not many contexts in which the choice of the language to be used in a multilingual setting is guided by different criteria? There certainly are.

First of all, deviation from the maxi-min criterion happens on a large scale for *didactic* reasons, precisely because of the importance of the opportunity dimension of language learning emphasized above. In foreign language classes, for example, teachers often know the native language of their pupils (which may well be their own) far better that the pupils know the language they are learning, but the mutually accepted rules of the teaching game will frequently entail the partial or total banning of the maxi-min language. Such deliberate deviation from maxi-min often stretches beyond the classroom. There are countless, often disapproving reports from around the world about the pupils' use of a local language or dialect at the playground being ridiculed or punished by the school staff. Such practices can be charitably interpreted as well-meant and effective language-teaching—rather than as sheer oppression and stigmatization of the native speakers of 'inferior' languages—in a context in which all or most pupils share a mother tongue distinct from the medium of education.[15] For analogous reasons, a Korean University created an 'English-only lounge', in which (Korean mother tongue) students were not allowed to communicate in Korean with one another.[16] And there are many stories about bilingual or multilingual people who choose to speak their mother tongue with their children in order to teach them that language, even though their children have been all along and they have themselves become significantly more fluent in at least one other shared language, typically a dominant language which would be displacing the weaker language in all contexts if it were not for such voluntaristic parental attitude.

Secondly, on a less massive scale but often in a highly sensitive way, deviation from the maxi-min criterion may also occur, even in informal settings, for *symbolic* reasons. You choose to speak or write in a particular language not because it is the one that enables you to communicate most effectively, nor because you want to learn or teach it, but because of what your choice expresses, given the context—place, time, occasion, other speakers, audience—about the value you ascribe or deny to the various languages among which you could have chosen. This symbolic deviation from the maxi-min criterion comes in four main variants.

The standard case is one where the concern for communication is trumped by the desire to assert, if not the superiority, at least the equal value of one's own language. Conforming to the rule 'Each speaks their own language' despite asymmetric bilingualism, as is commonly the case in Belgium, Switzerland, or Canada, can be interpreted along these lines. The native speakers of the less widespread language feel that speaking the dominant language would amount to recognizing the latter's superior status. Consequently, they stick to their own language at the cost of running a greater risk of being misunderstood, or not understood at all, by part of the audience. The communication cost remains limited as long as a passive knowledge of the language being spoken can be assumed. This can be realistic in contexts in which two or three languages are involved. But as the number of languages increases, the cost of generalizing this practice cannot fail to quickly become prohibitive in terms of communicative efficiency.[17]

The second variant is the reverse of the first one. Allegiance to the superiority of a dominant language leads the native speakers of some stigmatized dialect or language to shun the latter and speak instead, even among themselves, a more 'distinguished' language which they master less well. As pointed out in connection with the didactic motivation, one by-product of this symbolically driven choice is improved competence in the dominant language, which may therefore end up being gradually lifted into maxi-min position even among native speakers of the same stigmatized language. Such symbolic denial has routinely contributed to the demise of countless regional dialects.

Thirdly, there are cases in which the maxi-min language to be shunned for symbolic reasons is not one's native tongue but a lingua franca linked to an ethnic group, a regime or an ideology from which one wants to dissociate oneself. Thus, there are stories of post-1989 Poles, Hungarians, and Czechs struggling to communicate with one another in English, even when it would have been (linguistically) easier for them to do so in Russian. A similar pattern may help explain the abandonment of the colonial language in some multilingual ex-colonies where it tended to be the maxi-min language, but also the persistence of the colonial language in contexts in which a dominant local language was the maxi-min, as linguistic minorities wanted to symbolically deny their being inferior to the locally dominant group.

Finally and most gracefully, deviation from maxi-min may be used to express the equal value of languages, though not, as in the standard case, by insisting on speaking one's own language. This is the case, for example, when a symbolic concern for fair time sharing makes a Francophone speaker agree to address a mixed Belgian audience in Dutch, despite the fact that all would have understood her adequately had she spoken in French while some do not if she speaks in Dutch.[18]

1.7. Maxi-min dynamics and power relationships

By assuming that language choice is essentially driven by the desire to communicate, albeit with the didactic and symbolic caveats just mentioned, is one not adopting a naïvely benign approach to language use? Is one not thereby overlooking a third source of deviation from the maxi-min choice, so powerful that, more often than not, the latter's grip is completely neutralized? Is one not blinding oneself to the grim yet very real fact that what dictates the medium of interaction is sheer *power*?[19]

Let us say that a relationship of communication involves a power relationship if what one of the communicating parties might choose to do can have a far greater impact on the fate of the other than the other way round. It is not hard to imagine that a power relationship, so defined, can trump the maxi-min logic.[20] Suppose that I am particularly anxious to be understood by you, because my interests can be seriously affected by your grasping or believing what I am saying, whereas for you nothing of any importance is at stake in our conversation. Both you and I are then more likely to use your better language, even if you are more fluent in my better language than I am in yours, that is even if my better language is the maxi-min language. Consequently, the wealthy will tend to be more often on the comfortable side than the poor, the bosses more often than the workers, the powerful more often than the powerless, the loved more often than the loving. However, the extent to which this will involve departure from the maxi-min criterion should not be exaggerated. For the effective exercise of power generally requires effective communication. I am sure some of my readers have heard, as I did, US-born native English speakers instruct their Hispanic employees in Spanish. The reason why few do is not that power trumps the maxi-min logic, but that in the overwhelming majority of cases of interaction between US-born bosses and Hispanic employees English is unquestionably the maxi-min language.

Consequently, power must be added to didactic and symbolic considerations as a third source of deviation from the maxi-min logic of communication, though only of minor magnitude. Whenever communication is the prime concern, that is in the bulk of spoken and written language use today, power will not prevent the maxi-min criterion from running the show any more than didactic or symbolic concerns. Yet it does not follow that power does not play a major role in the dynamics of languages. The way it works, however, is not by affecting the choice of the language of communication against the background of a given pattern of linguistic competences, but by affecting the probability of meeting people with a particular type of linguistic competence: the directions of invasion, migration, economic cooperation, trade, or student exchange are strongly affected by military, political, and economic power and strongly affect in turn the statistical distribution of multilingual encounters. By affecting through such channels the intensity of interaction, power affects the probability with which people can expect to interact in various languages, hence their motivation and opportunity to learn it, and hence also eventually which language will tend to emerge as the maxi-min language.

Even after due attention is given to didactic, symbolic, and power considerations, the simple analysis in terms of probability-driven learning and maxi-min use remains a very convenient way of capturing the core mechanism of language dissemination under contemporary conditions. A more explicit and rigorous modelling of this mechanism and its implications would certainly be welcome, for example to provide a precise characterization of the conditions that trigger convergence towards a single lingua franca, and of the factors—such as the degree of residential segregation, the rate of mobility, or the average size of interactive gatherings—that accelerate it or slow it down.[21] However, the simple analysis sketched above is sufficient, for example, to make sense of the slow agony of small languages, of the language-crushing effect of cities or of the slowness of the Hispanics' linguistic assimilation in today's United States no less than of the dominant trend in the Europeans' linguistic repertoires (§1.1). Once one language is ahead and multidirectional communication develops, the analysis proposed easily explains the observed stampede towards English, without needing to invoke any British or American conspiracy.[22] But even if the maxi-min dynamic accounts fully for the trends observed, it operates against a background deeply shaped by power relations, struggles, victories, and defeats, in the case of the spreading of English as in any other language.

1.8. Power and the rise of English

There have been many regional lingua francas in the history of the world, with several of them shrinking back to the comparatively small group of their native speakers. Greek, for example, once served as the common medium for people with countless different native languages in the Eastern Mediterranean area: it was the language in which Christ had to stutter with Pilate. Unlike Latin, however, whose offspring now span the world, it imploded back to the area in which it is learned as a native language. Today there are still a large number of regional lingua francas, such as Swahili in large areas of sub-Saharan Africa, Hindustani in the Indian subcontinent, standard Arabic in North Africa and the Middle East. But for the first time, one language is in the process of establishing itself as a universal lingua franca. As we saw above (§1.2), English is the language that now has the largest number of secondary speakers.

Indeed, one can safely conjecture that no other language, in the whole history of mankind, has ever had as many non-native speakers competent in it. Most revealing perhaps: using a not too demanding criterion of competence, it can today be said that, for the first time in history, a language has more people competent in it beyond the borders within which it enjoys official status than it has native speakers.[23] As we also saw above, no other language, whether at European level or worldwide, gives any sign of rivalling English as a universal lingua franca, and the snowball effect currently unfolding is such that one can safely predict that no language will ever do.[24]

So, why was English picked, among the many thousands of languages that are and have been spoken by human beings, to play this unique historical role? Not because of anything like the superior rationality, the *génie* which Julien Benda (1933: 78, 81) was claiming for French when advocating its adoption as Europe's language.[25] Nor because of the particularly hybrid character of its lexicon, even though this can sometimes be used as a selling point.[26] Nor because of any ethnic superiority of its native population—by now a rather mixed bunch of people that owes its large size far less (and ever less) to the reproductive zeal of the fifth-century Angles' remote offspring than to the efficiency of the gigantic immersion language course offered daily to millions of migrants in US schools and streets, workplaces and shopping malls. Why then? Basically because of a haphazard sequence of events that could easily have led elsewhere.

English was modestly born out of a set of Germanic dialects akin to Frisian and Dutch that were carried over the Channel around the fifth century by hordes of Angles, Saxons, and Jutes. It was later packed with thousands of French words by Scandinavians who had spent several centuries on a language course in Normandy. The hybrid outcome of this ruthless mixing was then left to stew, solidify, and slowly spread throughout Europe's largest island. By the time it had more or less managed to overcome the contempt of the island's French-speaking elite and to gain currency in high circles, technological advances unexpectedly provided it with the opportunity to invade some comparatively underpopulated areas much further afield. With the assistance of gunpowder and lethal bugs, it engaged there in an impressively effective job of linguistic cleansing among locals, followed by the linguistic assimilation of all newcomers. The sequencing of the populations' movements was essential here: more people migrated into the United States from each of Germany, Italy, and Mexico than from England, but they did so massively only at a much later stage, and it was therefore into English, rather than into German, Italian, or Spanish, that linguistic assimilation proceeded.[27]

The direction, pace, and size of these population movements were themselves determined by countless chance events, especially of a military sort, which have nothing to do with features of the English language, indeed many of whom do not even involve any English speaker. Had the British of the fifth century been able to resist Germanic invaders as effectively as their twentieth-century successors or the British of the twentieth century as ineffectively as those of the fifth, the linguistic landscape of Europe and of the world would no doubt be quite different from what it has turned out to be. But had William the Silent managed to save Brussels and Antwerp from Spanish reconquest and to turn into the first thriving liberal democracy the whole of the Low Countries, not just their poorer and less populated Northern part, it is most likely that the linguistic make-up of the New England puritan settlers would have been quite different, and that it is not in English that Nieuw Amsterdam would have developed into what has now become the unofficial capital of the world.[28] More recently, had Stalin lost the battle of Stalingrad, and Hitler as a result won World War II, Europe's graph of linguistic competence would definitely look quite different from the one shown above (§1.1). And had India's Southern states not fiercely and successfully resisted the planned adoption of Hindi as the Indian Union's sole national language, it is not unreasonable to believe that the attraction of English in today's China would be far less than it currently is.

Thus, the chaos of violent battles and the power imbalances that determined their outcomes have a large share in explaining the current configuration, in particular the prevalence of English, by impacting not only population movements, but also patterns of trade or education systems. Events of this sort do not obliterate the socio-linguistic dynamics, but define the parameters within which it operates. They provide a background for the relentless work of the micro-mechanisms described above. The latter's cumulative interaction in a high-mobility, intense-communication world, has now snowballed English into a European and universal lingua franca position from which it could be dislodged only by some unforesee-able apocalyptic event—or by a concerted and persistent Europe-wide or worldwide endeavour to block or reverse the convergence process just analysed.

1.9. Lingua franca and justificatory community

For such an endeavour to take off, however, there must be sufficient agreement that this emergence of English as a lingua franca is undesirable. Hence our next question: Whether in Europe or in the world, do we want to have a lingua franca? Is it, all things considered, a good thing that we should all—all Europeans or all human beings—have a language in which we can communicate directly with each other? My answer to this question is emphatically yes, and the bulk of this book is an attempt to take seriously and tackle the main problems triggered by this answer.[29] But I first need to explain what justifies this answer ultimately—that is why the pursuit of justice, properly understood, demands that we should favour the spreading of a European and global lingua franca. To introduce the first step in this justification, let me start with the story of a brief encounter in Owerri, Imo State, Nigeria, in early November 2005.

As I was walking in a busy street, a small crowd of children gathered around me as usual shouting 'Onye Ocha', 'White man'—hardly surprising since I had seen no white person myself for several days, apart from a couple of albinos. Far more surprising was that we could communicate with each other so easily, on a variety of subjects, notwithstanding the fact that these primary school kids had never before met any native speakers of any European language. We talked enough for them to learn that I was coming from 'Belgium', there commonly known—I soon discovered—as a German city from which Nigeria's better second-hand cars are imported, and hence as a pretty wealthy place. So when I said that I had to leave because I needed to catch a plane back home, one of the boys—whom I shall call 'Stanley', as every third boy in Igboland seemed to be called that—said he wanted to come with me. His mum would never let him, I replied. Not true, Stanley said, she would love it if he moved to wealthy 'Belgium'. Anyway it is not

possible, I then told him, and he asked me why. I stuttered something, which neither he nor I found convincing and which I hastened
to forget. But as I was travelling away from the busy street, from
Owerri, from Igboland, from Nigeria, from Africa, I remained
haunted by the feeling that I had given a fair question a dishonest
answer.

Had Stanley tried to come along, he would have been forcibly
prevented from doing so. That would have been the honest answer.
Borders exist in our world. Their location and their significance are
determined by human beings. They are coercively enforced. And
they massively affect people's prospects in life, even increasingly so:
when world inequality indices are decomposed into an intra-coun-
try and an inter-country component, the latter keeps growing in
both relative and absolute terms.[30] Even in the absence of anything
like global institutions, therefore, the existence of borders is sufficient to constitute, in John Rawls's (1971: §2) language, a worldwide
'basic structure', that is a set of social institutions that 'distribute
fundamental rights and duties and determine the distribution of
advantages from social cooperation' and that need to be made the
subject of justice because their effects 'are so profound and present
from the start'.

However, should worldwide justice not be conceived, as Rawls
himself recommends, from a standpoint quite different from the
egalitarian one appropriate in a domestic context?[31] Taking as a
point of departure that we need to regard each other as free and
equal persons may be natural enough for citizens deliberating with
each other in a democratic state, that is precisely in the context in
which egalitarian conceptions of social justice have developed. But
is it not out of place at a global level? No, it is not. This is where the
Stanley experience kicks in. For those of us who accept that Stanley
and his likes cannot be dismissed as human beings living in such a
different mental universe that communication with them is bound
to remain as rudimentary as with primates from other species, it is
hard to uphold the view that Stanley should be content with a
justification for our immense privileges fundamentally different
from the one we owe to people who differ from him simply by
virtue of having been born of different parents or on the other side
of a particular border. Once Stanley has made his way into our
'justificatory community', there is no way back.[32] All attempts to

restrict egalitarian justice to 'our people', 'our nation', our 'demos', our 'ethnos', our 'fatherland', our 'community' will then look like pathetic self-serving efforts to dig shallow trenches or build flimsy fences, soon to be swept away by the following conviction: any honest attempt to think seriously about justice for our century must downgrade nations and states from the ethical framework to the institutional toolkit.

This leads us straight to the first of two reasons why the spreading of lingua francas matters to justice—what I shall call ethical contagion. The more people have the Stanley experience, the more people communicate with each other across national and hence linguistic borders, the more they perceive each other as more than sheer curiosities or trade partners, the more they accept each other as equal participants in a real conversation, as entitled to question and obligated to justify, in a spirit of openness and honesty, the more quickly their 'reflective equilibrium' will converge to some version of egalitarian global justice. A picture of mankind consisting of neatly distinct peoples which worldwide justice simply requires to cooperate on fair terms cannot resist the recurrent experience of genuine cross-border inter-individual conversational contact. As such contact becomes part of our routine experience, such a picture of mankind as fundamentally a set of peoples will quickly start looking as bizarre as a picture of a country as a set of neatly distinct families and a conception of social justice as fair cooperation between these families.[33]

Now, actual direct contact of the Stanley type is not strictly required for one's reflective equilibrium to settle on egalitarian global justice. One does not need to meet a Stanley in order for us to imagine that he could question us, or in order for us to acknowledge that we should not try to get away by ignoring him or by offering him justifications that would be unworthy of the people with whom we actually have this sort of conversation. But actual inter-individual contact of this sort, as facilitated by travel, migration, and the internet, clearly helps. And the sharing of a language is essential for it to happen at any depth. Of course, this language need not be a lingua franca, let alone always the same lingua franca. Had I been proficient in Igbo, the conversation with Stanley and his friends would have been even smoother. But convergence to one or a small number of lingua francas makes it massively more likely that this will happen across all combinations of countries. This major contribution to ethical contagion is a first reason why the spreading of a worldwide lingua franca is *prima facie* a positive and important trend from what I regard as the ultimate standard: egalitarian global justice.

1.10. Lingua franca and trans-national demos

The spreading of an egalitarian conception of global justice in the ethical convictions people hold in reflective equilibrium across the globe is one thing. Progress towards the implementation of such a conception is quite another. Egalitarian global justice will no doubt require the creation and strengthening of worldwide institutions. But if we try to rush, we are bound to trip. Incremental moves are wise, indeed unavoidable. Regional entities like the European Union are therefore essential stepping stones. By creating large areas in which goods, capital, and people can freely cross national borders, they weaken the domestic institutions' ability to pursue egalitarian justice. But they also constitute arguably an essential precondition for the development of egalitarian-justice-promoting institutions at a higher level, closer to the global one. We urgently need structural forms of trans-national redistribution which will both substitute and assist national institutions: substitute by organizing some inter-personal redistribution at a supra-national level, and assist by reducing the pressure of the race to the bottom to which nation states are exposed.[34]

At the level of individual nations, egalitarian-justice-promoting institutions could not have developed in the absence of society-wide deliberation and mobilization.[35] Similar conditions need to be met if such institutions are to emerge and stabilize at the global or the European level. There needs to be a trans-national common *demos*, in the sense of an arena for both deliberation and mobilization. An effective and inclusive deliberative forum—of which Stanley-like conversations are only a very inchoative, tenuous, haphazard preview—must rely on some form of representative democracy, with all the difficulty of making it work when hundreds of millions of citizens are meant to be represented. But it need not reduce to it. It can include a combination of transparency and civil society activism that disciplines public and private agents, using a wide variety of sanctions, formal and informal, starting with the sheer exposure of both honourable and shameful behaviour, and thereby forcing political rulers and other decision makers to justify their decisions and, in the best case, to make justifiable decisions.

Whether use is being made of the conventional channel of representative democracy or of less conventional tools, the deliberative forum will not work in the service of egalitarian justice without the demos also involving effective mobilization of—or at least on behalf of— all layers of the population, especially those most vulnerable to injustice. At a trans-national no less than at a national level, progress will not drop from the sky as the neat conclusion of an elegant argument. It will require tough and obstinate struggles by those who stand to gain from greater justice. This crucial mobilization, no less that the broader deliberative process into which it fits, can only hope to fulfil its purpose at a trans-national level if people and associations, especially those representing the weakest, can communicate, coordinate, and mobilize effectively and cheaply across language borders, if they can address effectively and cheaply the relevant media and thereby reach the relevant sections of the European or global public opinion.

This provides us with a second fundamental reason—for short, political feasibility—for welcoming the spreading of a lingua franca throughout Europe and beyond. Progress towards egalitarian justice requires the emergence of a trans-national *demos*—of the possibility for all categories of citizens to effectively deliberate and mobilize across national borders—and the emergence of such a demos is facilitated, indeed made possible, by the availability of a common language.[36]

This claim echoes an old thesis to the effect that a viable or a healthy democracy requires a common language. This thesis can be found, for example, in John Stuart Mill's (1861: 291) famous (near) indictment of multilingual democracies: 'Free institutions are next to impossible in a country made up of different nationalities. Among a people without fellow-feeling, especially if they read and speak different languages, the united public opinion, necessary to the working of representative government, cannot exist.'[37] Along the same lines, some of the first people to call for the creation of a Europe-wide democracy emphasized the key importance of a common language. As early as 1911, the Francophone Russian sociologist Jacques Novikow (1911: 138) stated categorically: 'Since federating Europe is of such considerable importance and since the triumph of French can accelerate it, we must work with all our strength towards the expansion of the French language.'[38] He was seconded, albeit in a less upbeat tone, by the French linguist Antoine Meillet (1918: 287): 'One has often been talking about the United States of Europe—which do not seem to be taking shape. Without some form of linguistic commonality, one cannot conceive of a genuine union.' And a few years later, Julien Benda's (1933: 77) *Address to the European Nation* proclaimed that 'if they want to unite, the people of Europe will need to adopt a common language, which will be superposed to their national languages in the same way as the national language got superposed to the local idioms in each of their nations and to which they will confer some sort of moral primacy.'

It is, however, important to stress that there are two crucially distinct arguments in support of the claim that a common language is a condition for a viable democracy.[39] One views language as a central component of a culture, of what constitutes a people in the thick sense of an *ethnos*. This is the sort of connection that can arguably be traced to a famous passage in Fichte's (1808: 190) thirteenth *Address to the German Nation*: 'Those who speak the same language are joined to each other by a multitude of invisible bonds by nature herself, long before any human art begins; they understand each other and have the power of continuing to make themselves understood more and more clearly; they belong together and are by nature one and an inseparable whole.'[40] In Fichte's view, it is the 'internal boundary' defined by the common language, not the 'external boundary' defined by a common territory, that determines the unit of political organization, the people on whose behalf popular sovereignty must be claimed.[41] If this is the case, Europe's linguistic diversity is simply incompatible with Europe-wide democracy. Only the linguistic and cultural homogeneity that would be needed for a genuine European ethnos to exist would make EU democracy more than a sham.[42] And the same holds, a fortiori, for a global democracy.

There is, however, another interpretation of the connection between language and democracy, which comes arguably much closer to Mill's view. On this interpretation, a common language is required not because democracy requires an *ethnos* with a homogeneous culture, but because it requires a *demos* with a shared forum, a common space for deliberation and mobilization. Language matters this time simply as a medium of communication, not as a core component of a culture. And the prospects for democratic functioning at the European or global level no longer need to be as gloomy. A common forum is consistent with the common language just being 'superposed' to the others—to borrow the expression used by Julien Benda (1933: 77) in the passage quoted above—rather than replacing them—as suggested by the Fichtean title he chose for his essay and the parallel he draws between Europe's common language and national languages. In other words, while not sufficient to turn a population into an *ethnos*, a shared language can suffice to turn it into a *demos*, albeit it one that can coexist with a multiplicity of *demoi* on a smaller scale.[43]

It is possible, however, to reject this optimistic conclusion, while agreeing that the reason why a common language is a condition of democracy is a matter of demos rather than ethnos, of public space rather than homogeneous culture. 'Put simply', Will Kymlicka (1999: 121) writes, 'democratic politics is politics in the vernacular. The average citizen only feels comfortable debating political issues in their mother tongue. As a general rule, it is only elites who have fluency with more than one language, who have the continual opportunity to maintain and develop these language skills, and who feel comfortable debating political issues in another tongue within multilingual settings.' Monolinguals, and in particular monolinguals in monolingual countries, are likely to find this position only too plausible. But most countries are multilingual, and many of their citizens' only option, if they want to participate in national politics at all, is to do so entirely, or mainly, in a language different from their mother tongue. Some of them are even pretty good at it. Just think of Nelson Mandela.

True, such active political participation at the national level is restricted to an elite. But is there ever more than an elite that 'feels comfortable debating political issues' even in their mother tongue? On a demanding interpretation of 'feels comfortable', certainly not. Learning the tone, concepts, and tricks which make for effective participation in the required variety of one's own tongue is far more difficult than learning another language to which one is frequently exposed. On a more modest interpretation, most ordinary people can 'feel comfortable' debating some political issues. But then, given appropriate socio-linguistic conditions, they can also quickly feel comfortable enough debating in a language distinct from their mother tongue. In some European countries, the democratization of competence in English has already reached such a level that the possibility of trans-national politics in the lingua franca does not look more—nor less—illusory than the possibility of national politics in the so-called vernacular.

This, then, is the second fundamental reason why we urgently need a lingua franca in Europe and, for analogous reasons, across the world. Its adoption and spreading creates and expands a trans-national demos, by facilitating direct communication, live or online, without the cumbersome and expensive mediation of interpretation and translation. It enables not only the rich and the powerful, but also the poor and the powerless to communicate, debate, network, cooperate, lobby, demonstrate effectively across borders.[44] This common demos, in turn, is a precondition for the effective pursuit of justice, and this fact provides the second fundamental reason why people committed to egalitarian global justice should not only welcome the spread of English as a lingua franca but see it as their duty to contribute to this spread in Europe and throughout the world.[45]

1.11. A vector of ideological domination?

There is, however, one aspect of such a spread to which no attention has been paid so far and which advocates of global egalitarian justice may have good reasons to be extremely worried about. It would be naïve, so the argument goes, to regard a language as nothing but a neutral medium, the spread of which should enable us to communicate more effectively across borders and thereby to help fulfil a crucial precondition for the effective pursuit of egalitarian global justice. Choosing English for this function is self-defeating: it amounts to endorsing ideological domination by the United States and to promoting convergence to an 'Anglo-Saxon model of society' which can hardly be sold as the best possible approximation of egalitarian justice.[46]

To make sure we focus on the best version of this argument, let us first note that there is of course nothing intrinsically 'neo-liberal' or 'pro-capitalist' about the English language as such, just as it is not because Karl Marx wrote all but one of his books in German that there is something intrinsically 'collectivist' or 'anti-capitalist' about the German language. Along with (presumably) all other languages in the world, English and German contain the means of expressing negation, so that whatever Karl Marx wrote in German can be denied in German and whatever Milton Friedman said in English can be denied in English. Recognizing this does not force us to deny that differences in grammatical structures, for example, may exercise a profound influence on the ways different linguistic communities tend to think. Sophisticated reasoning is so dependent on language that the so-called Sapir–Whorf hypothesis—or some other version of the proposition that some aspects of a community's world view are causally affected by structural features of its ancestral language—is plausible enough. But I am not aware of any argument or piece of evidence that would make even the most modest step towards establishing a causal connection between linguistic structure and political conception, which is all that matters to the present argument. To convince ourselves that this line of thought is not worth pursuing, it should suffice to ponder for half a minute about the linguistic distance between Pinochet's and Castro's Spanish on the one hand, between Swedish and Finnish on the other.

The real problem, aptly detected by those who worry about the ideological bias involved in the adoption of English, has nothing whatsoever to do with the English language as such. It rather stems from the fact that the typical political content of English-language discourse—as reflected for example in academic textbooks, newspaper articles, TV series, and web content—tends to differ significantly in ways the critics regard as undesirable from the typical content of what is originally published in at least some other languages, or from what this typical content would be in the absence of Anglophone influence. To be more specific, what 'makes sense' in terms of public policy in the United States even at the best of times has arguably been strongly shaped by the heavy dependence of access to public office on the collection of large private contributions to electoral campaigns. Moreover, what is being formulated and actively disseminated by native Anglophones can be expected to be systematically biased in favour of the economic and geo-political interests of the United States, where 70 per cent of the native Anglophones live. Such facts arguably skew the realm of the politically thinkable and hence of the politically feasible in all Anglophone countries, thereby contributing to shaping the contours of the 'Anglo-Saxon model of society'. With the worldwide dissemination of competence in English, English-language discourse is now flooding non-Anglophone countries, whether in the original language or in translation, whether in spoken, printed, or digital form. Consequently, so the critics plausibly argue, the deplorable ideological bias is less and less confined to Anglophone countries and is gaining a global grip.

When the argument is based on contingent connections of this sort, rather than on intrinsic features of the English language, it ceases to be ludicrous to claim that the adoption of English as a European or worldwide lingua franca threatens more than it helps the pursuit of egalitarian global justice. There is a real problem here, but its solution cannot be defensive retreat. On the contrary, the appropriate response consists in appropriating the emerging lingua franca in order to disseminate with its help whatever content we see fit. It is not shrill whispering in provincial dialects that provides the way forward, but the uninhibited grabbing of the global megaphone. Throughout the world people must acquire the ability to say: 'English is our language, even when it is, as for many of us, only one of our languages and one we use less comfortably, less fluently, less elegantly, less "correctly" than its native speakers. But there are as many legitimate ways of using it as there are people who bother to use it. We can, must, and will use English in the way we choose and to say what we choose to say in it, including—indeed especially—when it diverges significantly from what the average Anglophone would say or from what North America's most influential think tanks would like us to say.'

To make this strategy effective, the worst one could do is to hold back and obstruct in all sorts of ways the learning of English by native speakers of other languages, especially the least advantaged among them and those least likely to collude with the powerful of the planet. Instead of panicking at the prospect of their becoming ever more receptive to 'Anglo-American ideology' by improving their understanding of English, one must encourage them to acquire as soon as possible the competence needed to talk and write in English, indeed to feed the web with English-language material and to produce English-language memos and blog entries, op-eds, and best-sellers. If people from all over the world want to be read or heard all over the word and help shape what is happening, including on the Anglophones' home ground, they must not proudly or shyly withdraw into their tiny linguistic niche. They must use the language that will enable them to reach out as widely as possible, albeit with distinctive accents and in distinctive styles, and in ways that may make the guardians of beautiful English cringe.[47] And they must not be intimidated into accepting that English native speakers should have more than their share of speaking time, functions, and influence at international gatherings and in trans-national associations.

In this globalized forum, there is even one respect in which not being a native speaker of English may ironically prove an advantage. The bulk of a worldwide audience consists of people who are not Anglophones. When addressing such an audience, it can be a serious handicap to use clever puns, sophisticated syntax, and wonderfully chosen idiomatic expressions. Non-native speakers competent enough to satisfy minimal phonetic, grammatical, and lexical conditions are therefore more likely to spontaneously adopt the appropriate style and tempo and to be sensitive to the specific needs of their audience than native speakers who tend either to forget that they are not among their own folk or to sound as if they were addressing half-wits.[48] Global English or, as it is now sometimes called, Globish is a dialect of English whose spoken form in particular is more difficult to master for some of those who grew up hearing nothing but Oxford or Dallas English than for many native speakers of Italian or Bengali.

So, is there nothing left of the risk of ideological hegemony by Anglophone countries, once the 'grab the megaphone' strategy is vigorously adopted in the rest of the world? Not quite, for two reasons. First, it will remain a permanent nuisance for non-Anglophones that the megaphone cannot be connected directly to the domestic wiring. They will need to keep switching linguistic codes as they move back and forth between domestic and international audiences.[49] And they will not be able to mobilize without further hassle what they produce for domestic purposes in the service of Europe-wide or worldwide endeavours. Hence, other things being equal, they will have less time and resources at their disposal to address a global audience, and their inputs into their national debates will not help feed and influence unwittingly, without additional effort, the global debates, as some inputs into the national debates of Anglophone countries can do.[50] This bias will persist as long as national contributions and debates do not shift entirely to using the global lingua franca.[51]

The second source of an irreducible bias is the residual link between the global lingua franca and the national cultures of Anglophone countries. It is of course absurd to refer to Globish as *la langue de Shakespeare* or to signal the English-language version of a website by using a British flag. As stressed, for example, by Ros Schwartz (2005: 73), the English that is being learned for the sake of transnational communication 'is, as it were, de-nativized' and 'does not convey a national, regional or individual identity'. It is not meant to be a 'language of culture'. However, in spite of possessing its own distinct norms and genres, it is linguistically far closer to the 'language of culture' of the Anglophone countries than to that of any other country. This means that, other things being equal, it will be more comfortable and more useful, and therefore more likely, that non-Anglophones will pay extended visits to Anglophone countries and be exposed, superficially or in depth, to their past and present cultural products (from poetry to design), whether during their visits or in their own countries. Along the way, some of the most talented among them may even be co-opted and assimilated into Anglophone culture and further swell its worldwide impact. As a consequence of such processes, there is now, and there will continue to be, an asymmetrical process of cultural diffusion, with inequalities in the cultural flows from and to the Anglophone countries far exceeding what could be expected on the basis of the relative sizes of their populations or cultural production. Arguably, a national culture is not ideologically neutral. It is rather suffused, albeit in a fuzzy and plural way, by a set of beliefs about what makes a good society. To the extent that this is the case, the asymmetry of intercultural flows intimately linked with the spreading of a lingua franca that is much closer to one language of culture than to any other, is another potential factor of ideological bias.

For these two reasons—non-Anglophones being hindered by the need to debate in two languages (or more), and Anglophones being backed by universal exposure to their culture—the risk of ideological bias will not be extinguished by the vigorous worldwide promotion of participation in the global debate using the global medium. Yet, nothing can better serve the prospect of everyone's interests and views being taken into account than the competent inclusion of all in the unavoidably messy trans-national conversation. If unwelcome domination is to be minimized, people all over the world must not resist but accelerate the appropriation of the lingua franca.[52]

1.12. Go English?

The presumption in favour of adopting a lingua franca therefore survives the objection of ideological bias. However, adopting a natural language as the lingua franca does confer privileges to its speakers and may generate injustices in turn, indeed injustices of such a nature and magnitude that they may offset the twofold *prima facie* case sketched in this chapter. The question of how these putative injustices can be characterized and must be addressed will be the subject of the next four chapters, that is of the bulk of this book.

Before proceeding, I want to turn specifically to those of my readers who share my conception of global egalitarian justice and my correlative belief in the importance and urgency of effective universal trans-national communication, while being convinced that convergence to a single natural language is not the best, let alone the only way of achieving this goal.[53] There are three alternative proposals often made for solving the problem of worldwide communication without relying on such convergence: technological improvements, an artificial lingua franca, and a plurality of natural lingua francas. If at least one of them works, we shall be able to avoid or substantially shrink not only the problem of ideological domination just discussed, but also the various forms of linguistic injustice to be discussed in the following chapters.

Many people, however, find these alternative proposals ludicrous. As far as they are concerned, no more than half a line should be wasted on dismissing each of them. Others find at least one of them so appealing that, if in the end it needs to be discarded, it should only be after an in-depth, well-documented discussion. By way of compromise between these (sometimes passionately held) conflicting attitudes, I shall discuss all three proposals at some length in the appendix to this chapter. I do believe it is important and instructive to take seriously and scrutinize the main arguments in support of each of them, even though I do not believe any of them comes close to offering a plausible alternative to the dissemination of competence in one natural language and its use as a lingua franca.

As emphasized above (§1.8), the fact that this language is English has nothing to do with any intrinsic superiority it might have possessed. However, as no other natural language can plausibly claim such superiority,[54] there is no good reason to take on the daunting task of undoing the huge advantage achieved by English (§§1.1–1.2) or of blocking the dynamics triggered by this advantage (§§1.3–1.5). Those saddened by the fact that this historical role was not bestowed upon the language they learned as infants will have to come to terms with it. Their narcissism should not jeopardize the achievement of what is required for the sake of pursuing global egalitarian justice.

Other readers may not question the instrument I propose, but the objective I assign to it. They may reject my basic normative premise that justice today must be conceived as global egalitarian justice. Most of them, however, are likely to accept that distributive justice needs to be conceived as egalitarian in a sense to be clarified below (§3.1) and that it increasingly needs to be pursued at the level of large multilingual entities, such as the European Union or the Indian Union, rather than at the level of small monolingual nation states, if only because immersion in a single market has made the pursuit of distributive justice at a lower, more homogeneous level, increasingly shaky. As long as some significant degree of linguistic diversity is present at the level those readers regard as appropriate for the pursuit of distributive justice, much of what I shall have to say will remain relevant to them. The larger the scale on which one considers that justice concerns need to be met, the harder it will be to relegate the issues addressed in this book to the margins of public debate and political philosophy, and the more they will move, willy-nilly, to the very centre of the stage.

Three alternatives to lingua franca convergence

1. Babel Fish

In Douglas Adams's (1979: 52) *Hitch-Hiker's Guide to the Galaxy*, an ear insert called the Babel Fish enables people to communicate orally with one another, immediately, effortlessly, and accurately. Has the mind-boggling development of computer technology in the last few decades not brought us very close to giving non-fiction birth to Babel Fish, and hence to making the adoption of a lingua franca entirely redundant? Is it not sufficient to combine the best softwares for voice recognition and the best softwares for translation to be able to convey instantaneously, through earphones, in any chosen language what is being said in any other?

Both kinds of software have apparently been making fast progress.[55] Nonetheless, there is every reason to be sceptical. First of all, the learning of the global lingua franca and the development of 'Babel Fish' technology are involved in a race for survival: the implementation of each of these options involves expensive investments with an impact that dramatically reduces the expected payoff of the other.[56] In the case of smaller languages, lingua franca learning is bound to win this race hands down as competence currently achieved or soon to be achieved in English and other widespread languages further shrinks the—already small—market for the very expensive development and fine-tuning of the sophisticated software required. But even in the case of language combinations that offer the promise of large Babel Fish markets, the technological alternative to the lingua franca is hardly promising. Why?

To start with, you may have experienced yourself some of the bizarre interpretations supplied by voice recognition software even under the most favourable acoustic conditions. You may also have experienced some of the oddities generated by sophisticated translation software (not just with Altavista's 'Babel Fish'), even when it has to cope with only slightly casual style. Now think of these two transformation devices (of sounds into sentences, and of sentences in one language into sentences in another) working in succession. Imagine them operating with background noise, false starts, interruptions, proper names, differences in accents, meaningful variations in pace and tone. And bear in mind the significant time lags needed by both devices, as they generally have to wait for what they take to be the end of a sentence before proposing an interpretation. You can then easily imagine how stilted and contrived a spontaneous exchange would need to become in order for its participants to feel reasonably confident that the meaning of what is monotonously entering their ears bears close resemblance to what the person in front of them had in mind when speaking half a minute earlier. Moreover, any group of human beings who interact for any length of time tends to quickly develop a small idiosyncratic culture, with words being used between inverted commas, as it were, or proper names turned into nouns, or short-lived imports from other languages.

Consequently, even very imperfect competence in a common language will generally provide for far better communication than impeccable command of one's own language coupled with two computer-operated transformations. However useful such software can be for some purposes and however ingeniously it can be further improved, communication relying on it will constantly be threatened by ludicrous rigidity if speakers bother to take account of the limits of the technology as they speak, and by hopeless misunderstandings if they do not.[57] Techno-geeks can and will keep dreaming about sparing the bulk of mankind the pains of language learning. But the (perhaps not so) sad truth is that there is no providential fix to be hoped for from these quarters.

2. Esperanto

If technology does not enable us to dispense with a common language, why not opt for an artificial language, a language that has not evolved 'naturally' as the native language of a particular community? This second solution is less fanciful. It was seriously considered in 1923 when Esperanto, the most famous and successful among these languages, was proposed as a possible official language for the League of Nations. Ever since it was concocted over a century ago, it has attracted the support of many great minds, from the French linguist Antoine Meillet to the German economist and Nobel laureate Reinhart Selten, and of a million or so enthusiastic xenophiles around the globe. It is still vigorously defended in both eccentric pamphlets and respectable reports.[58] The two key advantages it claims are neutrality and simplicity.

(a) Neutrality

Take neutrality first. Choosing as the common language a natural language, that is a language for which there exists a community of native speakers, is clearly not 'neutral': it creates a variety of advantages for that community (to be identified and discussed in later chapters) and therefore smacks of unfairness. Choosing an artificial language, like Esperanto, does not present this defect and there is therefore a strong prima facie case for claiming that a concern for linguistic justice should make us opt for Esperanto rather than for a natural language. Why is this not the route taken here?

First and most obviously, Esperanto is very far from being neutral in the demanding sense of being equidistant from all existing languages. It belongs unambiguously to the Western group of Indo-European languages, with identifiable Latin, Germanic, and Slavic ingredients in very unequal proportions. Even within Europe, with Hungarian, Finnish, Estonian, Maltese, and Basque as part of the picture, it cannot make any claim to 'neutrality' in this strong sense. But Esperanto's claim to lingua franca status is not restricted to Europe, and sensibly so: one cannot reasonably expect Europeans to learn one additional language for communication with fellow Europeans, and yet another for communication with the rest of the world. However, when advocated on a world scale, it must lose all hopes of being sold as anything like an approximation of linguistic neutrality in this strong sense. Think of the millions of Indians, Nigerians, South Africans, or Chinese who have invested heavily in the laborious learning of one Western language. Will they not understandably show little patience for this new Eurocentric gimmick which they are enthusiastically invited to digest? As a Latin-Germanic-Slavic hybrid, Esperanto can be defended within Europe as being, not equidistant, but significantly more equidistant than a Germanic-Latin hybrid such as English or *a fortiori* any other European language. Once the relevant space is meant to include all the languages of the world, there is still some difference between Esperanto and English in this respect, but it has shrunk into insignificance.

Most Esperantists will readily concede all of this. But it is still possible for them to argue that, unlike English and other natural languages, Esperanto is neutral in a second, more modest yet important sense that follows trivially from its being an artificial language: it is the native language of nobody and would be a secondary language for everybody. Even this far weaker claim, however, needs to be qualified. First, even though the numbers involved would not lift Esperanto out of the category of threatened languages, it is it no longer strictly true that it is no one's mother tongue.[59] Secondly, if Esperanto were to spread successfully, as its advocates hope, this would gradually cease to be a marginal phenomenon. For

Esperanto will then start being used in a growing number of contexts, including by mixed couples in the upbringing of their children. Nothing would then prevent it, after some generations, from thickening from a learned language for all its users into the mother tongue of a significant proportion of them—as happened, for example, deliberately to Hebrew in Israel, and less deliberately to Swahili in a large part of sub-Saharan Africa. Even in this more modest sense, neutrality would then be lost again, and the whole process of designing a neutral language would need to be relaunched from scratch.

More importantly, one must ask why neutrality in this more modest sense should matter. I can think of two plausible answers to this question. One is that a neutral language, so defined, does not belong to any particular people, to any community of native speakers. Consequently, no national authority will be in a position to adopt a possessive attitude towards it, to decree how it should be used or taught, to fix its standard form and reform its rules. Such a status of a 'no man's language', of a denationalized idiom contrasts sharply with that of some national languages. France, for example, has a tradition of centralized control over grammars and dictionaries and the city from which the French language originated has remained by far the most important centre, demographically and economically, of the area in which it is the main mother tongue. But the contrast is far less sharp with the status of English, at least since the United States replaced the United Kingdom as the Anglophones' main homeland, and it tends to vanish altogether with the status of 'denativized' Globish, at least if people around the world appropriate it as they should, that is as a handy instrument of communication across all borders, and not as the *langue de Shakespeare* which can only properly belong to its cultural heirs.

There is, however, a second answer to why Esperanto being more neutral in the modest sense may matter: not because it belongs to nobody, but because it needs to be learned by everybody. It has already been pointed out above (§1.11) that the variety of English that operates as a lingua franca is distinct from the mother tongues of native speakers of English and therefore needs to be learned by the latter too. It also follows from our discussion of neutrality as equidistance that people with native languages very close to Esperanto will find the latter easier to learn. Moreover, even if Esperanto were equidistant from all existing native languages, Esperanto's being no one's native language does not mean that access to it would be equally easy for all. Although French is the native language of practically no one in the Democratic Republic of the Congo, for example, the ease with which it can be learned varies greatly depending on how frequently one's family and social circumstances provide cost-less opportunities for effective exposure. Similarly, if Esperanto were to operate as a lingua franca, there would be significant inequalities between those whose cosmopolitan family background provides plenty of opportunities to practise it and thereby to learn it effortlessly and impeccably from an early age and those who grow up in closed, linguistically homogeneous communities and will need far more effort to reach a far lower level of fluency.

The upshot of all this is not that the choice of English as a European or global lingua franca is more fair than the choice of Esperanto would be, nor that the two options are equally fair, or that that they are incomparable in terms of fairness. Esperanto does have some fairness advantage over English based on greater 'neutrality' understood either (overambitiously) as equidistance or (modestly) as non-nativeness. But this advantage, huge at first sight, shrinks dramatically once scrutinized. If Esperanto's fairness advantage over English as a global lingua franca is only marginal and/or ephemeral, it can be easily overridden by efficiency considerations. The argument for English (or any other natural language) against Esperanto (or any other natural language) has never been, and could never have been, that it is more neutral or more fair, but that going for it would be far more efficient in providing us with the effective communication tool we urgently need at the European or the global level. Since some variety of English is already the mother tongue of a few hundreds of millions of human beings and a second language for several hundreds of millions more, choosing English rather than an artificial language to be learned by everyone would seem to save a considerable amount of laborious learning effort and scarce resources.

(b) Simplicity

This is where the second key argument for Esperanto kicks in: simplicity. The fairness argument based on neutrality may be weak. But it is combined with an efficiency argument based on simplicity, and the simplicity advantage reinvigorates the fairness argument because, it is claimed, far less effort is required to learn Esperanto than to learn English as a foreign language. Opting for English or rival natural languages amounts to inflicting very unequally a huge learning cost. As argued above, opting for an artificial language such as Esperanto rather than a natural language cannot pretend to inflict equal costs. But the costs, with Esperanto, will be far smaller and the unfairness, therefore, greatly reduced. Put differently, the difference the choice of Esperanto would make in terms of fairness has far less to do with making journeys to proficiency in the lingua franca more equal than with making them much shorter. Can simplicity provide the decisive argument which neutrality could not yield?

When compared to languages like English and French with a spelling established long ago and conservatively managed, and even more so when compared to languages using a non-alphabetic writing system, Esperanto undoubtedly possesses the great advantage of offering a particularly straightforward relationship between oral and written forms. More crucially still, syntactic and morphological rules are exception-free in Esperanto, and therefore undeniably far simpler to learn from a grammar book than are those of natural languages, all plagued with exceptions of all sorts. Esperanto, therefore, is and will remain far easier to learn. Or at least so it seems. But here again, appearance can be misleading.

First, it is worth reminding ourselves of the mechanism, well-documented in natural languages, that leads to the regularization (and lengthening) of forms that become less frequent and to the shortening (and irregularization) of forms that become more frequent. Through such a mechanism—in which mislearning by children plays a key part—natural languages are able to operate complex trade-offs between the minimization of memory effort and the minimization of pronunciation effort.[60] The more intensively a language is used, the more the latter matters relative to the former. A written, formal-learning-controlled language—such as Esperanto has been, unlike natural languages, from its birth—can be expected to be shielded against such creative adjustments and hence less responsive to the functional pressures that prompt them. However, once turned into a really living language—and especially once learned from childhood onward—it can be expected to be subjected to similar pressures, with the longer, more regular forms being gradually driven into obsolescence by the shorter and less regular ones.

Secondly, if Esperanto is to be made suitable for all contexts, it will need to beef up its lexical stock massively. Its internal resources make it possible to create an indefinite number of words by combining roots, but these long compounds have to compete with shorter imports from other languages, especially from those languages widely known among Esperanto speakers. If Esperanto is to become a medium of lively mass communication, rather than a venerable work of art cherished and displayed by people with plenty of time at their disposal, there is little doubt as to which side will win. Consequently, like all Western languages today, Esperanto will massively borrow from English, possibly more than other languages because of its smaller initial stock. Hence, it will not take that long for the dictionaries of Esperanto to start looking as bulky as those of other major contemporary languages, with a slim core of Esperanto roots that can be learned in a matter of days and a huge periphery of borrowings. As meanings become more complex, owing to metaphorical and other deviant uses, the Esperanto lexicon, its many subtle nuances and countless local variants would soon take about as long to be mastered as that of any other language equally distant from one's mother tongue.

If this analysis is correct, a far greater morphological and lexical simplicity is only a transitional advantage. There is, however, a much more serious objection to the claim that Esperanto is and will remain significantly easier to learn than a widespread natural language. The strong prima facie plausibility of this claim rests on a bookish picture of language learning, which may be realistic enough as a depiction of how most twentieth-century Esperantists learned Esperanto, but is completely out of touch with the bulk of effective language learning in today's world. As argued earlier (§1.3), the achievement of competence in a language is above all a matter of having the opportunity to play, whisper, and quarrel, listen to music, watch TV, and browse the web in that language, and of being motivated to do all these things, especially at an early stage in one's life. If this more realistic picture of large-scale language learning replaces that of studious pre-TV, pre-internet devotees confined to grammar manuals and vocabulary lists, the decisive question to ask, when assessing how easy it is to learn a language, is not how beautifully simple its rules are but how widely it is used in situations one is likely to be in or in media one is likely to be exposed to, whether intentionally or not. If ease of learning, so conceived, is the crucial criterion for deciding, under present conditions, between Esperanto and English, then it is obvious what the answer should be.

One could legitimately object that a Europe-wide or worldwide movement to invest massively in the learning and use of Esperanto could quickly make this answer far less obvious. It is therefore important to understand the nature and size of the obstacle to any voluntary, bottom-up, decentralized movement of this sort. In the case of widespread natural languages, such bottom-up movements are quite common because of the secure minimum return guaranteed to any investment in their acquisition. There is, first of all, a formidable written and now increasingly audio-visual corpus available in these languages, centuries old and every day richer, to which one can be sure one will gain access by virtue of learning the language in which it was originally produced or into which it has been translated. It would take a long time before an equivalent repository of novels and poems, songs and films, scientific articles, and political manifestos could be built up in an artificial language. But this is not what matters most. If one chooses to learn a natural language, there are those tens or even hundreds of millions of native speakers with whom one can be sure one will acquire the capacity to communicate: a powerful incentive and a huge reservoir of opportunities. In the case of an artificial language, there is no similarly firm guarantee. Whether the effort will redeem itself crucially depends on whether a sufficient number of other people (or governments) will be willing to make and keep making the deliberate effort of learning and using the same artificial language, say Esperanto, which is itself dependent on how confident they are that others will make that choice and stick to it.[61]

To provide everyone—individual or government—with the guarantee that everyone else—or at least enough others—will make a similar investment and thereby make the investment of those who made it worthwhile, one needs a coercive, centralized, top-down approach. An encouraging precedent seems to be provided by the transformation of Hebrew from a dead language into the native language of a majority of Israelis. The operation succeeded because it could rely on the commitment of a strong state endowed with the power and authority to impose the medium of education and administration.[62] Nothing of the sort exists at either the European or global level, or is likely to emerge soon. Moreover, for an agreement to emerge at that level, one must be able to make a powerful case for the collective switch to the proposed artificial language. Neutrality considerations, however, turned out to be far weaker than seemed at first blush even in the European context, and exceedingly weak from a global standpoint. Esperanto's simplicity advantage over English, on the other hand, is genuine but, in large part, temporary and anyway of little weight, as regards ease of learning, against the disadvantage of its incomparably more modest presence in people's current competence and environment worldwide. This disadvantage could be remedied, but only through the vigorous coordinated action which the consensus aimed at is meant to bring about but cannot presuppose. In the meanwhile, the clock is ticking. As competence in English keeps spreading, Esperanto's handicap keeps growing in terms of both opportunity and motivation to learn. Consequently the efficiency case for sticking to English gets stronger by the day, and the prospect of ever reaching the degree of consensus required for the indispensable top-down strategy, perhaps not so illusory at the time of the League of Nations, can safely be said to have vanished nearly a century later.

Where does this leave us? Neutrality considerations confer some slight advantage to Esperanto over English in terms of fairness. This advantage would be considerably amplified if it could be shown that Esperanto is far easier to learn than global English. But its superiority in terms of (sustainable) simplicity is generally overstated, and the relevance of greater simplicity is overshadowed by the opportunities and motivation that derive from the sheer amount of competence and material currently available. The ever growing advantage English has achieved in this respect weakens— possibly even reverses—the argument in favour of Esperanto (and *a fortiori* any other artificial language) in terms of fairness of access. At the same time, it provides an ever stronger efficiency-based argument in favour of

English, which the ever weaker fairness-based argument is less and less likely to override. Anyone concerned with the pursuit of global justice—not only linguistic justice—in the twenty-first century and aware of its linguistic preconditions (as spelled out in §§1.9–1.10) should have no hesitation recognizing that, in choosing a lingua franca, considerations of linguistic fairness narrowly conceived, especially as weak as they turn out to be, must yield to efficiency considerations. The urgent need for a European and worldwide lingua franca demands that we exploit to the full the tremendous asset, in terms of both motivation and opportunity, associated with the existing stock of competence in English and with the widespread expectation that it will keep growing.

Esperanto is a wonderful way of linking up a fantastic bunch of generous and hospitable people around the world. For people eager to hook into this network, its learning is well worth the trouble. As an alternative Europe-wide or worldwide medium of communication, it is no more hopeful than clever software.[63] And luckily so for Esperanto enthusiasts: would their language retain its flavour and their community retain its warmth once appropriated by capitalists and bureaucrats?

3. Lingua franca pluralism

Having granted that we need a natural language, perhaps we should not rush into asserting that we need only one. Why not have two, three, or more lingua francas side by side, with an identical status, as is occasionally proposed in the European context? Unsurprisingly, support for this proposal is overrepresented among the native speakers of the few languages that stand a chance of being added to English, should some variant of a plural regime be implemented. There are two crucially different ways of understanding a plural lingua franca regime.

(a) Disjunctive plural regime

On the *disjunctive* interpretation, this pluralism consists in viewing one or more lingua francas as substitutes for each other: each person is expected to learn only one of them. Reflection on some very modest arithmetic exercises should suffice to make us quickly discard this version of the idea.

Admittedly, if the members of some population all learn one out of two languages—say, English or French—random sets drawn from this population will be able to communicate far more frequently than would be the case were their second language chosen at random among a larger number of languages. As illustrated in Box A.1, the percentage of random groups of six people with a language in common is nearly doubled from 26 per cent to 58 per cent as a result of adopting this double lingua franca regime if the choice is between three languages, and it is lifted from 1 to 17 per cent of the cases if the choice is between six languages.[64] However, as Box A.1 also shows, the percentage of the groups which the double lingua franca regime provides with a common language decreases quickly as the size of the groups and the number of native languages in the population increase.

By contrast, the learning by all of one and the same lingua franca obviously provides a common language in 100 per cent of the cases, whatever the size of the groups and the number of native languages. Thus, in the example with six languages, a random group of four or more has far less than a fifty–fifty chance of having one language in common under a double lingua franca regime, whereas it is certain to have one under a single lingua franca regime. Moreover, this far superior result can be achieved with a sizeable discount (one third of the cost with three languages, one sixth with six), as those whose native language functions as the lingua franca can be exempted from learning a second language without any impact on the percentage of groups with a common language.

Compared to a single lingua franca regime, therefore, a disjunctive plural regime performs badly despite a higher cost even with a small number of languages and for encounters involving few people, and it performs abysmally when the encounters involve many people with many different languages.

(b) Conjunctive plural regime

There is, however, another interpretation of lingua franca pluralism that performs just as well as the single lingua franca option in ensuring inter-communication in all groupings. This *conjunctive* interpretation consists in viewing the two or more languages granted lingua franca status not as substitutes but as complements. In other words, the rule is no longer that each person must learn one of the lingua francas, but that she must know them all. This may sound at first sight like an absurdly expensive overkill: two or three times more learning without any gain in inter-communication, since one lingua franca is sufficient. Advocates of this formula argue, however, that it is easier to acquire (though admittedly even easier to believe or pretend that one has acquired) a passive knowledge of a language than an active knowledge of it.[65] And all this conjunctive pluralism requires is an active knowledge of one of the lingua francas and a passive knowledge of the other(s).

Little reflection suffices to understand, however, that as the number of native languages increases beyond a very small number, this second version of lingua franca pluralism also becomes unpromising. In the European context, French is keen to share the lingua franca status of English. But if it did, Germans would need to achieve an active competence in either French or English, while in addition having to acquire a passive knowledge of either English or French. As they form the largest native language group, they would understandably find this hard to accept. If Francophones are to have a chance of winning their case, they therefore realize that they need to broaden their alliance by proposing that French should share the lingua franca status not only with English but also with German.[66] But how will the Spanish, the Italians, and all the rest feel? Making life more comfortable for the Germans and the French by exempting them from achieving an active competence in English makes things considerably worse for each of the others, now compelled to acquire a passive knowledge of two more languages without being exempted from the obligation to acquire an active competence in at least one of them.

Consequently, however rhetorically packaged, any attempt to press for the adoption of one's own native language as a additional lingua franca in

---

Box A.1 Probability of at least one language being shared by all members of random groups under three language regimes

Regime 1. No lingua franca: Native speakers of each language learn a second language chosen with equal probability among the other native languages.

Regime 2. Double Lingua Franca: Two languages are picked as lingua francas (LF). Native speakers of each LF learn the other LF as a second language. Native speakers of a non-LF learn either LF with equal probability.

Regime 3. Single Lingua Franca: One language is chosen as the LF. Native speakers of other languages learn the LF. Native speakers of the LF learn no second language.

Case A: Three native languages

Group size	2	3	4	5	6
(1) No Lingua Franca	1	0.78	0.56	0.38	0.26
(2) Double Lingua Franca	1	0.89	0.78	0.68	0.58
(3) Single Lingua Franca	1	1	1	1	1

Case B: Six native languages

Group size	2	3	4	5	6
(1) No Lingua Franca	0.60	0.22	0.07	0.03	0.01
(2) Double Lingua Franca	0.83	0.57	0.39	0.26	0.17
(3) Single Lingua Franca	1	1	1	1	1

this conjunctive sense will immediately be perceived and denounced as what it is: trying to get greater comfort for oneself, quite legitimately at the expense of increasing the burden on those who currently enjoy the privilege of having had their own native language picked as the only lingua franca so far, but far more problematically also at the expense of further increasing the burden on all other linguistic communities currently not better situated than one's own. Broadening the alliance by adding one or more further lingua francas unavoidably further increases the burden on any linguistic community still left out and further boosts the global cost of the language regime. Moreover, it quickly runs the risks of turning the net benefit expected from the inclusion of one's language into a net cost: a passive competence of yet another language may be less burdensome to acquire than an active one, but it still requires quite a large investment if the language to be learned is not very close to one's own. Hence, in the context of today's European Union or any other context in which many linguistic communities would be left out under any realistic conjunctive plural lingua franca regime, there is no way in which the latter could be defended on grounds of either fairness or efficiency. Though more effective in terms of ensuring universal inter-communication, it is therefore no more promising than the disjunctive regime.

CHAPTER 2

Linguistic justice as fair cooperation

2.1. Anglophones as free riders

In Chapter 1, I argued on two grounds—ethical contagion and political feasibility—that commitment to egalitarian global justice justifies a strong presumption in favour of the spreading, in Europe and throughout the world, of a single lingua franca, that is of one language which should enable us all to communicate with one another, irrespective of our mother tongues. In this light, it seems that the powerful dynamics that currently drives the spreading of competence in English should not be resisted or reversed, but on the contrary welcomed and accelerated. However, this can only be a provisional conclusion. For the spreading of the lingua franca itself may be a source of injustice. If so, there may be ways of removing or alleviating such injustice, and—possibly under some conditions—the spreading of a lingua franca may remain, all things considered, a trend to be cheered and fostered. But this cannot be taken for granted. The challenge needs to be taken seriously.

I shall address this challenge by discussing in turn three interpretations of the putative injustice generated or amplified by the adoption of a lingua franca. The interpretation that is the subject of this chapter is perhaps the most obvious one. It certainly fits the way many people perceive and articulate the linguistic injustice they believe they suffer and occupies a significant place in Europe's current language debates. However, of the three interpretations it is the least important from my standpoint.[1] Discussing it in depth will yield surprises and prove instructive, but nothing in this discussion is essential, except negatively, to the main conclusions of this book.

This first way in which the putative linguistic injustice can be captured is in terms of unfair cooperation. Competence in a shared language provides a major *public good* by virtue of enabling communication between all those who share that competence. A lingua franca satisfies the two standard conditions commonly held to define a public good in the technical sense economists give to this expression. First, it is *non-rival*, in the sense that 'consuming' the lingua franca—by using it in order to communicate with a native speaker of a language different from one's own—does not reduce its amount. Indeed, because of the opportunity dimension of language learning stressed earlier (§1.3), 'consuming' a lingua franca increases its amount: it improves or at least preserves competence in the lingua franca for those thereby given the opportunity to practise it. Secondly, it is *non-excludable*, in the sense that it would be prohibitively expensive to monitor the 'consumption' of the lingua franca so as to be able to make people pay individually in proportion to how much they benefit from its use.

Non-excludability paves the way to *free riding*. The latter consists in some people enjoying a public good without sharing in the cost of producing it. In the case of a lingua franca that is a natural language, large-scale free riding looks pretty much unavoidable. While not contributing to the production of the public good of potential communication across linguistic communities, its native speakers benefit from it no less than those who brought it about by learning a second language. This free riding by the the native speakers of the lingua franca is often experienced and denounced as a major form of linguistic injustice by those who had to put a lot of time, effort, and money into the learning of a language which they may still speak, understand, write, and read with considerable difficulty.[2] That some may find this situation frustrating is understandable enough. But is it unfair? After all, those who choose to learn the lingua franca in addition to their native language do so voluntarily, in their own interest. In support of the view that fairness does require some degree of burden sharing, consider the following analogy.[3]

A number of years ago, I spent a few months, together with my family, living with my father-in-law. After a while, one feature of our common life started bothering me: as soon as any amount of dust became visible, my father-in-law got the vacuum-cleaner out of the cupboard to get rid of it. As a result, all the cleaning was done before the level of dirtiness reached would have triggered my doing the cleaning myself, and my standards of cleanliness were permanently more than met without any work on my part. No power relationship or altruism was involved, or at least needed to be. Yet, the structure of the situation was such that I systematically benefited from my father-in-law's toil without contributing myself in any way to the public good he produced. Even on the generous assumption that neither I nor my offspring were responsible for any of the dust, this seemed unfair to me, and to restore my peace of mind (and enhance the probability of my remaining welcome?) we soon struck an explicit deal involving some compensatory performance—toilet cleaning, if I can trust my memory.

Lingua franca learners find themselves in a situation analogous to my father-in-law's. By learning a second language in their own best interest, they are producing a public good which others enjoy at no cost to themselves, just as my father-in-law is doing when cleaning the floor. To simplify, just think of two linguistic communities, each with its distinct native language, living together in a country, on a continent or on a planet, in the same way as my father-in-law and I had to live, albeit for a while, in the same house. The cohabitation of the two communities leads to many types of interaction in which the availability of a shared language, produced by asymmetric learning, proves highly useful. For example, the native Anglophones who read these words benefit from my having laboriously learned from age fifteen how to understand, pronounce, read, and write the words they happily learned as toddlers and how to order them more or less the way they do. Had it not been for this learning effort, they would never have had access to the insights I am in the process of sharing with them. Big deal, they must think. But they will have no difficulty imagining situations in which the linguistic competence acquired by others would make a far more dramatic difference to your welfare. Just think of them in a Spanish or Sri Lankan bar trying to articulate as clearly as possible 'I think I swallowed my spoon'. How salutary for them that the waiter put enough effort into his English lessons to be able to identify without delay the nature of their discomfort. This is one of the innumerable ways in which all of us potentially benefit from the existence of a lingua franca, and some of us—the native speakers of the lingua franca—without contributing to the cost of making it exist.

The question is whether fairness requires that non-contributing beneficiaries be asked to share the cost of producing the benefit. If it is just a one-off thing, or if the benefit is tiny or uncertain, or if the beneficiaries are doing all they reasonably can to avoid enjoying the benefit, there is a case for not bothering with cost sharing. Displaying geraniums on your window ledge does not make it fair, let alone sensible, for you to collect a fee from any passer-by. But what we are talking about in the case of a worldwide lingua franca is massive and protracted interaction with substantial contributions that are systematically one-sided and produce benefits that are eagerly (though often unwittingly) enjoyed. Under such conditions, if only to avoid embarrassment or resentment, or to make our inter-action smoother, more relaxed, and thereby, quite possibly, more profitable for both, all things considered, it makes sense to think together about what could count as a fair arrangement. The latter need not entail equal contributions to the cost of producing the joint benefit. It may even allow free riding to continue in one domain of interaction, providing it is offset by compensatory free riding in another. But whether in the cleaning anecdote or in the linguistic case, assessing the fairness of the pattern of interaction requires us to specify an appropriate criterion of cooperative justice.

2.2. Indefinite learning versus one-off conversion

Before turning to a critical discussion of what this criterion might be, it is important to spell out and scrutinize one potentially contro-versial feature of the way in which the question of fair cooperation has been understood so far. As formulated, this question is not about how much the non-lingua-franca-speaking communities—or, as I shall call them for the sake of brevity, the *peripheral* communities—need to get by way of compensation for switching to the lingua franca as the home language they will transmit as a native tongue to the next generation. It is rather about how much of the language-learning burden will need to be shared on the assumption that peripheral communities stick to their native languages while learning another one later in life, generation after generation. But why should the latter formulation be preferred to the former?

Here again, an analogy may prove useful. Suppose the dwellers of both a city and its surrounding countryside all benefit greatly from spending most of their days side by side in the city, for example by working together. It therefore makes sense for the country dwellers, spread in all directions around the city, to do the commuting. It may also make sense to ask how much it would be fair for city dwellers to contribute to the cost of the commuting, at least supposing that country dwellers did not deliberately choose to settle in the country, but happened to live there at the time the potential benefit from spending days side by side arose. However, beyond the short term, the acknowledgement of this joint benefit and of the legitimacy of co-financing it unavoidably prompts the question of whether the right thing to do is to subsidize permanent commuting or to fund a one-off move. The former is bound to be cheaper in the short run but more expensive in the long run, and its adoption therefore needs to be justified.

Cooperative justice between linguistic communities could analogously be conceived either as a fair sharing of the cost of permanent commuting—that is of the learning of the lingua franca by the present and all subsequent generations of speakers of the peripheral languages—or as a fair sharing of the cost of a one-off move—that is of the replacement of the peripheral languages by the lingua franca as a common native language. In this case too, the former formula—funding the asymmetric bilingualism of many generations—is bound to end up more expensive than the latter—the conversion process of one or two. If the world were to be turned, linguistically speaking, into a Republic of Ireland writ large, its linguistic communities might be entitled to a far more generous compensation from today's Anglophone countries than what the Irish people got from the United Kingdom as English replaced Irish as their mother tongue, but this is bound to be far less, in a sufficiently long run, than the cost sharing of permanent second language learning would require.

So, how can one justify using the more expensive formula for framing the issue of fair cooperation? In the commuting case, one would need to invoke, in addition to the collective good of spending days close to each other, either the collective good of spending nights and weekends spread over a broader space (maintenance of the rural landscape, better social control in smaller towns?) or some general right to keep living in the same place with extra costs, if any, picked up by all. In the absence of either a further collective benefit or a strong entitlement of this sort, it seems fair that the part of the cost of indefinite commuting that exceeds the cost of moving once and for all should be entirely borne by those with an expensive taste for living far from the centre.

Analogously, in the lingua franca case, one could try to argue that the undeniable convenience of linguistic homogeneity is offset by at least one of the following two considerations: each peripheral linguistic community is entitled to the preservation of its language with the extra cost, if any, to be supported by all and/or linguistic diversity can plausibly be expected to generate significant beneficial consequences for every affected party. Both these lines of argument raise serious problems, which will be discussed later on (in §§5.7 and 6.5, respectively). But neither is necessary, in the linguistic case, to justify the particular framing of the question of fair cooperation proposed in the previous section, because of a third possibility, not captured by the analogy between country dwellers and peripheral speakers.

The country dwellers with whom the cooperative deal needs to be made can decide where to live, and hence where to commute from. And if they choose not to move, they cannot legitimately charge the additional cost to the others who do move, or who do not need to move because they grew up in the city. It seems that the same could be said about peripheral linguistic communities: if they choose not to switch to the lingua franca as their native language, they cannot legitimately charge the additional cost to those who do switch and to those who do not need to switch because the lingua franca happens to be their native language. But this analogy relies on an illegitimate personification of linguistic communities.

It is between the current generations of the various linguistic communities that a fair deal is being sought. Members of the current generation of peripheral speakers cannot choose their own native language, and hence cannot be regarded as having inflicted upon themselves any part of the cost of learning. They do have some grip on the language in which the next generation will grow up, and reducing the number of peripheral native speakers would reduce the cost, including the part to be imputed to the lingua franca native speakers, but only in the next generation. If the deal is not between trans-generational communities, but between the present generations of each community, fairness cannot require the present generation of lingua franca speakers to pay higher compensation to the peripheral speakers on condition that they bring up their children in the lingua franca and thereby make the next generation as a whole better off.

When thinking about fair linguistic cooperation, it is therefore appropriate to take each generation of speakers with the native languages they happen to have and compute the cost of learning and the fair contribution by non-learning beneficiaries within this single-generation time horizon. This is at any rate what I shall assume in the remainder of this chapter. This reasonable assumption may prove unnecessary if an adequate case can be made either for a right of linguistic preservation the cost of which needs to be borne by all or for linguistic diversity as such being in the general interest. Whether or not such a case can be made, the discussion of the present chapter remains meaningful if a single-generation framework is deemed appropriate.

2.3. A stylized picture

Against this background, let us turn to the chief task of this chapter, which is to specify the most defensible criterion of linguistic justice understood as cooperative justice. Consider two linguistic communities, whose native languages are called F(ranca) and P(eripheral), with respectively N and n (smaller than N) native speakers. Suppose that the cost c of learning a second language is the same for all speakers of both languages and can be measured using the same metric as the one used for benefits.[4] The learning of the other language generates a gross benefit B for an F-speaker, and a gross benefit b for a P-speaker. This gross benefit will be supposed to be given simply by the number of speakers the learning enables a person to communicate with, that is $B = n$ for each F-speaker and $b = N$ for each P-speaker. The net benefit for one person is the gross benefit (B or b) minus the cost of learning (c) in the case of those who do the learning.

A more sophisticated index of the gross benefit could meaning-fully incorporate a comfort coefficient that reflects superiority or inferiority in the interaction: the per capita benefit is higher if communication occurs in one's own native language, it is lower if it takes place in an idiom learned later, in which one never feels quite as comfortable. The index could also be adjusted upward or downward so as to reflect how likely it is that one will interact with a member of the other linguistic community, for example by being made a negative function of physical distance. Or it could be adjusted to reflect how useful this interaction is likely to be, for example by being made a positive function of per capita wealth. To keep things as simple as possible, however, I shall abstract from this more fine-grained characterization of the benefit and simply assume that, irrespective of whether the P-speakers or the F-speakers do the learning, the benefit created for each speaker by the fact that all are now able to communicate with each other is exactly given by the number of new potential speech partners each speakers has acquired as a result.

Language learning is efficient from the standpoint of the population as a whole if and only if it generates, in the aggregate, a surplus, that is if and only if the total benefit deriving from one of its two communities learning the other community's language exceeds the total cost of this learning. I shall call β the total gross benefit, given by $N.B + n.b$. Under the simple assumptions made about the measurement of each speaker's benefit, this total benefit is equal to $N.n + n.N = 2N.n$, or twice the number of pairs of people who become able to communicate with one another as a result of the whole of either of the communities learning the language of the other. This gross benefit is the same, irrespective of which of the two communities does the learning. The total cost, by contrast, is affected. It is $n.c$ if the learning is by the n P-speakers, and $N.c$ ($>n.c$) if it is by the N F-speakers. The necessary and sufficient condition for the possibility of the overall net benefit being positive is therefore that the total gross benefit $2N.n$ should exceed the minimal total gross cost $n.c$, or equivalently that $2N > c$.

It is crucial to observe that the necessary and sufficient condition for either of the two communities to derive a positive net benefit from learning the other language is unavoidably more demanding than this condition for the possibility of an overall surplus. F-speakers will benefit from learning P if and only if $B = n > c$, while the P-speakers will benefit from learning F if and only if $b = N > c$. Obviously, it is arithmetically possible for the per capita cost c to fall short of $2N$ (and hence being worth paying overall) while at the same time exceeding N and *a fortiori* n (and hence not being worth paying for the members of either community). This is what opens the possibility of a discrepancy between on the one hand laissez-faire, decentralized individual choice to learn or not to learn without any collective intervention, and on the other hand efficiency in the minimal sense of Pareto optimality. In other words, the uniform individual cost of learning (c) can exceed the benefit from learning for every potential learner (N or n), thus killing any individual or community-wide incentive to learn, even though the overall potential gain from learning ($2N.n$) is such that some could be made better off without anyone needing to become worse off if the learning were performed (at total cost $n.c$).

To illustrate this possibility with a simple numerical example, suppose the F-speaking community consists of Frank and Frances, while the P-speaking community has a single member Petra. The gross benefit (i.e. abstracting from the cost, if any) to one of them of the learning of a second language (by him/herself or someone else) has been posited above to be 1 for each of the speakers with whom this learning enables him/her to communicate. Let us now stipulate that the *gross cost* (i.e. abstracting from the benefit) of learning the other language is 3 for the person who does the learning. The net benefit for each is given by the difference between gross benefit and gross cost. The total net benefit or cooperative surplus is the sum of gross benefits minus the sum of gross costs. This yields:

Benefit for each of the Fs of being able to communicate with Petra: $B = n = 1$.

Benefit for Petra of being able to communicate with the Fs: $b = N = 2$.

Total gross benefit: $\beta = N.B + n.b = 2 \times 1 + 1 \times 2 = 4$.

Per capita cost of learning and total gross cost if Petra does the learning: $c = 3$.

Cooperative surplus if Petra does the learning: $\beta - n.c = 4 - 3 = 1 > 0$.

Thus, the total benefit exceeds the total cost. Yet neither for Petra nor for the Fs is the benefit expected from being able to communicate sufficient to make their own learning worthwhile.

2.4. Efficient cost sharing: Church and King

With this stylized picture of costs and benefits in mind, I shall consider the question of how fairness requires the cost of learning to be shared among all those who benefit from the learning. I shall do so by presenting and discussing four criteria, some versions of which can be found in the fields of public economics, political science, moral philosophy, and social psychology, respectively. I shall reject the first three and argue in favour of the fourth one.

What motivates the first of these criteria can easily be explained by reference to the numerical example just given. What would happen there under laissez-faire, that is in the absence of any intervention? Frank and Frances will not learn P, since the net benefit of doing so would be negative for each of them $(1 - 3 = -2)$. Nor will Petra learn P, for the same reason $(2 \times 1 - 3 = -1)$. But this outcome is inefficient once account is being taken of communication externalities, that is of the benefits derived by some from the language-learning by others. True, if Frank and Frances were learning Petra's language, the overall net benefit would remain negative, as the costless benefit for Petra $(2 \times 1 = 2)$ would not offset the net cost to Frank and Frances $(2 \times (-2) = -4)$. But if Petra were learning the language of the majority, the costless benefit for Frank and Frances $(2 \times 1 = 2)$ would exceed the net cost to Petra $(2 \times 1 - 3 = -1)$.

Under such circumstances, there is an obvious case for intervention, and a no less obvious suggestion as to its level. Efficiency can be reconciled with individual voluntary choice if Petra's willingness to learn the Fs' language earns her a subsidy at a level sufficient to induce her to do so. In our example, a minimally sufficient sharing of the cost of learning will need to take the form of a tax of slightly more than 0.5 on both Frank and Frances to fund a subsidy of slightly more than 1 to Petra. Added to the direct benefit of being able to communicate with the Fs $(= 2)$, this subsidy will just exceed Petra's gross learning cost $(= 3)$. Relative to the no-learning situation, the total net benefit is then 1, and each of the three speakers is better off. This corresponds exactly to the cost-sharing rule proposed by Jeffrey Church and Ian King (1993) as an appropriate way of internalizing the 'network externalities' of language learning, that is the benefits generated for any user of a network by the fact that one more user joins it.

Note that, from this pure efficiency standpoint, there are many situations in which communication externalities do not need to be compensated. Suppose that there are four Fs instead of just two. Petra's gross cost of learning remains unchanged (= 3), but her gross benefit doubles (= 4 × 1), thus yielding a positive net benefit for her (4 − 3 = 1), even in the absence of any cost-sharing by the Fs. Hence, Petra will learn the Fs' language even if she has to bear the entire cost. No Pareto-improvement could be achieved through the introduction of a subsidy and consequently no such subsidy is justified from Church and King's pure efficiency standpoint.

What our criterion is meant to capture, however, is not linguistic efficiency but linguistic justice. And the distribution of costs and benefits endorsed by Church and King's criterion is, to put it mildly, not self-evidently fair. Just reflect on what it mandates in our example. In the initial version of our example (with two F-speakers), Petra ends up, after subsidies, paying most of the cost of producing a net benefit nearly 100 per cent of which is enjoyed by Frank and Frances. In the variant with four F-speakers, each of them enjoys the same net benefit (= 1) as Petra (= 4 × 1 − 3), but Petra bears alone the entire cost. In this linguistic example, just as in the cleaning analogue used above (§2.1), the fact that the benefit is voluntarily produced is surely not enough for it to be fairly produced. Is there any criterion around that could make a more credible claim to expressing the demands of cooperative justice, as distinct from cooperative efficiency?

2.5. Equal cost sharing: Pool

Identifying a language regime that could reconcile efficiency and justice is precisely the chief objective of an interesting essay by Jonathan Pool (1991). His point of departure can be presented as follows. In a situation in which there are two or more distinct native languages, it is easy enough to identify a choice of one official language that would be fair: for example, no one learning any other language, or everyone learning all other languages, or each learning one language picked at random, or everyone learning the same other language, either natural or artificial, so remote from each of the native languages involved that it can be regarded as equidistant from all of them. It is also easy to identify a solution that would be efficient: the language with most native speakers being learned by the native speakers of all other languages—at least if it does not happen to be exceptionally difficult to learn. But the fair solutions seem bound to be inefficient, while the efficient solution is clearly unfair. Is there a way of escaping this dilemma between fairness and efficiency?[5]

Pool thinks that there is, providing one selects the most wide-spread native language as the common language and organizes transfers to those who learn it as a second language—for their own benefit but also everyone else's—whether or not the personal benefit they derive from learning it is sufficient to motivate this learning. What is the criterion that determines the fair level of transfers? Necessarily one that is more demanding than Church and King's efficiency-guided rule: Pool's proposal is that the cost of learning is to be shared by the various linguistic communities involved in proportion to their sizes. In other words, the per capita contribution to the production of the lingua franca must be the same for all the linguistic communities involved. Assuming, if only for simplicity's sake, that there is no reason to treat differently different members of each community, this implies that each of the beneficiaries needs to contribute an equal share of the cost. In the version of our example with two lingua franca speakers, Petra will do the learning, but the cost of this learning (= 3) will need to be divided equally among Frank, Frances, and Petra (1 each).

This criterion certainly looks far more plausible than Church and King's as a characterization of the fair sharing of the burden of producing a public good. Or at least it does so as long as one's attention is not drawn to the way in which the total net benefit of the learning is distributed among the three speakers. As it happens, Petra appropriates 100 per cent of this benefit, since Frank's or Frances's contribution (= 2×1) to the cost of Petra's learning is exactly equal to the benefit each derives from being able to communicate with her (2×1). Indeed, had Petra's learning cost been even very slightly higher (say, 3.3 instead of 3), the total net benefit would have remained positive ($2 \times 1 + 1 \times 2 - 3.3 = 0.7$), and hence the learning would still have been worth doing, but Frank and Frances's net benefit would have become negative ($1 - 3.3/3 = -0.1$), as the cost sharing required of them by Pool's criterion would have made them worse off than if Petra had not bothered to learn their language.

Consequently, Pool's criterion of equal per capita cost does reconcile efficiency—the adoption of the learning pattern that maximizes the overall net benefit—with some attractive egalitarian conception of burden sharing, but it overshoots the mark: it inflicts a net loss on some, which makes it an unacceptable criterion of cooperative justice, that is of the fair distribution of a cooperative surplus which should leave none of the cooperators worse off than in the absence of cooperation.

2.6. Equal benefit sharing: Gauthier

To solve this difficulty, it is worth considering a third criterion that can be gleaned from a very different corner of the existing literature. After the economics of networks and the politics of language policy, let us turn to moral philosophy. As a general criterion for the fair distribution of the benefits from voluntary cooperation, David Gauthier (1986: 271–2) proposes that the relative benefits of all parties be equalized. More explicitly, fairness requires that one should equalize the ratio of each cooperator's actual benefit from the cooperative venture (relative to what her situation would have been in the absence of cooperation) to the maximum benefit she could have derived from it (consistently with the other cooperators not being made worse off than they would have been in the absence of cooperation).[6]

The level of production of the public good chosen, in the calculation of each of the cooperators' maximum benefit, needs to be the one that maximizes the total net benefit. In our example with three speakers, this corresponds to the pattern in which Petra learns F while the F-speakers learn nothing.[7] Petra's maximum benefit then consists in her appropriating 100 per cent of this total net benefit (1), thanks to a transfer of 1 from both Frank and Frances, which leaves each of them indifferent between the production of a lingua franca thanks to Petra's bilingualism (1 − 1 = 0) and universal monolingualism (0). On the other hand, Frank's maximum benefit is achieved when he appropriates 100 per cent of the total net benefit (1), by letting Frances alone contribute a transfer of 1 towards Petra's learning costs, thus leaving both Frances ($1 - 1 = 0$) and Petra ($1 \times 2 - 3 + 1 = 0$) no better or worse off under Petra's bilingualism than under universal monolingualism (0).

Given that the maximum benefit is necessarily the same for all three—namely the whole of the cooperative surplus under the surplus-maximizing regime, equalizing their relative benefits will obviously require that each should achieve the same absolute improvement relative to universal monolingualism, that is an equal net benefit of 1/3. This requires, in our example, a pattern of transfers to the language learner less stingy than under the Church and King regime—just enough to prompt the learning—but less generous than under the Pool regime—an equal contribution by learners and non-learners alike. To lift Petra's net benefit to the level of their own, as demanded by Gauthier's criterion, Frank and Frances will both have to pay her 2/3, so that Petra ends up with a total subsidy of 4/3 towards her learning effort, and hence a net benefit of 1/3 ($= 2 \times 1 - 3 + 2 \times 2/3$). The risk of overshooting inherent in Pool's criterion has now vanished. For as the cost of learning increases (while remaining less than the total benefit, and hence worth incurring), the subsidy by non-learners will increase, but it will never make them worse off than in the absence of cooperation, that is under universal monolingualism. Each cooperator's equal net benefit will remain strictly positive as long as the learning is worth doing.[8]

This is an improvement, but still not good enough for us to be at peace with our intuitions. One may start suspecting that there is still something not quite right when noting that even after having received the transfer mandated by Gauthier's criterion, Petra is still bearing a disproportionate share of the learning costs—more on her own (5/3) than the other two together ($2 \times 2/3$). However, this imbalance is getting worse as the inequality in the sizes of the two linguistic communities increases. For example, if the number of F-speakers is doubled (from 2 to 4), the total gross benefit of Petra's learning F swells from 4 to 8, while the gross cost remains unchanged ($= 3$). The equal division of the total net benefit ($8 - 3 = 5$) attributes 1 to each of the five speakers, and since this is precisely what emerges in this case in the absence of any transfer, Petra can be left to bear the whole of the learning cost by herself. If the number of F-speakers swells even further, the Gauthier-inspired criterion

of equal net benefit requires us not only to let the F-speakers get a
free ride and leave Petra to do all the work unsubsidized; in addition
Petra needs to pay a fee to the F-speakers, as a reflection of the large
communication potential the Fs jointly offer to Petra.[9]

As in the case of Pool's criterion, it would be possible to get rid of
the most extreme counterintuitive implications by adding an ad hoc
stipulation, in this case the condition that the learners must not be
worse off under the deal than they would be under laissez-faire.[10]
Laissez-faire is not equivalent to absence of cooperation: if the
learning is happening spontaneously for the benefit of others than
the learner, there is cooperation under laissez-faire. Such a restriction would not prevent Gauthier's criterion from condoning free
rides by the F-speakers on Petra's learning, but it would prevent it
from requiring Petra to pay a fee. However, it is also possible to
formulate a distinct criterion, which avoids in one swoop the under-
shooting of Church and King and the distinct overshootings of
unrestricted Pool and Gauthier, while also getting rid of a number
of less extreme counterintuitive implications.

2.7. Equal ratio of cost to benefit: Homans

I now turn, finally, to the 'rule of distributive justice' formulated by
the sociologist George Homans (1961: 72–8, 232–64) and subsequently used in the social-psychological literature under the name
of 'equity'. Homans' empirical conjecture is that in many contexts
of human cooperation (or 'exchange') feelings of fairness and resentment are guided by a rule of proportionality between 'investment'
and 'profit', with 'investment' understood very broadly to cover
age, seniority, or gender as well as effort or skills.[11] The criterion
I am proposing as a normative criterion of cooperative justice is a
particular specification of this rule. It simply requires that one
should equalize the rate of return to investment for each cooperator,
or conversely the cost–benefit ratios for all those involved in the
cooperative venture.

The cost is understood as before as consisting either in the amount
of resources (teacher time, textbooks, classrooms) and personal time
invested in the process of learning the shared language, all translatable
into an equal cash amount for all learners or in a tax paid by

non-learners to learners. The benefit is here most conveniently understood as the gross gain from cooperation, that is the gain abstracting from any cost incurred. But if gross benefit is proportional to cost, so is net benefit.[12] For the sake of maximal simplicity, the benefit, like the cost, is supposed to be uniform for all members of the same community and to be given by the number of speakers of other languages with which learning the shared language makes communication possible. The proposed criterion amounts to requiring the cooperative surplus to be distributed in proportion to each party's contribution to the cost of producing it.[13] Since the learning is only worth doing if the total (gross) benefit exceeds the total (gross) cost, the ratio of total cost to total benefit must be strictly smaller than 1. What the proposed criterion requires is that this overall ratio should apply to each speaker involved, and hence also to each of the two linguistic communities taken as a whole.[14]

As a criterion of cooperative fairness, this criterion has decisive advantages over each of the criteria examined so far.[15] In contrast to the Church and King criterion, it implies that as soon as someone needs to bear some cost for the public good to be produced, no one can fairly derive a benefit without making some contribution. In contrast to the Pool criterion, it implies that the cost can never exceed the benefit for some unless it exceeds the benefit for all, in which case the learning is pointless. And in contrast to the Gauthier criterion, it implies that learners will never be required to subsidize non-learners, since fairness will always require the latter to make some contribution.

As the number of F-speakers increases—and hence also the potential overall benefit from the learning of language F by the P-speakers—the adoption of the proposed criterion requires a total subsidy from the F-speakers to the F-learning P-speakers the size of which remains fixed at exactly half the learning cost, whatever the absolute or relative number of speakers.[16] This equal cost sharing between linguistic communities reflects the fact that the aggregate gross benefit increases to exactly the same extent for the P-speaking community and for the F-speaking community, in proportion to the number of F-speakers with whom the learning enables the P-speakers to communicate. Under our rough but not absurd assumption that equates benefit and number of potential speech partners, the equal cost–benefit ratio criterion thus supports a simple 50/50 cost-sharing rule between the two linguistic communities: the native speakers of the lingua franca need to support half the cost of its learning by the native speakers of the other language.[17]

Rather than rushing into applying this simple cost-sharing rule to the learning of English in the real world, it is essential to first consider, again in stylized form, the more general case in which there is more than one F-learning linguistic community. The learning of F is then not only a way for F-learners to get access to F-speakers (and provide F-speakers with access to the F-learning non-F speakers). It also becomes a way for subsets of non-F-speakers to get access to each other. In this general case, our criterion still requires the equalization, across all members of all linguistic communities, of the ratio of the cost to the gross benefit. And this cost is given, as usual, by the cost of learning the lingua franca (for those who do the learning), minus the subsidy (for those entitled to positive transfers) plus the tax (for those liable to negative transfers). But the gross benefit for each speaker is given by the aggregate size of all linguistic communities except her own, and this is now no longer the same as the size of the F-speaking community. The required equalization is achieved when taxes and subsidies are calibrated in such a way that the ratio in each community is equal to the ratio of the aggregate cost (still simply assumed to be given by the uniform per capita cost of learning multiplied by the size of the non-lingua-franca population) to the aggregate gross benefit (still simply assumed to be twice the number of pairs of people which the availability of the lingua franca enables to communicate with one another).

Suppose, for example, that the F-learners now belong to two distinct linguistic communities of equal sizes, with P and Q as their respective native languages. The benefit of any P-speaker learning the F language is the same from the standpoint of any member of F as when all F-learners belonged to the same linguistic community. But any F-learning P-speaker is now enabled by the learning to communicate not only with F-speakers but also with F-learning Q-speakers, thereby also bestowing a benefit upon these Q-speakers. The implication is that the gross benefit accruing to each of the F-learners is higher than in the two-language case, without the per-capita cost of learning having increased. Consequently, our criterion of proportionality between cost and benefit will entitle them to transfers from the F community that now amount to less than 50 per cent of the cost of their learning. The more linguistically divided the F-learners, the greater the benefit they get from being able to communicate with other non-F-native speakers, and the smaller therefore the contribution that can be fairly expected, according to the criterion proposed, from the F community. For example, with an F-speaking community twice the size of the set of all other communities taken together, the share of the learning cost to be borne by the F-speaking community can be shown to fall from 50 per cent to 40 per cent as the number of distinct non-F communities increases from 1 to infinity.[18] To generalize: under the simplifying assumptions made, if the F-speaking community is very large relative to all others, our criterion will still require it to pay a considerable fraction of the learning cost, never more than half of it, but never much less.

2.8. Why the small may subsidize the big

More surprising and at first sight more embarrassing is another implication of our criterion: a subsidy may be owed to some F-learning communities not only by the F-speaking community whose language they are learning, but also by some other peripheral F-learning communities. To understand why this may happen, consider first the case in which the lingua franca picked by two linguistic communities is not the native language of either of them, but a third language, say Esperanto, which I shall suppose can be learned at a dramatically reduced cost $c = 1$.[19] Take again Petra, Frank, and Frances, who now all make the same effort to learn Esperanto. Having learned Esperanto (while the other two do the same) gives Petra a gross benefit of 2 and a cost–benefit ratio of 1/2. Frank and Frances, instead, each end up with a gross benefit of 1 and a cost–benefit ratio of 1/1 = 1. The equalization of cost–benefit ratios therefore requires that Petra, in addition to making the same effort as Frank and Frances, should make a transfer to each of them.[20] The underlying idea is simply that those who gain most from the equal universal effort in which the cooperation consists should cover part of the cost incurred by those who gain least from it.

Once we understand why some learners may have to subsidize other learners in the Esperanto case, it is not difficult to understand why this may happen too when the language learned is the native language of one of the communities involved. Of course, the native speakers of the language that is being learned will have to do much of the subsidizing. But if the learning communities are very unequal in size, the members of the smaller ones among them may gain so much from the existence of the lingua franca compared to the members of the bigger ones, that making cost proportional to benefit may require the former to help subsidize the latter. This will happen when one of the learning communities is very large relative to the rest, including the community of native speakers of the lingua franca. The ratio of cost to benefit for a small learning community can then easily be smaller before transfers than the overall ratio of cost to benefit, because the ratio of cost to benefit for the very large community is very high. To equalize this ratio across all communities will then require that the lingua franca speakers should be taxed, but also the smaller linguistic community.[21]

Is this subsidy owed by small F-learning communities to larger ones an embarrassing implication, in the same league as the one that led to the rejection of the Gauthier-inspired criterion in the previous section? It would certainly be if this chapter were dealing with distributive justice, not with cooperative justice. For what our equal cost–benefit ratio criterion mandates is a tax to be paid by some of the producers to others who expend the same effort but derive a smaller benefit, as measured by the number of speech partners they get access to. Is it not unfair that one should receive a smaller subsidy for a given effort, or even be taxed, just because of belonging to a smaller community, and hence suffering the disadvantage of being provided 'by birth' with less speech partners, while others are getting a higher subsidy (or are being subsidized at all) because they belong to a larger community, and hence enjoy the advantage of being provided 'by birth' with more speech partners?

The perspective adopted here, however, is not that of correcting language-based distributive injustice through transfers from one community to another. This is, for example, why, in the discussion of Pool's criterion (§2.5), it was taken for granted that no community should be made worse off, not relative to the laissez-faire situation—which would amount to endorsing the free riding of the lingua franca speakers—but relative to the absence of cooperation. For a discussion of cooperative justice, that is of the fair sharing of the surplus from cooperation, to get off the ground, the distribution of entitlements that holds in the absence of cooperation must be assumed to be just, or its being just or unjust must be abstracted from. Our concern is not with correcting any distributive unfairness in the pre-cooperation baseline—that will be our concern in the next chapter—but with correcting unfairness in the allocation of the surplus from cooperation. And the proposal is that this surplus should be allocated to the cooperators in proportion to their contribution to the cost.[22]

As a member of a small community benefits more, other things equal, from the existence of a lingua franca, it is fair that she should contribute more to its production, by being subsidized less than members of larger communities, possibly even by paying a tax. This simply guarantees that all cooperators contribute in proportion to how much they benefit. By contrast, the Gauthier criterion rejected earlier condones a tax to be paid by the producers of the public good to those who enjoy it without making any contribution to its production. Unlike this subsidizing of non-learners by learners, the possibility of small learners having to subsidize big learners should not be regarded as fatally counterintuitive once we take care to switch off any intuition unrelated to the cooperation context.[23]

2.9. Estimating the cost of language learning

In this discussion of linguistic justice *qua* cooperative justice, I have examined four possible criteria, each with at least some prima facie plausibility, but with strikingly different implications.[24] By formulating what I regard as decisive objections to the first three criteria, I have indicated why I believe the fourth criterion to make most sense. Suppose we adopt it. What, then, are the chief policy implications of linguistic justice so conceived in the real world?

Whether coerced or spontaneous, asymmetric bilingualism of the sort captured in stylized fashion in our simple illustrations has been a frequent phenomenon in many places for a long time. But as schooling, mobility, and communication expand and intensify, it is becoming more ubiquitous and more massive than ever. Abram de Swaan (1993, 2001) has aptly described our speaking species as forming a worldwide language system firmly held together by asymmetric plurilingualism: native speakers of peripheral languages learn the central language of their area; native speakers of central (or lesser) languages learn one of a dozen supercentral languages, that is regional lingua francas; and native speakers of supercentral (or lesser) languages learn the emerging hypercentral language, that is the worldwide lingua franca. This structured plurilingualism is arguably quite efficient: it generates a huge cooperative surplus. However, by the standards of our proposed criterion, it is very unfair. To make it fairer, transfers are required. Can one make some intelligent guesses as to how high they would need to be?

One possible point of departure is the average time required to master adequately a non-native natural language. One guess is 10,000 hours,[25] which can be compared to a standard school year totalling less than 1,000 hours in the classroom. But this sort of estimate is intrinsically problematic. In the first place, the notion of 'mastering' a foreign language is very fuzzy. Once the basic syntax and morphology are learned, hundreds of hours may be needed for tiny improvements in pronunciation, fluency, use of idiomatic expressions, and respect for grammatical exceptions, as well as for expanding one's lexical repertoire. At what stage should the timer be stopped? Secondly, the number of hours required through a classroom method for any given level of competence is obviously affected by the linguistic distance between one's mother tongue (and other languages learned previously) and the language to be learned. Should all combinations of languages be considered, or only some of them, and if so which, and how should they be weighted to provide an average? Thirdly and most importantly, as emphasized earlier (§1.3), the effectiveness of what happens inside the classroom is very sensitive to motivation and opportunity and hence to what is going on outside the classroom. The 'average' time needed to achieve any level of proficiency in a language is therefore crucially dependent on the way in which the countless combinations of native language, learned language, and socio-linguistic context are being weighted—an exceedingly tricky matter, both conceptually and empirically, to say the least.

A more promising point of departure can be sought in estimates of the cost of actual language learning. Here again, pitfalls abound. But a convenient conjecture can reasonably be made on the basis of the difference between the annual cost of foreign language teaching in state schools in France and in the United Kingdom. This difference is estimated to amount to about €100 per inhabitant (not per pupil or per proficient speaker).[26] This is quite rough, and there are no doubt many factors that bias this estimate both upward and downward. In particular, it does not incorporate the resources spent on private language lessons both at home and abroad, nor the opportunity cost of the time devoted to language learning by the learners themselves.[27] For present purposes, however, it would be futile to look for an exact figure. The exercises we are about to consider could easily be rerun with a higher, lower, or more differentiated figure. All we need is an order of magnitude in answer to the following question: Had a language other than English been picked as the European and global lingua franca, how much would the UK have had to spend per capita to achieve the average level of proficiency in the lingua franca currently achieved by the French in English? This will give us an idea of how much our criterion of cooperative justice would require the Brits to pay and the French to receive under various assumptions that will gradually take us closer to the situation actually obtaining in the real world.

Before doing so, however, I should mention three important complications relating to this estimate of the cost of learning that will be deliberately ignored in the exercises to follow. First, the cost of learning a completely alien language—as English is for the Chinese—can be expected to greatly exceed, for any indicator of oral or written proficiency, the cost of learning a language that is just a variant of one's own—as English is, comparatively speaking, with respect to French. Taking this complication into account would require the cost estimates to rise overall and to vary considerably across combinations of languages. As a consequence, the overall level of subsidy entailed by our criterion of cooperative justice would increase at the expense of native Anglophones, who would be better off with more native speakers of French and less native speakers of Chinese in the world. Moreover a greater proportion of this subsidy would need to be directed to populations with non-Indo-European languages: the French would lose, the Chinese would gain.

Secondly, how high the cost of learning is and how much it differs from one language to another depends on the learning method used. The bookish learning of grammar and vocabulary by adults may cost a lot more, for a given level of proficiency, than immersion, media exposure, and other interactive methods at a young age. What must be used as the basis for calculating the Anglophone community's fair liability—and everyone else's fair entitlement—is arguably not the actual cost incurred, however inefficient the learning method used, but rather the cost implied by the most efficient of the methods to which the community can reasonably be assumed to have access. If some linguistic communities choose not to avail themselves of effective tools used by others, both fairness and efficiency recommend that they should not be compensated for these choices. Whether through increased contributions (from the non-learners) or reduced subsidies (to the learners), other linguistic communities cannot be expected to foot any portion of the resulting extra bill.

Thirdly, note that the learning cost is endogenous to the very diffusion of the lingua franca. As competence in English spreads worldwide, the quantity of learning may be rising, but its unit cost is likely to fall. This is not immediately obvious, as one might think that the first segment of a population to learn a foreign language is also the one with the greatest aptitude for learning it. There are, however, two good reasons to expect falling marginal costs. First, the dissemination of competence in English, both globally and locally, makes it possible to provide prospective learners far more cheaply with the competent teachers they need: it is no longer necessary to import native speakers at high cost or to send children to immersion courses in native territory.[28] Secondly, and even more importantly, as the number of (non-native) potential English speech partners expands along with the likelihood of meeting them, there are more and more opportunities to speak, listen, read, and write in English, and there is nothing like the expansion of costless opportunities for speaking a language to cheapen the learning of it. Consequently, the swelling of the global cost of lingua franca learning is likely to be far less than proportional to the swelling of the amount of learning.[29] At the limit, if it ever became as easy and natural to learn the lingua franca as it is to learn one's mother tongue, linguistic injustice, understood as the unfair distribution of the burdens of lingua franca production, would vanish altogether.[30]

2.10. Real-life approximations

For the time being, however, the learning of a lingua franca does involve a significant cost, and our present task is to figure out what a fair distribution of its cost would mean in the real world. By way of a first approximation, suppose that the world reduces to the French and British populations (of about equal sizes), each supposed to be linguistically homogeneous, and hence that the learning of English by the French serves no other purpose than to enable the two populations to communicate, actively and passively, with one another. Suppose further that the benefits of this learning are enjoyed symmetrically by both sides. This ignores various real-life complications and involves biases in both directions. For example, the Brits are able to chat, correspond, bargain, argue, etc. with the French using a language in which they feel more comfortable. On the other hand, language learning provides the French with an access to English-language material accumulated by British people throughout the centuries, and such access is of little benefit to the present generation of Brits. Assuming equal levels of benefit may therefore be reasonable enough. Under these assumptions, our criterion of proportionality between cost and benefit implies that half the cost of €100 per capita should be billed to the British population, and hence €50 per capita or roughly €3 billion transferred annually as a fair contribution to the current learning of English by the French.

However, the British and the French are not alone on the planet. Very roughly again, there are five times more native Anglophones than there are people living in the UK, and one hundred times more non-Anglophones than there are people living in France. Assuming, for simplicity's sake, that the level and cost of the learning of English is the same in the rest of the non-Anglophone world as it is in France, the total cost is multiplied by one hundred, and hence also the part of it to be funded by the Anglophone countries, now up from €3 billion to €300 billion. Fortunately for the UK, this amount is to be shared with other Anglophone countries. But unfortunately for all of them, this makes only five times more people, and the per capita subsidy our criterion says they owe to the rest of the world therefore seems to have to be multiplied by 100/5 = 20, up from €50 to a hefty €1,000 per capita.

Is this what our criterion of fair cooperation implies? Far from it. This conclusion would follow only if the lingua franca learners consisted of one big community of six billion people who share the same native language, and hence for whom the benefit of learning English reduces to communication with Anglophones. But the six billion non-Anglophones are split up among six thousand distinct native languages, and even for the many among them who know a non-native language other than English that enables them to communicate with some non-Anglophones, access to English is a major potential benefit to them by virtue of the many other non-Anglophones with whom convergence towards English enables them to communicate. Because of this huge additional benefit accruing to English learners, achieving proportionality between cost and benefit necessarily requires a smaller transfer from native Anglophones to English learners. How much smaller?

To answer this question, we need to specify the proportion of each linguistic community that is assumed to become proficient in the lingua franca as a result of the learning whose cost needs to be fairly shared, or at least proficient enough to be able to communicate with its help with Anglophones and other non-Anglophones. Such a specification was not needed as long as we had only two linguistic communities: whether the proportion of the Francophones that have been made proficient with €100 per capita is 1, 50, or 100 per cent of the Francophone population, the Anglophones have to foot half the bill. But when there is more than one learning community, the benefit to each depends on how effective the learning is in each of the other learning communities. If the proportion of people made proficient in each linguistic community is negligible, most of the benefit to each will come from being able to communicate with native lingua franca speakers. If it approaches 100 per cent, by contrast, most of the benefit will come from talking with each other, and the fair contribution of the lingua franca community to the cost of learning will be accordingly reduced. If only for arithmetic convenience, let us suppose that at the cost of €100 per capita 10 per cent of each linguistic community achieves the relevant level of proficiency in the lingua franca.[31]

Suppose now that the non-Anglophone population of the world consists of 100 linguistic communities of 60 million speakers with a learning cost of €100 and a proficiency rate of 10 per cent. Our criterion can then be shown to imply that only a quarter of the learning cost, rather than half should be borne by the Anglophones, and hence their tax liability would shrink (relative to the incorrect prima facie conclusion formulated above) from €1000 to €500 per capita.[32] At the limit, if 100 per cent of all 100 linguistic groups became competent, the percentage contribution legitimately expected from the Anglophones would even drop to 5 per cent of the total. But, assuming the per capita cost of learning remains unchanged, the total cost would grow tenfold, and we would therefore be back to a per capita contribution of €1,000 by each Anglophone.[33]

Let us now make one more step towards the real world by departing from the assumption that all non-Anglophone communities are of equal size. As we saw above (§2.8) group size inequality justifies differentiation in the per capita levels of subsidy. It may even justify transfers from smaller to larger communities. The subsidy to the learning by large communities might therefore need to be co-funded by the Anglophones and by small non-Anglophone communities. Given the distribution of potential learners among linguistic communities in our real world, however, this latter situation is unlikely to arise. Subsidies could only be required from small learning communities if the biggest learning community—the Mandarinophones— formed a even bigger proportion of the total population than it actually does. But differences in size do lead to differences in subsidy levels: the smaller the linguistic community, the smaller the per capita level of the subsidy to which it is entitled.[34]

2.11. A linguistic tax?

However many refinements we may wish to add, the pattern of transfers that can be justified by our criterion of equal cost–benefit ratios will involve some considerable contribution from Anglophones. If proportionality between cost and benefit is the right criterion and if the empirical assumptions made above (§2.9) are not too far off the mark, a country like the UK can safely be expected to have to pay an annual amount of no less than €500 per capita. This amount will increase or decrease over time depending on how fast the volume of learning increases relative to the predictable decrease of its cost per unit. On the other hand, a country like France can, on the same assumptions, expect to receive annually a subsidy in the order of €25 per capita. This amount can be expected to fall over time, however, despite increased learning and cost in France, because of increased learning elsewhere.[35] How can one imagine implementing the transfer scheme thus shown to follow from cooperative linguistic justice?

Most straightforward would be to charge a global tax to the native English community and leave it to allocate this tax among its members, while distributing the proceeds among other linguistic communities so as to equalize all ratios of cost to benefit. But linguistic communities are not political communities endowed with a formal power to tax. Nor do they usually have the sort of informal grip on the wealth of their members which many religious communities can boast. A more plausible though rougher approximation consists in taxing countries, that is politically organized communities, in proportion to the number of English native speakers they house. One may, and probably should, exempt the countries with a small proportion of English native speakers, not only because this would not be worth the administrative trouble, but also because whatever English native speakers they have may be presumed to be particularly mobile, and hence likely to largely elude whatever allocation of the tax burden might be designed.

This leaves us with a sizeable tax to be levied on the few countries in which the bulk of the English native speakers live—in particular the United States, home to 70 per cent of them—and to be spread by these countries among their citizens. When distributing this tax, these countries may understandably baulk at the prospect of targeting the native English speakers among their residents, if only because this would have the implication of perversely penalizing those immigrant families that assimilate most successfully. But in all those countries in which there is a significant degree of interaction between native Anglophones and non-Anglophones, there would be little harm done in failing to differentiate between them for two main reasons: first, non-Anglophones living among Anglophones generally enjoy particularly favourable conditions for learning English, and hence tend to incur a lower cost of learning; secondly, a public school system funded mostly by native Anglophones is likely to provide effective language teaching to local non-Anglophone children, who thereby enjoy sizeable in-kind transfers.

So far so good. But is it not pointless to speculate about the most sensible way of sharing the burden of a tax that is most unlikely to ever come about. This is not the sort of tax that is going to be imposed by force. Hence, the governments of the Anglophone countries will need to be persuaded—in English, of course—that this is a fair tax for them to pay. Why should they provide massive subsidies for the learning of English all over the world, when such learning is happening anyway on a grand scale, powerfully driven by the individual and collective self-interest of hundreds of millions of people? Providing a persuasive answer to this question is a daunting challenge, however you approach it, even if all governments concerned were able to understand and willing to accept the general claim that massive free riding on other people's efforts is ethically problematic. But perhaps we should not give up too quickly.

One possibility would be to bring the matter up whenever supranational organizations need to be financed. The most massive supranational budget is that of the European Union. For over twenty years the debate on the way in which contributions should be distributed between member states was dominated by the so-called 'UK rebate' which Margaret Thatcher managed to bring home, after much bickering, in 1984. When part of it was cancelled and a new compromise was reached on this issue in December 2005, would it not have been appropriate to bring up the implicit transfer to the UK from the rest of the EU as a result of asymmetric language learning?[36] The British rebate under discussion was in the order of €4.5 billion annually. But under the assumptions made in the previous section, the UK owes €30 billion annually to the non-Anglophones of the world, while the non-Anglophone EU population is owed €10 billion by the Anglophones of the world.[37] So why not forget about the 'UK rebate' and even ask the UK for a little additional effort? A fair contribution to the worldwide production of a mutually beneficial lingua franca requires far more to be done, by Brits and others, to subsidize the learning of English throughout the world. But contributing an additional €5 billion to the EU budget would be a promising start, while leaving the USA, Canada, Australia, and New Zealand to do their fair share of the job in other continents.

2.12. Compensatory poaching?

If this looks too haphazard, too dependent on contingent opportunities, what about compensatory free riding? To understand the huge potential of this alternative avenue, it is important to bear in mind a powerful trend. As English increasingly suffices to get by wherever one happens to be, both the incentive and opportunity to learn English will increase, whereas the incentive and opportunity to learn any other language will decrease. As a result, English will become more and more a globally public language, whereas other languages will remain or increasingly become globally private languages. 'Private' is not to be taken here in the sense of being restricted to people's domestic sphere, but in the sense that what is uttered in it is accessible to only a relatively small proportion of the people one has some chance of interacting with, whereas what is uttered in the public language is immediately accessible to all. Those who have no language other than the public one are far more liable to give away information to any outsider who cares to listen or read. This may take some minor forms. For example, whatever your mother tongue, you may benefit from overhearing two American tourists telling each other, in the queue to the museum, that the door to the toilet is locked. Had they been Finnish, you might have lost in vain your place in the queue.

Such trivial asymmetric benefiting may seem hardly worth mentioning. But as more and more information gets uploaded onto the web, easy to access, copy and use worldwide, this asymmetry is taking gigantic proportions. Whatever the web makes available to the three or four hundred million native Anglophones is being made available simultaneously to the hundreds of millions of non-Anglophones who bothered to learn English or are learning it now, and are likely to be seriously over-represented among web users from their respective countries. By comparison, very little of the information that these hundreds of millions are putting on the web in their own native languages can be 'overheard' by Anglophones—or indeed by the native speakers of any language but their own—because so few of these, comparatively speaking, know languages other than English and their own.[38] As long as a significant proportion of potentially useful content is produced and made available in a wide variety of languages,[39] a deep asymmetry remains. This asymmetry should at least partly cancel the advantage derived from one's language having become the lingua franca. Indeed, it may provide the only realistic chance of ever cancelling that advantage to a significant extent.

Whereas the political prospects of a trans-national linguistic tax are dim, it is trivial to observe that poaching—here understood very broadly as accessing useful information without compensatory payment—is already happening on the web quite massively.[40] Protecting intellectual property rights effectively is far more difficult now that most information is accessible in electronic format through the web and no longer attached to a physical medium. Consequently, such poaching, tolerated or not, will assume ever growing proportions. In the internet era by far the most effective lock on the dissemination of information is the language in which it is expressed. But it operates selectively: it works only for those who do not understand it, and therefore cannot detect it, nor browse it efficiently, nor read it properly without great expense. As English spreads, all English material gets unlocked for the world—not least through the language-specific operation of powerful search engines—and poaching becomes increasingly asymmetric. True, once competence in English has spread at a high level throughout the world, English-language material of more than local interest may be produced proportionally as much by non-Anglophones as by Anglophones, and the perpetrators of the poaching will coincide far more than now with its victims. But by then, the learning of English may have cheapened to such an extent that there will be little to compensate for.

Admittedly, this is only rough justice. For a start, even assuming all of the information accessed in this way is identified, it is not exactly easy to assess its value. And unless we do so, we are unable to state at some stage that the poaching of English material by, say, the French must stop, because they have had access to their annual quota of free Anglo-produced material (€25 × 60 mn = €1.5 billion), in exchange for the language learning they do at their own expense for everyone's benefit. So, how should the material accessed be valued? The price the owners of the information are trying to get for it cannot serve as a standard of valuation: what is deliberately made accessible on the web free of charge is not *ipso facto* unworthy of being taken into consideration in the accounting of fair compensation. How convenient or awkward it would be to make beneficiaries pay for a public good, or how keen or reluctant the producers of the public good are to avail themselves of this possibility, should in no way affect the assessment of the benefit level relevant to the application of our criterion of proportionality between benefit and cost. Nor is the fact that the information producers would have produced it even in the absence of an expectation of reward by non-Anglophones sufficient to make it count for nothing—just as the voluntary nature of language learning does not disqualify the possibility of free riding. In analogy to the case of language learning (or floor cleaning), something like the cost of production must be used. On the benefit side, something like each linguistic community's aggregate willingness to pay is presumably the least bad reference point.

Another difficulty is that the match between the beneficiaries of the linguistic free riding and the victims of the compensatory free riding may be very poor. Does the compensation proposed not amount to stealing blindly from a large number of people on the ground that some of them do not pay their due? Those who lose out through the plundering of the information they worked hard to produce may only very approximately coincide with those who benefit from the hard work that is being put worldwide into learning English. This lack of coincidence should not be exaggerated, and the poaching strategy is unlikely to be much less well targeted than the least badly targeted of all feasible schemes for taxing Anglophones. For the English native 'symbol analysts' who are losing out in fees and royalties also tend to be among the cosmopolitans who most benefit in a wide variety of ways from the spreading of the lingua franca. And if less revenue can be collected abroad as a result of permissive legislation or lax enforcement in matters of intellectual property, they will have to recoup their costs and secure the profitability of their activities on Anglophone territory, which will be a way of sharing the cost with a far wider constituency of Anglophones.

Consequently, taking it very easy with the pecuniary aspect of intellectual property accessible on the web may provide the least bad way, admittedly quite messy, of organizing fair compensation for asymmetric language learning. Free access to English-language content on the web—or indeed in (increasingly obsolete) printed form—can plausibly be advocated on grounds of cooperative justice. When no intellectual property rights protect them, no moral self-restraint should be exercised. When intellectual property rights do protect them, no vigorous efforts should be deployed to enforce them in non-Anglophone countries. Nor can collaboration be legitimately expected for the sake of redressing the resulting asymmetric (net) benefiting by non-Anglophone individuals and countries. For this is nothing but compensatory (if not retaliatory) free riding, a rough compensation for the massive benefit offered free of charge to Anglophones by the hard learning of non-Anglophones. To return to the spatial metaphor (§2.2): when it is in everyone's interest that everyone should always meet in the same place, it is fair that those who do not need to do any travelling should be charged part of the travelling expenses. If they are not, they can fairly be expected to compensate by offering dinner. And if they fail to do so, the others might as well help themselves from the fridge.

Where does this leave us? Under contemporary conditions, there is a problem that can be characterized as language-based cooperative injustice in the form of free riding by the native speakers of the lingua franca. But as the very spreading of the lingua franca makes its learning less hard, the free riding associated with asymmetric bilingualism should become less significant. Less and less asymmetric poaching of English web content will be justified as a result. But less and less asymmetric poaching will be happening anyway, as more and more English content will be coming from non-Anglophones. Even if we were to give central importance to linguistic justice as cooperative justice, therefore, we would have good reason to be very relaxed about it: all that can and must be achieved in this dimension is rough justice, for which no more is needed than a benign attitude towards the asymmetric flows of information that are the correlate of the spreading of the lingua franca.[41]

However, what has been presented in Chapter 1 as the ultimate standard is not fair cooperation, but global egalitarian justice. And from this standpoint, all we have been discussing in Chapter 2 is no more than wrinkles on the surface, cooperative deals between communities against the background of entitlements that are unjustly distributed, and indeed even more so as a result of the adoption of a lingua franca. Linguistic justice in this distinct distributive sense will be addressed systematically in the next chapter. It is nonetheless worth noting that those committed to global egalitarian justice have some reason to welcome the policy implications that emerge from the present chapter. This would have been the case had we stuck to financial compensation as the best conceivable implementation of cooperative linguistic justice, on the safe assumption of an imperfect yet strongly positive correlation between the wealth of a country and the proportion of its residents who have English as their mother tongue. But this is even more the case with the more realistic alternative implementation we ended up with. Not only does the plundering of English-language internet content contribute to the further spreading of the lingua franca, to be cheered for the reasons developed in §§1.9–1.10. In addition, global egalitarians are most unlikely to bemoan the recommendation that one should resist or circumvent any attempt by greedy fingers to lock what is no longer linguistically locked, any attempt to fetter the free worldwide flow of knowledge and ideas to which the spreading of a global lingua franca is giving a wonderful unprecedented boost. Global egalitarians may have only limited patience for the mean accountancy that goes into determining how the cost of language learning by (sometimes rich) communities needs to be shared in order to satisfy a plausible criterion of fair cooperation. But they will not protest if it leads more people to support policies that will help the world move in the direction they believe is right.

Formal expression of the four criteria of fair cooperation in the case of two linguistic communities

Under the simplifying assumptions made in §§2.1–2.3, let us consider the case of two linguistic communities, one consisting of native speakers of the lingua franca F and one consisting of a peripheral language P. Each of the four criteria introduced and discussed in §§2.4–2.7 can then be compactly restated as a formula for the size of the subsidy to each of the F-learning P-speakers.

The per capita gross benefits of there being a shared language, respectively for each of the N F-speakers (Frank and Frances in our example) and for each of the n P-speakers (Petra in our example) are given by $B = n$ and $b = N$. The per capita cost of the P-speakers learning F is given by c, the per capita subsidy (to P-speakers) by t and the per capita tax (on F-speakers) by $T = (n/N).t$.

(1) According to Church and King's criterion of efficient cost sharing (§2.4), the transfer must very slightly exceed the difference between the per capita cost and the per capita benefit for P-speakers, subject to this difference being positive and to the learning of F by P-speakers generating an overall surplus. The conjunction of these two conditions simplifies into requiring c to be larger than N but smaller than $2N$. Hence:

$$Church \ \& \ king : t = c - b + \epsilon$$
$$= c - N + \epsilon, \text{ subject to } N < c < 2N.$$

(2) Pool's criterion of equal cost sharing (§2.5) demands that the tax paid by each (non-learning) F-speaker be equal to the gross cost of learning borne by each P-speaker minus the subsidy each of them receives. Given the budget constraint $(N.T = n.t)$, this amounts to subsidizing a proportion of the cost of learning equal to the share of F-speakers in the total population. Hence:

$$Pool : t = c - T = c - (n.t/N) = c.N/(N + n).$$

(3) Gauthier's criterion of maximin relative benefit simplifies, in the cooperative venture under consideration, to the equalization of net benefits

(§2.6). The subsidy to each P-speaker must therefore be equal to the difference between the cost of learning and the gross benefit of each P-speaker (as in Church and King) plus the net benefit (after tax) of each F-speaker. Bearing in mind again the budget constraint, this amounts to demanding that one should subsidize the cost of learning in the same proportion as under Pool's criterion, but only after deduction of the difference between the (higher) per capita gross benefit of the lingua franca community and that of the peripheral community. Hence:

$$Gauthier: t = (c - b) + (B - T) = (c - (N - n)).N/(N + n).$$

(4) Lastly, the Homans criterion of equal cost–benefit ratios (§2.7) requires the gross benefits derived from the learning by each person (and hence by each community) to be proportional to her contribution to its cost, that is the gross cost of learning minus the subsidy (for P-speakers) plus the tax (for F-speakers). Whereas Church and King subsidies cover only the gap between gross cost and gross benefit, the subsidy implied by the proposed criterion covers the gap between the gross cost and a proportion (smaller than 1) of the P-speakers' gross benefit corresponding to the F-speakers' ratio of contributions to benefits (T/B). Whereas Pool subsidies cover the whole of the gap between the P-speakers' per capita learning cost and the F-speaker's per capita tax, the subsidy implied by the alternative proposal covers only the gap between the learning cost and a proportion (higher than 1) of the per capita tax given by the ratio of the P-speakers' to the F-speaker's per capita gross benefits (b/B). Bearing in mind again the budget constraint ($n.t = N.T$) and the simple assumptions about gross benefits ($b = N$ and $B = n$), this reduces to requiring a per capita subsidy corresponding to half the cost of learning. In brief:

$$Homans: t = c - (T/B).b = c - (b/B).T$$
$$= c - (b/B). (n.t/N) = c/2.$$

The key factual assumption that generates this simple result is that the communication links opened up through a language learner's toil are symmetrically valued by the members of the two communities thus connected, and hence that proportionality between cost and benefit requires the community of those who become able to communicate with the learner to jointly foot half her bill. If a comfort factor had been introduced to reflect superiority/inferiority in competition and other forms of interaction, the subsidy would have needed to be higher than $c/2$. If one had heeded the differential importance attached to communication, for example owing to inequalities in wealth or power, the required subsidy, in most circumstances, would have been lower.

APPENDIX 2

Equal cost–benefit ratios with many linguistic communities

Our criterion of equal cost–benefit ratios entails a fifty–fifty rule for sharing the cost of learning only when there is just one community of learners of lingua franca F. As the number of linguistic communities that make up the F-learning population (supposed to be of unchanged total size) increases, the contribution to the total learning cost required from the F-community gradually falls. This can be shown as follows.

When instead of having a single F-learning community of size n, we have many communities i with a varying number n_i of native speakers, the contribution to the cost of learning that can be fairly requested from the natives of the lingua franca is given by the general formula:

$$N.\sum n_i \Big/ \Big(N.\sum n_i + \sum n_i \Big(N + \sum n_i - n_i \Big) \Big),$$

that is the ratio

- of the gross benefit accruing to the F community, that is the number of F natives N multiplied by the number of non-F natives $\sum n_i$)
- to the gross benefit to the whole population, that is the gross benefit $N.(\sum n_i)$ accruing to the F community plus the sum of gross benefits accruing to F-learning individuals by virtue of being able to communicate with the F natives (N) and the natives of non-F communities other than their own $\sum n_i(N+\sum n_i - n_i)$.

In the extreme case in which linguistic diversity is minimal, there is only one non-F community: $\sum n_i = n_i\, i = n$, and the formula simplifies into $N.n/(N.n + n.(N + n - n)) = \frac{1}{2}$.

In the extreme case in which diversity is maximal each of the non-F communities has a negligible number of speakers. Learning the lingua franca is then necessary and sufficient to enable it to communicate with the whole population, and the formula reduces to:

$$N.\Big(\sum n_i\Big) \Big/ \Big(N.\sum n_i + \sum n_i.\Big(N + \sum n_i \Big) \Big) = N/\Big(2N + \sum n_i \Big)$$

With $N=20$ and $\sum n_i = 10$, this contribution by the native F community under maximum linguistic diversity among non-F speakers is $20/(2 \times 20 + 10) = 40$ per cent of the cost of learning. As one moves from a linguistically homogeneous set of lingua franca learners to a maximally diversified one, the share of the lingua franca native community thus shrinks smoothly from 50 to 40 per cent. The larger the total size of the population of F learners relative to the population of F natives, the lower this minimum percentage.

CHAPTER 3

Linguistic justice as equal opportunity

3.1. Liberal-egalitarian justice

In our second interpretation of linguistic justice, language is viewed as an individual asset, not as a public good, and linguistic injustice is understood as a departure from an egalitarian distribution of resources rooted in the diversity of native linguistic equipments, not as a deviation from fair cooperation between linguistic communities. The conception of justice which enters the picture at this stage is the egalitarian conception of global distributive justice which was appealed to in Chapter 1 to articulate a twofold case in favour of the adoption of a lingua franca—ethical contagion and political feasibility (§§ 1.9–1.10). It is not part of the purpose of this book to justify this conception, except by showing that it is useful and meaningful when handling linguistic issues.[1] Nor is it part of the purpose of this book to argue for a particular version of this conception, except again in so far as handling linguistic issues may bring to the fore some shortcomings or difficulties specific to one or more such versions. It is nonetheless important to start this discussion of linguistic justice as distributive justice by spelling out more precisely the egalitarian conception of distributive justice on which it will rest.

This conception is *egalitarian* in the sense that it takes the equal distribution of whatever resources are relevant to enable us to achieve a good life as the fundamental baseline any deviation from which requires justification. More specifically, it allows for justified deviation from equality of resources on two grounds. (1) *Responsibility-sensitivity* makes room for some people to be entitled to more resources than others as a result of the preferences they have or the choices they made. (2) *Efficiency-sensitivity* makes room for some people to be entitled to more resources than others because reducing what they are entitled to would involve an unreasonable cost to others. The first of these grounds for justified inequalities makes the conception *opportunity-egalitarian* (formulated in terms of endowments, luck, capabilities, real freedom, etc.) as opposed to *outcome-egalitarian* theories (formulated in terms of income, welfare, achievements, etc.). The second ground makes the conception *lax-egalitarian* (typically using a criterion of sustainable maximin) as opposed to *strict-egalitarian*.[2]

In addition, this egalitarian conception of distributive justice is *liberal* in two distinct senses: (1) it does not rely on any particular conception of what constitutes a good life, but is committed to respecting equally the variety of conceptions of the good life characteristic of our pluralistic societies (*impartiality*); and (2) it gives some priority to the equal protection of everyone's formal freedom (or 'self-ownership', or 'fundamental liberties') over the equalization of other resources relevant to the achievement of a good life (*liberty constraint*).[3]

The theories of distributive justice developed by John Rawls (1971, 2001), Ronald Dworkin (1981, 2000), Amartya Sen (1985, 2009a), G. A. Cohen (1989, 2000), Richard Arneson (1989), John Roemer (1999) and the one I proposed myself (Van Parijs 1995) are all *liberal-egalitarian* theories of distributive justice of the *lax opportunity-egalitarian* variety, or can easily be construed as such.[4] I shall describe all of them, and not only my own version, as illustrating a conception of distributive justice as *real freedom for all*. The choice of this expression is meant to highlight first that distributive justice is a matter of freedom, but not only of formal freedom, also of real possibilities or opportunities open to individual people (as distinct from the outcomes into which these possibilities are being turned by them); and secondly that this real freedom must be granted not equally but to the greatest extent possible to all. The question I now want to address is whether convergence towards one lingua franca systematically generates distributive injustice understood in this way and, if so, how this injustice needs to be addressed.

3.2. Language, religion, and rights

At first sight, the implications of any liberal theory of justice for language policy are straightforward, just as straightforward as they are for religion. Language, like religion, tends to be transmitted within a community from one generation to the next, as a major component and determinant of that community's culture and as a major feature of people's individual and collective identity. Just as the religion people choose to practise, the language(s) or dialect(s), or idiolect(s) they choose to use when speaking or writing, singing or vociferating, broadcasting or publishing are obvious candidates for protection under the liberty constraint. Perhaps the freedom to learn and use any language one wishes should be viewed as part of the fundamental freedom of expression, or as a self-evident component of self-ownership, namely the right to move one's tongue and lips to produce sounds that obey one set of rules rather than another or the right to move one's fingers on a keyboard in a way that systematically produce sequences of signs drawn from a strongly constrained small subset of possible sequences rather than from another such small subset. The fact that some people may switch from one language to another therefore seems to raise no more issues of justice than the fact that some people may convert from one religion to another. People should simply be left free to make their own choices at their own expense, without interfering with the choices of others nor expecting others to understand them whatever linguistic choice they make. Beyond this guarantee of fundamental rights of toleration, it seems that an institutional framework that aims to meet liberal-egalitarian standards should do nothing, in matters of language just as in matters of religion. In particular, any bias it may show in favour of one language or one religion over another would fall foul of the constraint of impartiality between diverse conceptions of the good life, of which language, like religion, is often a central part. Freedom of choice and benign neglect, therefore, would seem to be all that is needed to guide language policy in a liberal-egalitarian state.[5]

However, there are a number of crucial differences between language and religion that make such a hands-off attitude inappropriate in linguistic matters. First of all, unlike religion, language cannot be 'disestablished'.[6] It is easy enough for public officials, in the exercise of their function, to abstain from praying, but not to abstain from talking. No legislation can be discussed or published, no instruction can be circulated, no declaration can be made without choosing a language in which to do it. States can function without choosing one or more churches, but not without choosing one or more languages.

This is an important difference, but one might think of handling it quite simply within a liberal framework by requiring the state to act not in a hands-off fashion—which it could not do without forfeiting its responsibilities—but in an even-handed way.[7] Since a state could keep away from religion, one could argue that it does not behave impartially when funding religious confessions in proportion to the numbers of their practitioners or religious schools in proportion to the numbers of their pupils. But given that a state cannot keep away from language, it can arguably achieve perfect impartiality as even-handedness by simply adjusting its official use of languages to the preferences of its citizens. If numbers make the added cost reasonable, legislation, official documents and procedures of all types should be provided in as many languages as citizens request. When the linguistic make-up of some country's population is altered by migration or when a language shift occurs spontaneously in some population—as is the case, for example, with the spreading of a lingua franca—official language use can simply follow (and thereby stabilize or amplify) the trend, albeit with some time lag.[8]

What seems to unfold smoothly along these lines is a liberal theory of linguistic justice in terms of *linguistic rights*: first the fundamental negative right to learn and use the language of one's choice for private purposes, and secondly the fundamental positive right to public services in one's preferred language—from education and the judiciary to administration and political participation—at least under reasonable cost constraints. This rights-based approach to linguistic justice—quite often conceived as a wonderful further expansion of a grand list of human rights—has proved the most popular so far among philosophers and also—unsurprisingly—among lawyers. But it fails to adequately capture the most specific aspects of linguistic justice. The whole of this book can be read as an attempt to provide an alternative in which rights (apart from those following from the liberty constraint) are not basic axioms but a heterogeneous set of consequences, some more contingent than others, of a coherent and defensible conception of justice. The divergence is intimately linked to the importance that is here being ascribed to three further ways—in addition to 'undisestablishability'—in which language differs from religion. These distinctive features of language generate issues of linguistic justice that have no parallel in terms of religious justice and cannot be addressed properly under the umbrella of multicultural rights.

One of these distinctive features supplied the point of departure of Chapter 2. Unlike a shared religion, a shared language is, by its very nature, a public good, the production of which has a cost that needs to be shared in a fair way.[9] There is no 'religio franca' pattern analogous to the 'lingua franca', if only because becoming bi- or pluri-religious is trickier than becoming bi- or pluri-lingual. Even if it were as trivial to add a second religion to one's native one as it is to add a second language to one's native one, the central point of doing so could not be in the sharing of this second religion. And even if it were—as perhaps one could argue it is in what could be metaphorically described as the patriotic religion of nation states—it is hard to imagine a problem of fair cost sharing arising between native and non-native practitioners. This is why linguistic justice makes sense as cooperative justice, whereas religious justice does not.

A second additional difference is that membership in a linguistic community, unlike membership in a religious community, is an economically relevant skill. This matters greatly to the opportunity dimension of justice as real freedom for all, and will be at the core of the present chapter. The third difference relates to a feature of language that can be viewed as a generalization of the state's inability to 'disestablish' it. Because of being essentially a medium of communication, language, unlike religion, cannot be abstracted from or left aside in practically any human interaction, however informal. This fact leads to an issue of mutual respect that does not arise in the case of religion and will be at the core of Chapters 4 and 5.

3.3. Language-based inequality of opportunities

Justice as real freedom for all is not only about fundamental formal freedoms, for example to practise the religion or speak the language of one's choice. It is also about the real possibility or opportunity to realize one's conception of the good life in all its dimensions. Both belonging to a particular religious community and belonging to a particular linguistic community may affect one's opportunities because of the discrimination, favourable or unfavourable, which membership in a particular community may trigger. Discrimination constitutes one mechanism through which opportunities are made unequal. It can be defined as differential access to desirable positions, typically jobs, according to some characteristic that is irrelevant to performance in that position. From a lax opportunity-egalitarian standpoint, the response is simple and, it seems, the same in both cases. Since there can be no justification for deviating from equality for the sake of greater efficiency in the case of characteristics that are by definition irrelevant to performance, the objective must be to eradicate discrimination, both religious and linguistic.[10] However, whereas most religion-based inequality of opportunities would be eliminated by such a ban, most language-based inequality of opportunities would subsist. The reason is simple: unlike religion, language is a major productive skill. Or, put differently, even in the absence of any discrimination, one's language, unlike one's religion, can be a major asset or handicap.

Once this feature of linguistic competence is perceived, a new dimension of linguistic injustice becomes visible. As a language becomes dominant in a linguistically diverse environment—for example, the dialect of the capital city in many processes of nation building, or English today in Europe or worldwide—those who have easy access to it, mostly though not only as a native language, arbitrarily enjoy greater opportunities than others. Even if these manage to achieve a high level of proficiency in the dominant language, they can only do so through efforts from which native speakers are exempted. This putative distributive injustice, as experienced and denounced with growing alacrity in connection with the place given to English in Europe, is said to arise through four main channels. In all four cases, what drives the alleged trend is that the increasing use of the lingua franca boosts the demand for the scarce skill of being proficient in it, and hence confers a growing advantage to those who enjoy privileged access to this skill, in particular to native Anglophones.[11]

The first and most obvious form taken by this phenomenon is the quick growth of specifically lingua-franca-related jobs that tend to be reserved for, or given preferentially to, its native speakers. Thus, there has been a surge in the worldwide demand for native teachers of English, for language schools run by native Anglophones and for residential language courses in an Anglophone environment.[12]

Whereas the French or German governments need to subsidize heavily the language courses taught by native speakers of French and German in their *Maisons françaises* or *Goethe Institute* in order to induce people to take them, English language courses are a lavish source of revenue. Even when the people directly involved are not native Anglophones, they make massive use of the products of the TEFL industry ('Teaching English as a Foreign Language') in the form of textbooks, CDs, DVDs, etc., most of them produced by Anglophones in Anglophone countries.[13] Next to the demand for teachers and teaching material, there is also an ever swelling private and public demand for English mother tongue drafters, editors, or proof-readers for reports, regulations, instructions, information boards, websites, broadcasts, advertisements, scientific journals, airline magazines, and countless other publications intended for an international audience. Moreover, the more the provision of translating and interpreting facilities moves away from strict symmetry between languages—the more one relies, in particular, on the audience or readership having at least a passive knowledge of English and the more one resorts to a relay language in order to reduce the number of language combinations to be catered for—the more the demand for interpreters and translators is biased in favour of native Anglophones.

On top of the specifically linguistic jobs that are reserved to Anglophones, there is also, secondly, a large and growing number of jobs that are not specifically linguistic in content and would exist anyway but are openly or tacitly restricted, or are far more easily accessible, to native speakers of English, because of the central importance of being able to communicate in that language in the internal or external relations of the organizations concerned.[14] Added to the biased expansion of language-related jobs, the biased linguistic desiderata for filling other jobs feed a booming demand for people proficient in the lingua franca and hence tend to boost the relative pay of people with native competence in that language. They can ask for higher fees for private language tuition, bargain for higher wages as secretaries, and expect quicker promotion in multinational organizations.[15]

Beyond differential access to jobs, a third channel of distributive inequality is rooted in the fact that whenever the lingua franca is picked as the medium of interaction, its native speakers tend to communicate with greater ease and effectiveness. Whether in private conversations, public debates, commercial negotiations or cultural events, they therefore tend to be more active, better understood, more persuasive, more impressive, more often intentionally witty and less often unintentionally funny than their non-native counterparts. If the language rules that govern a particular event allow for more than one language being spoken (without adequate interpreting), what is gained in greater ease by non-lingua-franca speakers is lost in lesser reach. Job interviews for multinational organizations form one type of interaction of this sort. But landing better jobs as a result of greater success in this context is only one of the many material or non-material advantages that thereby tend to accrue, by virtue of their greater ease, to native speakers of the lingua franca.[16]

A fourth channel emerges as one moves from face-to-face interaction to interaction through the media. Those who write or speak, sing or act in English have access to an ever wider audience relative to those who do so in a different language. This is the case in the first place because more is heard, read, or watched directly in English by non-Anglophones, relative to what is heard, read, or watched by Anglophones in languages other than English. This shows up, for example, in the growing gap between the net export of French and British books and other publications. This primary bias is further amplified by an even larger derivative bias in the flow of translations: for any given language, an ever greater proportion of what is produced in English is translated into it than of what is produced in any other language.[17] This should come as no surprise: the very spreading of competence in English among those who have to make decisions about what to publish in any particular language gives a far greater chance of being spotted and hence of being adapted or translated, for any given level of quality or relevance, to anything that is available in English.[18] And once the process in on the way, marketing strategies focusing on known names will further amplify the process. Of course, many non-Anglophones understand this and a growing number of them undertake to write, speak, sing, or act in English rather than in their native language.[19] But they do so, on average, far more laboriously and far less effectively than native speakers. Here again, there is a massive economic advantage being gained by Anglophones—only a portion of which is reducible to privileged access to jobs—through the sales of their cultural industry, the royalties and fees of English mother tongue authors and singers, actors, and directors. And this massive economic advantage is again only part of the story: the prestige and influence associated with effective dissemination is no less important a dimension of the unequal opportunities associated to different native languages.[20]

3.4. Tinkering with the language regime

In this light, it is clear enough that those whose native language has been picked as the lingua franca enjoy, on average, an arbitrary privilege by virtue of some or all of the four channels characterized and illustrated in the previous section: language-related jobs, linguistic requirements for other jobs, face-to-face interaction, media-amplified audience. This privilege is understandably perceived as a serious distributive injustice by those who do not enjoy it—not least in our little academic world. What should be done about it?

Obviously, people's native linguistic competences form only one of the many advantages or disadvantages whose unequal distribution may demand correction or compensation on grounds of distributive justice. It would make no sense to pursue distributive justice in each of these dimensions separately: linguistic justice for unfair inequalities rooted in linguistic competence, geographic justice for unfair inequalities stemming from one's place of birth, physiological justice for unfair inequalities associated with health predispositions, etc. To get linguistic injustice as distributive injustice into focus, nothing of the sort needs to be assumed. But it is convenient to imagine a point of departure reckoned to be just from the standpoint of our favourite interpretation of justice as real freedom for all and then ask how this conception will require us to respond, if at all, as the native language of a subset of the population establishes itself—whether abruptly or gradually, whether as a result of a deliberate political choice or as the unintended outcome of many independent decisions—as socio-economically more valuable than others, thereby generating language-based inequalities of opportunity along the four channels identified in the previous section.

A first possible response starts from the observation that the advantages and disadvantages associated with various native languages can be significantly affected by alterations in the prevailing official language regime. Particularly striking evidence for this assertion has been provided by the study of the earnings differentials in Québec and in Canada as a whole before and after the 1970s legislation which strengthened the obligation to know and use French in various official and professional contexts within the borders of the Province of Québec. In the province itself, between 1971 and 1981, monolingual Francophone men saw their earnings deficit with respect to bilinguals shrink from 8.1 per cent to 1.6 per cent (after controlling for a number of factors such as level of education, experience, working time, etc.), while monolingual Anglophone men saw their 6.5 per cent earnings advantage over bilinguals vanish into insignificance. For Canada as a whole, being French-Canadian-born was turned in the same period from a disadvantage of 2.3 per cent of earnings to a 3.3 per cent advantage relative to being English-Canadian-born.[21]

This is just one particularly well-documented illustration of the general fact that the market value or economic rent associated to competence in a particular language is highly sensitive to the legal framework. This sensitivity is by no means unique to language skills: a legal ban on corridas or the introduction of a compulsory computer science course in all secondary schools also affects the market value of the very different sorts of talents and skills needed by toreros and computer science teachers, respectively. What makes language legislation quite unique is how powerfully and easily it can affect the economic rent associated with a skill highly concentrated in a distinct section of the population. Hence, the obvious suggestion: could and should one not address the inequalities that emerge from the rise of a dominant language by altering the language regime up to the point where the presumptively unjust advantage is turned into a handicap?

This strategy is tempting, especially in those cases in which a local majority within a particular territory—say Québec, Catalonia, or Flanders, but also any single-language nation state—would gain from a democratic decision that would grant a formal privilege to its native language or strengthen it.[22] But not much reflection is needed to identify its limits. First, the advantage enjoyed by native speakers of the initially dominant language is simply replaced by another advantage, which could be greater, now enjoyed by the native speakers of the language given a new or more exclusive official status. And secondly, the new regime may create new hurdles for native speakers of languages other than the two rival ones. In post-language-legislation Québec, for example, not only was the rate of immigration less than in the rest of Canada, but the earnings deficit for the foreign-born relative to the Canada-born was higher in Québec than in any other province.[23]

Thus, it is true that changing the language regime by requiring competence in some local language in a particular territory can improve considerably the opportunities of the local-born relative to others, by imposing linguistic 'custom tariffs' on these others, as Benedict Anderson (1993: 615) puts it, while they had to pay such tariffs in their own homeland as long as the dominant language prevailed. It is also true that this may provide, in some cases in which the native speakers of the language promoted into a stronger official position are significantly less affluent than average, a quick and effective immediate way of equalizing opportunities. But if the sole concern is egalitarian distributive justice as the equalization of opportunities, tinkering with the language regime is a pretty clumsy instrument, which will only durably improve things under particularly lucky circumstances. Moreover, in the typical case in which one effect of the change in language regime is to slow down the spreading of a lingua franca, this sort of response presents the further disadvantage of hindering the materialization of what was argued earlier (§§1.9–1.10) is a pre-condition for significant progress towards worldwide egalitarian justice.[24]

3.5. Transfers to the linguistically handicapped

Is there an alternative? Certainly. The most straightforward way in which a conception of justice as real freedom for all can be expected to deal with an emerging language-based inequality is simply by recommending redistribution from the linguistically privileged to the linguistically handicapped. The extent and pattern of this redistribution will depend on the specific version of the conception considered.

Consider, for example, John Rawls's theory of distributive justice. His principle of fair equality of opportunity demands that people with equal talents should have equal access to all social positions, while his difference principle requires that, subject to the constraint of the previous principle, the average level of social and economic advantages (income and leisure, wealth and powers) associated with the worst among these positions should be as high as is sustainable.[25] As a result of one language becoming dominant, native competence in that language becomes a more valuable asset, and one can therefore expect those who possess it to form a shrinking proportion of the incumbents of the worst social positions, that is those positions with the lowest indices of expected social and economic advantages, and a growing proportion of the incumbents of the better social positions. Native speakers of other languages, by contrast, can be expected to gather in larger numbers in the worst social positions and to be fewer than before in the best ones. From Rawls's standpoint, it is important to distinguish two reasons why such a reallocation may happen.

In one case, a person's mother tongue—or her 'accent' when speaking the standard idiom—is an economically irrelevant characteristic, and the advantage conferred to the native speakers of the dominant language is sheer discrimination. This violates the principle of fair equality of opportunity just as much as racial, religious, or gender discrimination. The outlawing of discriminatory practices, the introduction of quotas or other forms of reverse discrimination may be appropriate to help correct this injustice. However, the inequality generated along the four channels sketched above (§ 3.3) is not of this type. Competence in the dominant language operates as a productive skill relevant to the adequate performance of many of the jobs that define social positions. Native competence in that language can therefore be assimilated, it seems, to an innate talent and the advantage it confers fails to be indicted by the principle of fair equality of opportunity, that is of equal access to all social positions for people with the same talents. On the other hand, by requiring the incumbents of the worst position to be made as well off as possible in terms of social and economic advantages, the difference principle mandates redistribution, whether in the form of cash benefits, wage subsidies, or other in-kind transfers. Without any need for linguistic targeting, a Rawlsian tax-and-transfer system

will therefore redistribute automatically from those made economically more successful by the increased market value of their native
language skills to the native speakers of other languages whose
access to better social positions is worsened as a result of the same
process.

Consider, next, Ronald Dworkin's theory of distributive justice.
At first glance, its implications for the treatment of language-based
inequalities seem quite different. The stylized picture of social
inequalities on which he relies is not formulated in terms of social
positions, but in terms of resources, both personal (physical and
mental abilities) and impersonal (entitlements to external goods). For
the sake of specifying what his version of opportunity-egalitarian
justice requires, we are invited to perform the following thought
experiment. First, we must forget what resources we happen to
be endowed with, while knowing our own preferences and the probability distribution over endowments of both internal end external
resources in the relevant community. On this basis, we are asked to
insure ourselves in an actuarially fair way, that is in such a way that the
premiums we commit ourselves to paying in case we turn out to be
favourably endowed (by the standards of our preferences) would
cover the indemnities we want to be able to claim in case we turn
out to be unfavourably endowed, with all possible cases weighted as if
the distribution of probabilities over all possible endowments were
the same for each of us. Native linguistic competences are included
in these endowments, on the assumption that the key distinction is
a distinction between those features (such as one's mother tongue)
one owes to brute luck and those (such as learned languages) one
owes to choice.[26]

Assuming it could be conducted, this intellectual exercise yields a
coherent set of individualized tax and transfer schemes. These
would incorporate what would amount to a language tax on those
who happen to grow up equipped with the dominant language and
a language subsidy to the native speakers of other languages.[27]
However, for a number of reasons—relating both to the principled
inaccessibility of some of the information such individualized
schemes would require and to the practical obstacles to their implementation—Dworkin recognizes that this elegant way of combining
'ambition-sensitivity' and 'endowment sensitivity' is not a real-life
option. He therefore settles for a rough approximation, based on

what he believes 'would seem reasonable to the majority of people in the community, or to the average person, or something of that sort'. This would include an insurance scheme for the lack of sufficient skills to earn some minimum level of income. Such a scheme could take a number of different forms, from unemployment benefits to training-and-jobs programmes.[28] Just like Rawls's difference principle, therefore, Dworkin's second-best scheme would involve transfers from the linguistically privileged to the linguistically handicapped as a language-blind consequence of their differential market success.

There is, however, at least one opportunity-egalitarian conception of distributive justice that would justify, in the circumstances under discussion, a specific linguistic tax and subsidy: John Roemer's (1999) theory of justice as equal opportunity, which can itself be understood as an ethical elaboration of Roemer's (1982) theory of exploitation as asset-based inequality.[29] The equalization of opportunities is here understood as the neutralization of the effect of an open-ended list of variables that affect people's welfare while being beyond their control—for example IQ, mother's educational level, parents' smoking habits, neighbourhood at birth, etc. A combination of (discrete) values of these variables Roemer calls a type. Distributive justice requires the neutralization of the impact of belonging to one of these types on people's achievement—for example, their educational performance or health status, or also their overall level of welfare. Ideally, Roemer would like to characterize distributive justice by the equalization of the levels of achievement for each level of effort within and across all types. As this is generally unfeasible, he proposes a complex second-best which is itself problematic in various ways.[30] A less sophisticated alternative, sufficient for our present purposes, consists in allocating lump sum taxes or subsidies to the various types so as to equalize expected achievement across types: equalizing the average educational achievement of all geographically defined types, for example, will require transfers from rich to poor neighbourhoods.[31]

The implication of this interpretation of distributive justice for linguistic issues is straightforward. First, there are specific achievements—most obviously educational achievement, but also, and not only as a consequence, access to a job, level of earnings, etc.—for which native language is a major causal factor. If justice is conceived as the equalization of opportunity for educational achievement, for example, a person's native language is a relevant type for specifying opportunity-equalizing transfer policies. This also holds if justice is conceived more broadly as equal opportunity for welfare. Any gap between the average welfare levels achieved by the members of different linguistic communities that does not vanish when controlling for other variables should therefore be handled by an appropriate transfer policy from the native speakers of the dominant language to the native speakers of the other languages.

My own preferred version of the opportunity-egalitarian conception of distributive justice is akin to Roemer's in adopting a completely open interpretation of what could make opportunities unequal, while joining Rawls and Dworkin in pursuing the equalization of opportunities through a transfer scheme that is not differentiated as to the factors that need to be neutralized. Instead of viewing society as a system of stable social positions or as a community of unequally endowed individuals, the underlying stylized picture presents it as a huge gift distribution machine, with the bulk of the gifts we receive being incorporated into the rewards for the jobs we perform. Distributive justice requires that these gifts be distributed so that the value of what is received by those who receive least be as high as possible. This requires taxing all incomes at rates and in ways that sustainably maximize the tax yield, and next distributing the proceeds equally among all as a universal basic income. This corresponds to a modest gift guaranteed to all, part of which could be given in kind on mildly paternalistic or externality grounds and the value of which is to be maximized according to this interpretation of efficiency-sensitive, responsibility-sensitive liberal-egalitarian justice, i.e. of real freedom for all.[32]

Access to social positions in Rawls's sense and endowments of resources in Dworkin's sense are important factors in determining the size of the gifts people end up with. But these factors interact in complex ways with many other factors, including people's place of birth or study, their friendships and connections, and many other more or less random events. Our native linguistic competence is one among the factors that affect the size of the market gifts that come our way, mainly but not only through the jobs it helps us get. Like Rawls's difference principle or Dworkin's second-best insurance scheme, the maximin gift principle will automatically adjust the flow of net transfers across language groups to a rise in the market value of competence in one language. The equal basic income given to all will be funded to a more significant extent than before by the native speakers of this privileged language, and less than before by the native speakers of peripheral languages, without any specific assessment needing to be made, either individually or collectively, of the change in the size of the economic rent accruing to the various languages.

3.6. Dissemination through immersion schooling

Compared to alterations of the language regime, corrective transfers, whether or not they are explicitly targeted at some linguistic groups, have the advantage of equalizing opportunities in a less haphazard way and of doing so without hindering the spreading of a common language enjoined in Chapter 1. Transfers to disadvantaged linguistic groups are actually happening on a large scale as one aspect of the general tax-and-transfer schemes that make up the welfare states of linguistically diverse countries. However, most of the corrective transfers called for by the adoption of a lingua franca would need to operate trans-nationally. Hence, they require the presence of powerful supranational redistributive institutions which are currently lacking and will not come about, as argued earlier (§1.10), until a sufficiently democratized lingua franca has created a sufficiently robust Europe-wide or wordwide demos. And this may never happen, or will only happen at a desperately slow pace, if outrage at the injustice of the emerging uncorrected language-based inequality of opportunities makes people stubbornly resist the adoption of an EU-wide or wordwide lingua franca. Put differently, we need an instrument to remove an obstacle to the creation of an institution which is itself needed to provide us with that instrument.

Yet we are not stuck, because there is a third possible strategy that comes in sight as soon as one questions one assumption too rashly made at the beginning of our discussion of the redistribution strategy. Language-based inequalities have been treated in the previous section in exactly the same way as talent-based inequalities, that is as inequalities that are relevant to the performance of productive tasks, but are arbitrary in their source and therefore need to be offset or at least mitigated through corrective transfers. However, a 'native' linguistic competence, unlike an innate talent, is learned, albeit at a very early stage and without conscious effort.

Bearing this in mind, let us consider again Rawls's version of opportunity-egalitarian justice. A native-language-based inequality is then no longer to be addressed by the difference principle, on a par with genetic-equipment-based inequalities. It is rather to be regarded as the outcome of unequal education and hence as a violation of the prior principle of fair equality of opportunity. People with the same talents for learning languages end up with unequal opportunities by virtue of being made to learn different languages, just as people with the same talents of any sort could enjoy unequal opportunities as a result of the unequal quality of the schools their different social backgrounds led them to attend. This analogy could be accepted, but its practical importance denied because of a point repeatedly made by Rawls: the irreducible deviation from fair equality of opportunity inherent in the very existence of the family, itself protected by the liberty constraint encapsulated in Rawls's prior principle of equal liberty.[33] Parents must be allowed to bring up their children themselves and cannot be assumed to be able to bring them up in whatever happens to be the most valuable language for children to learn. The so-called 'native' language can therefore after all be assimilated, for all practical purposes, to the genes parents transmit to their children.

This conclusion would hold if learning a language unwittingly by interacting with one's parents as a baby and learning it painstakingly by studying its grammar and vocabulary at a later age were the only two options. But there are two more options, and the availability of at least one of them is sufficient to invalidate the reduction of native language to talent, with important implications for the pursuit of linguistic justice as distributive justice.

First, under appropriate pedagogical and socio-linguistic conditions, the handicap suffered by children whose mother tongue is different from the dominant one can easily be removed by early immersion schooling, that is by having children schooled from an early age using partly or exclusively a medium different from the home language. This is easy and cheap when the children with *the same* home language different from the school language are thinly scattered among other children, when the living environment outside the school operates in the school language and when teachers can easily be found among native speakers of that language. The maxi-min dynamics in the peer group and beyond then powerfully reinforces the learning impact of exposure to formal teaching in the dominant language. Under such conditions, children can easily and quickly become at least as fluent in the school language as in their native language. If instead many children with the same native language distinct from the school language are concentrated in the same classes, if the school language is hardly present in the environment and if teachers with the school language as their mother tongue are lacking or hard to recruit, effective immersion schooling may still possible, but then unavoidably far more expensive to achieve.

Immersion schooling so understood has been the strategy routinely used in nation states. Initially, most of their citizens spoke local dialects that differed notably from the one picked as the national language. Whether for the sake of political cohesion, labour mobility, or equality of opportunity, their governments undertook to spread competence in the national language through compulsory schooling in that language. In many cases, the school language gradually became the native language of the bulk of the population, with the help of urbanization and the maxi-min dynamics that fostered the use of the national language in linguistically mixed urban and suburban populations. In those areas in which socio-linguistic conditions were unfavourable, the cost of effective immersion schooling was considerable, but was routinely covered by nationwide funding. In most countries, this process of linguistic integration is still at work, sometimes on a massive scale and at great expense, as linguistic diversity and hence language-based inequality of opportunity keep being recreated by more or less concentrated new waves of immigration.

An educational system of this type is unambiguously required by Rawls's interpretation of opportunity-egalitarian justice, which gives priority to a distinct principle of equality of opportunity for given talents. But it is also required, albeit more contingently, under the other interpretations discussed above (§3.4), which give no priority to the neutralization of inequalities stemming from social origin (including linguistic background) over the neutralization of talent-based inequalities. Under these other versions of opportunity-egalitarian justice, the relative cost of lifelong transfers versus educational investment in those less well equipped by their class and family background will be decisive. Dworkin's cost-conscious hypothetical insurance scheme, for example, is bound to cover the acquisition (if sufficiently cheap) of proficiency in the dominant language (if sufficiently valuable), rather than higher cash transfers to cover situations of low earning power. Similarly, there is nothing in Roemer's objective of neutralization of the impact of types on achievements that forces him to rely on compensatory lump-sum taxes and transfers rather than on effective remedial education. And the maximum sustainable universal basic income justified by my own real libertarianism will be given in-kind, in particular in the form of basic education that would involve acquisition of competence in the dominant language, to the extent that there is a strong case—mildly paternalistic or externality-based, taking costs into account—for doing so.[34]

Dissemination through effective immersion schooling thus seems the way to go if language-based opportunities are to be equalized in a national context. But this looks like an unpromising model for dealing with the inequality of opportunity that arises as a result of English gradually becoming just as much of a trans-national requirement as the dialects of capital cities became a national requirement. The problem is not that the linguistic distance between today's national languages and English is generally greater than between local dialects and the national languages. Effective and quick early learning of a very different language through immersion schooling is perfectly possible if the socio-linguistic conditions are favourable. The problem is rather that, in the case of a trans-national lingua franca, unfavourable socio-linguistic conditions are the general rule rather than the exception: pupils who share a native language distinct from the lingua franca are heavily concentrated in the same class, the environment operates mostly in that distinct language, and native teachers of the lingua franca are not easily available. Effective immersion schooling is still possible under such conditions, but at a high cost.[35] And we are then back to a difficulty strictly analogous to the one that proved fatal to our second strategy for dealing with language-based inequality of opportunity, namely the strategy relying on corrective transfers. The implicit redistribution to the linguistically disadvantaged that tends to operate in national contexts through the national funding of more or less effective education for all is out of reach in the trans-national context, at least as long as the preconditions, linguistic and otherwise, for trans-national redistribution are not met. And this will take a long time, especially if the spreading of the lingua franca is resisted because of the distributive injustice it is perceived as generating.

3.7. An inexpensive instrument of dissemination

Immersion schooling, however, is not the only way of acquiring a language distinct from one's mother tongue at an early age. Under contemporary technological conditions, one must look more than ever beyond schools for the systematic learning of foreign languages. One can no longer identify, as has been done here all along, one's 'native language', that is the linguistic competence one is unwittingly equipped with from an early age, with one's 'mother tongue', that is the linguistic competence one owes to one's parents. With foreign television and now also the internet invading living rooms and bedrooms, every child can have, linguistically speaking, more than one mother. If children can acquire fluency in a second language in this way, then language-based inequality is neither an unavoidable consequence of the very existence of the family, nor one that can only be corrected, under favourable socio-linguistic conditions or at great expense, through immersion schooling in the dominant language. It is one that can be dramatically reduced at low cost, if not removed altogether, using new technological possibilities particularly relevant to the learning of a lingua franca.

To substantiate this claim, one can start by observing that competence in the lingua franca is growing quickly throughout the European Union as one moves from the older to the younger cohorts (see §1.1). True, even in the younger cohorts, proficiency in English remains—at the level of the EU as a whole and even more at the world level—a minority feature and on average falls far short of the competence of native speakers. However, the average level of proficiency in English varies greatly from one European country to another, and the best simple predictor of this level is not the linguistic distance between the country's national language and English, but rather the size of the linguistic community to which (the bulk of) the national population belongs: the larger the community, the poorer the average competence.[36] This is no doubt in part simply the reflection of the general fact that the larger one's linguistic community, the smaller the urge to find speech partners outside it. But it is even more, I conjecture, the effect of something more specific: the fact that the dubbing of broadcasting of foreign-language series, films, and other programmes is profitable and hence viable only when the target audience is sufficiently large.

As dubbing is far more expensive than subtitling,[37] the threshold number of viewers from which it starts making sense to incur the cost of translation is far lower in the case of subtitling than it is in the case of dubbing. Consequently, it is not surprising that the extent to which English-language productions are subtitled rather than dubbed is far higher in countries whose language is spoken by comparatively few people, such as Denmark, Sweden, Finland, Greece, and the Netherlands than in countries populated by the members of larger linguistic communities.[38] Moreover, there is some experimental evidence to the effect that the watching of non-dubbed foreign programmes provides, under appropriate conditions, a powerful way in which children can learn foreign languages.[39] No wonder, therefore, that we should find a strong negative correlation between size of the language group and competence in English.[40]

My factual claim is not and does not need to be that no other factor, such as linguistic distance or frequency of interaction with foreigners, affects the speed and extent of lingua franca learning. All I am asserting, as the available evidence strongly suggests I can, is that language learning through the watching of subtitled films and other broadcasts is a powerful factor in this process, including through the incentives it creates to engage in more structured forms of learning and more active modes of interaction and through systematically increasing the chance that the lingua franca will be in maxi-min position and hence be used and improved when interaction happens. We cannot do much about linguistic distance between languages, nor about the numbers of native speakers of the various languages, nor therefore about the relative profitability of subtitling and dubbing. But we have the ability to recognize that language learning is at least as much the task of our media as it is of our schools and to take appropriate action on this basis, most radically by outlawing dubbing.

I shall consider and refute in the next section a number of objections to the legitimacy and effectiveness of such a measure. Assuming it can be implemented and works, we can begin to imagine a situation in which competence in the lingua franca will be as thoroughly democratized all over Europe and beyond, thanks to exposure to today's media in all social classes, especially the least advantaged, as it is today in countries like Sweden or Finland. As has been happening in these countries, once subtitled film watching will have lifted competence above some threshold, trans-national browsing, blogging, chatting, skyping, tweeting, and real encounters—often in English between non-Anglophones with different native languages—will complete the job, and in the space of one generation, competence in English will become all over Europe even less of a problem than it now is in the most English-literate parts of the European continent.

The key difference, in terms of trans-national distributive justice, with lingua franca dissemination that relies exclusively on schooling, is simply the cost involved. Effective immersion schooling under unfavourable socio-linguistic conditions would only be realistic and fair if its high cost were funded collectively, as it is in national contexts. But the combination of some formal learning with frequent early media exposure in the lingua franca can be regarded as having a negligible *net* cost, if one bears in mind that watching subtitled films and programmes at an early age appears to have a positive effect on reading capacities in one's mother tongue.[41] Moreover, precisely because the main tool of dissemination is not domestically funded schooling but undubbed TV or internet content that is only party funded domestically, the various forms of 'compensatory free riding' discussed earlier (§2.12) can be viewed as so many modes of co-payment by native lingua franca speakers. This makes for the possibility of a 'trans-nationally subsidized' acquisition of competence in the lingua franca long before it becomes politically feasible to organize anything like trans-national transfers to those who lack it.

Consequently, once the language-learning potential of today's media is realized and mobilized, there is something far more accurate and realistic than ad hoc adjustments of official language regimes or compensatory transfer schemes, as a strategy for trans-national linguistic justice as distributive justice: dissemination of the lingua franca far beyond its native speakers and the non-native elite that has acquired it so far, by making full use of its presence in visual media. Moreover, unlike the first two strategies, this third strategy has the advantage of not only lifting a possible source of resistance to the acceptance of a lingua franca, but of contributing by itself to its dissemination, and thereby to realizing a key linguistic precondition for global egalitarian justice (see §§1.9–1.10).

3.8. A ban on dubbing?

As presented so far, this third strategy for pursuing linguistic justice as distributive justice is attractive enough. It is already well under way in countries with comparatively 'small' languages. However, given the general public's current widespread preference for dubbed versions in other countries, it could only be swiftly generalized through a vigorous measure: the banning of dubbing and its replacement by subtitling on television, in cinemas, on DVDs, and on the internet. Given the key role such a simple and cheap measure could play, it is worth reviewing the very different types of objections that have been or could be formulated against it.

First, there are a couple of freedom-related principled objections. A ban on dubbing, it is sometimes argued, would violate the fundamental freedom of expression. The ban, however, would involve no restriction whatever on the content of what is being conveyed. Moreover, since an alternative mode of screen translation remains available, namely subtitling, it would not deprive anyone from addressing a foreign audience directly through the media. Indeed, a ban on subtitling would be far more problematic than a ban on dubbing as regards the freedom of expression, because dubbing can be and has been used for censorship purposes.[42] By contrast, the ban on dubbing guarantees that the original sound track remains audible, and hence that there is a way of checking that words are not being skipped or distorted, whether intentionally or not. The freedom of expression arguably involves not only the right to utter words, but also the right not to have one's words distorted before they reach the ears of the audience. This right is better protected when dubbing is banned than when it is not. Finally and most fundamentally, the point of the measure is to enable a large proportion of the population to express themselves better in a language in which it will be increasingly crucial for them to be able to communicate if they are to be heard by those by whom they need to be heard. Any attempt to incriminate the proposal by appealing to freedom of expression can therefore be safely dismissed.

A second principled objection is that such a ban would unacceptably restrict consumer sovereignty, our freedom to consume whatever other people are willing to produce at a price we are willing to pay. Given that the point of the measure is didactic, it needs to be compared to other didactically motivated obligations. For example, there is compulsory schooling with a constrained curriculum. If the learning of algebra is regarded as essential for all members of society, pupils and their parents are not allowed to opt for hai-ku instead in the name of consumer sovereignty. The analogy has its limits, as the ban would apply to all, including retirees for whom the learning of the lingua franca may be of precious little usefulness. Perhaps the best version of the ban would therefore be one restricted to times of the day and evening when minors are most likely to watch. Or perhaps, one should go instead for a heavy tax on dubbed broadcasts, films, and DVDs and a subsidy for subtitled ones so as to foster the substitution without forcing it. Or even more modestly, one could systematically make the subtitled version the by-default option. The right to watch *Desperate Housewives* dubbed in French or Italian is not a fundamental liberty that can claim lexical priority over the equalization of opportunities. So, if it makes a significant difference for the sake of distributive justice, let us happily outlaw it. But if the milder measures just mentioned suffice to achieve about the same outcome, let us not frustrate TV viewers unnecessarily.

Next, there are some objections stemming from some sectional interests. Thus, a sudden ban or heavy tax on dubbing would directly hurt the interests of professional actors, who use dubbing as a way of securing a more regular income than film or theatre contracts can provide. There will undoubtedly be an effect of this kind, but it will be buffered, if not offset, by a significant increase in the demand for local production as long as it remains the case that a significant part of the population does not like subtitling, and hence will prefer watching films produced in a language they understand.

A residual net negative effect on professional actors taken as a whole cannot be ruled out. But the vested interest of a tiny minority cannot legitimately block a move that would massively benefit a large, comparatively disadvantaged majority, and thereby further distributive justice.

A second interest-based objection, which egalitarians may find congenial, is that the banning of dubbing would harm people with reading difficulties. One obvious response is that dubbing is as unfair to the deaf as subtitling is to the blind. Moreover, for people with serious sight difficulties, it seems plain that television is not the appropriate medium, and that the radio is the best alternative. For those with serious hearing difficulties, there is no such alternative medium, and adjusting TV communication to their specific needs by providing subtitles therefore makes plenty of sense. However, reading difficulties are not restricted to people with serious sight impairment. It also affects the illiterate, and those too young or too old to be able to read quickly. For the young, however, the difficulty encountered is essential to the learning process, including as an incentive to improve their knowledge of the foreign language through different means. And for the old, most of the problem encountered is transitional: once exposed to dubbing from a young age, one can expect to do far better up to an advanced age, both in directly understanding the foreign language and in managing to read subtitles fast enough. To address the concern that one should not 'sacrifice' a generation, one could imagine phasing in the ban smoothly, starting with children's peak TV times.

Further, some are seriously concerned that the ban would overshoot. It is argued in various places, for example, that the dubbing of foreign films can provide a tool for the protection of weaker languages. Thus there have been repeated attempts by the Catalan government to impose dubbing in Catalan (instead of Spanish) for some proportion of films shown in local cinemas in order to reinforce local competence in Catalan. Analogously, there is a concern in Latvia that the large Russophone minority consumes too many Russian films (or American films dubbed in Russian), thereby impairing the learning of Latvian. What is perceived as a problem here is not excessive but insufficient dubbing into a local language that is competing with a more powerful neighbour.[43] Note, however, that in both cases mentioned, the ban on dubbing itself would get rid of much of the pressure, as English-language productions would no longer be shown dubbed in Spanish or Russian, but subtitled. And in many cases, subtitling in the local language, unlike dubbing, should be economically viable. If local authorities find it important enough, they may wish to spend their resources subsidizing the dubbing of particularly popular series or films. The ban or heavy tax on dubbing could conceivably allow this as an exception, or even be restricted to what is produced in the lingua franca. But once dubbing into the competing languages is banned, it would be surprising if this use of public resources would make more sense than subsidizing what is being produced directly in the local language.[44]

A quite different concern with overshooting arises from the anticipation of the long-term effects. Once English has become sufficiently familiar to non-Anglophones—partly as an outcome of such a measure—the ban on dubbing may no longer negatively affect the foreign demand for English-medium broadcasts and films, with or without subtitles. But it will keep depressing the foreign demand for films produced in other languages: Bollywood will lose out to Hollywood. This does not seem fair. However, there are now so few non-Anglophone films being dubbed that this effect of the ban, if any, is likely to be negligible, and therefore by no means sufficient to offset its advantages. If it were not negligible, one could again conceivably restrict the ban to what is being produced in the lingua franca.

Finally, there are down-to-earth objections relating to the practicability of the ban. First, would a ban or heavy tax on dubbing in cinemas and on TV not induce a shift to dubbed DVDs or downloaded films with multiple sound tracks? Or, if this can be effectively outlawed, could it not make people shift entirely to films and cartoons in their native language? Although some shift in each of these directions can be expected, it is most doubtful that it would inhibit a lasting and expanding impact, especially as DVD and teletext technology makes it possible to open a wide range of individual choices for the language of the subtitles and to optionally get rid of subtitling altogether as competence in English (or any other non-native language) makes it superfluous for a growing proportion of non-native people and for a widening range of broadcasts.

Secondly, would an effective ban on dubbing for what is broadcast or produced in one country not simply boost the demand for foreign dubbed productions accessible through cable and satellite TV and through the internet? For all the large linguistic communities, this is a serious difficulty, which could only be overcome through coordinated international action. In Europe, it is therefore obvious that the EU should take the lead, and it is most encouraging that proposals along these lines are getting a hearing in some national political arenas[45] and even more—as well as more importantly—at the level of the European Commission[46] and the European Parliament.[47]

To sum up: the principled and interest-based objections to a ban or heavy tax on dubbing are weak, the concern for overshooting, if founded, could be handled by fine-tuning the measure, and the practical difficulties should be solvable if addressed at a high enough level. Moreover, international comparisons showing a strong correlation between the practice of and the preference for dubbing versus subtitling suggest that the ban would only be needed in a transitional period.[48] The direction of the causal link underlying this correlation is not in doubt. Subtitling countries do not use as much subtitling as they do because they have preferred it all along, but because dubbing was prohibitively expensive for their small markets. Why such a strong preference for subtitling now? With their children exposed to it from an early age, it has given them at all ages both a far greater ability to understand directly much of what they hear in the foreign language and a far greater ability to read quickly whatever needs reading in their own language, thereby minimizing the drawbacks of subtitling. Hence, once a threshold is reached, even in the largest markets, a new stable equilibrium is likely to emerge from which there will be no way back. We shall then have extinguished for good a practice that amounts to needlessly inflicting a linguistic handicap on the most disadvantaged layers of the population. Refusing to tread this path in those countries in which dubbing is currently common practice amounts to perpetuating the privileges of the fortunate few who happen to enjoy an easier access to the lingua franca through quality schooling and foreign contacts.[49]

3.9. Disadvantage reversed?

The substitution of subtitling for dubbing is not the only instrument available for democratizing competence in the lingua franca. But it is particularly cheap, and raises no decisive objection. As trans-national mobility and communication intensify, partly as a result of the spreading of competence in the lingua franca, the multiplication of opportunities for active interaction in that language will take over as the main mechanism, thereby making the learning ever easier and cheaper. At the limit, the learning of the lingua franca will be as natural as that of one's native language. In the meanwhile, using the right media in the right way is the way to go. This is how the circle can be broken: because of the low cost of the instruments now available, the possibility of a vigorous spreading of the lingua franca is not contingent on the emergence of trans-national redistributive institutions which it is itself meant to help make possible.

Thus, lingua franca dissemination through cheap media exposure feeding into the maxi-min dynamics is the most feasible and most advantageous way of addressing the problem of global linguistic justice as distributive justice. But there is one corollary of this dissemination process about which it is worth pondering. As competence in English spreads worldwide, there are less and less circumstances, for maxi-min reasons, in which native Anglophones will have a natural opportunity to speak another language and improve or simply maintain their knowledge of it. How many times does it happen that some awfully nice Americans or Brits (not of the 'If English was good enough for Jesus Christ, it should be good enough for you' type), after managing some laborious but much appreciated sentences in the local language, are rewarded with a 'Now, let's get down to business' in an English so competent that carrying on in the local language would not only feel like pointless masochism, but also burden the local speech partners with unnecessary trouble or even insult them by questioning their linguistic competence or ignoring their good will? The advantage of being able to use one's own language in a growing number of contexts therefore has the side effect of making it increasingly difficult to learn other languages.

Even though the importance of knowing other languages for communication purposes decreases as the lingua franca spreads, this is a genuine disadvantage. Those non-Anglophone countries that manage to opt for an effective and ever cheaper English-learning policy—through exposure and interaction—will therefore soon put their people in an advantageous position relative to Anglophones—on the assumption (to which I shall return at length in Chapter 5) that

English is not displacing other languages in local uses too, as the dominant languages have tended to do in national contexts. At the limit, non-Anglophones, including the 'heritage bilinguals' living in Anglophone countries, will be on average the more advantaged the more widespread their own native language. Abstracting from situations of easy tri- or plurilingualism, language-based inequality will therefore ultimately have the Mandarinophones at the top, next the Hispanophones, etc., until we reach the smallest surviving linguistic communities and finally the Anglophones, essentially condemned to monolingualism. One major aspect of this inequality is that Anglophones will face competition on their home labour markets with everyone else in the world, while being effectively barred from those labour markets in which another language remains required.

At the end of the dissemination process of English as a lingua franca (as distinct from a substitute for local languages), it may therefore be conjectured that the advantage of the Anglophones will not only be removed, but reversed: it may be more valuable to be fluent in English than in any other language, but it is more valuable to be fluent in two languages, providing one of them is English, than in English alone. True, Anglophones are genetically no less well equipped for bilingualism than are native speakers of any other language, and it may therefore seem that the inequality in question cannot be characterized as an unfair inequality of opportunity. But the ability to learn a language is not only a matter of mental capacity but also of socio-linguistic opportunity, and as the maximin rule drives languages other than English out of spontaneous interaction between native speakers of different languages, the cost of learning English for non-Anglophones keeps falling while the cost of learning or maintaining other languages for Anglophones— and indeed for everyone else—keeps increasing.

Having pointed out this paradoxical corollary, it is now time to summarize our discussion of linguistic justice as distributive justice. The spreading of English as a lingua franca does create new language-based inequalities of opportunities (§3.3). From an opportunity-egalitarian standpoint, the best way to address them is not by hindering the progress of the stronger languages and the advantages they confer by tinkering with the language regime (§3.4) nor through transfer schemes, whether targeted or language-blind (§3.5). It is rather by accelerating the dissemination of the lingua franca beyond the elite of each country (§3.6). This has become a genuine possibility in a technological context in which school no longer needs to be the main instrument of foreign language learning for the bulk of the population. If appropriate measures are taken, we can safely expect that the language-based inequality will soon start melting, as it already has in some non-Anglophone countries (§3.7). One such measure is the prohibition of dubbing, which faces difficulties but no decisive objection (§3.8). The process can even be expected to lead to the inequality being eventually reversed, unless English spreads all over the world not just as a lingua franca but also as a native language—a possibility to be discussed in the next chapters.

When this reversal starts showing, we shall need to talk anew about what distributive justice requires to be done for the linguistically disadvantaged Anglophones. Dissemination and regime tinkering will not be relevant options. But the possibility of a transnational redistribution system should have emerged, and it is then being a non-Anglophone, and no longer being an Anglophone, that will boost, other things being equal, one's chance of being a net contributor. This prospect, however, is still a long way off. For the time being, all that our concern for the equalization of language-based opportunities dictates is happily just the same as what we were led to by our concern for the political feasibility of global justice generally: disseminate the lingua franca!

CHAPTER 4

===

Linguistic justice as parity of esteem

4.1. Equal respect

Things, so far, look nearly too good to be true. The maximal spreading of an egalitarian conception of global distributive justice and the maximal feasibility of the institutions that could implement it require the dissemination of competence in a single lingua franca, whether on a European or on a global scale. The privilege thereby granted to English would risk strengthening a global ideological hegemony hostile to such a conception. But the only way of fighting this hegemony effectively consists in learning and using the megaphone language, not in boycotting it. On the other hand, the advantage given to the native speakers of the language picked as the lingua franca creates a language-based injustice. But whether this linguistic injustice is characterized in terms of unfair cooperation or unequal opportunities, the best response to it consists precisely in a set of policies that will contribute to the spreading of competence in the lingua franca.

For many of those most incensed by the growing dominance of English, however, such measures make things worse rather than better, because they further accelerate the primacy given to one language and the associated collective identity. And this clashes, these people feel, with some notion of justice as equal respect or equal dignity crucially different from and no less important than those considered so far. This is a dimension of justice commonly ignored in theories of distributive justice, including my own, as developed in *Real Freedom for All*.[1] It is precisely by reflecting on and empathizing with feelings of linguistic injustice that I was forced to try to accommodate it in my 'reflective equilibrium'. This chapter and the next one contain the outcome of this attempt: the way in which I propose to make sense of this distinct conception of linguistic justice and to spell out its institutional implications, starting with the following anecdote.[2]

One afternoon in August 2008, Stéphane Bern, a journalist for France's national television channel, enters a bar in the Flemish (and hence officially Dutch-speaking) city of Bruges and orders a drink in French. The waiter refuses to serve him unless he repeats the order in Dutch. When Bern points out that he is a Frenchman and not a francophone Belgian, the waiter retorts: 'You all say that.' What is it that prompts the waiter to react in this way, at the expense of his self-interest? Not a communication difficulty of any sort, but what the waiter perceives as a lack of respect for his language and hence for himself. This explains why, paradoxically, (someone believed to be) a foreigner could get away more cheaply than a fellow citizen. What the waiter perceives as offensive is not that some customers do not address him in Dutch, but that members of his country's Francophone minority systematically turn out to be unable or unwilling to address him in Dutch and take it for granted that communication will take place in French, even in the waiter's own Flemish town. Hence the response 'You all say that' rather than 'And so what?': if deemed trustworthy, Bern's reply would have provided an acceptable excuse.

I do not need to take a stance on whether Bern was rightly denied his Flemish pint, or on whether he would have been rightly denied it had he really been what he was believed to be, namely a Francophone Belgian, rather than the unfortunate French victim of statistical discrimination. I just want to use this anecdote in order to illustrate and motivate two claims that will be central in this chapter. One adds an important dimension to social justice, as characterized so far. The other one links this dimension to asymmetric linguistic practices.

First, a just society, whether national or global, is not only one whose institutions organize cooperation and distribute opportunities in a fair way. It is also a society whose members treat one another with equal respect. Arguably, the demand that cooperation should be fair and even more the demand that resources should be fairly distributed from a liberal-egalitarian standpoint can themselves be construed as expressions of a requirement of equal respect.

But whether or not one accepts this construal, there is a dimension of equal respect that is irreducible to the equalization of opportunities. In a just society, people must not be stigmatized, despised, disparaged, humiliated by virtue of their collective identity, that is of the social category to which they happen to belong in their own eyes and the eyes of others, for example their gender or their race, their religious or linguistic community.[3] It is certainly possible for such stigmatization to affect opportunities, either directly through discrimination or indirectly by depressing people's self-esteem and self-confidence, and thereby their capacity to seize whatever opportunities are formally open to them. But whether or not it does, it violates justice as equal respect. This aspect of equal respect irreducible to the distribution of opportunities I shall here call *parity of esteem*.[4] Deviation from this parity of esteem, unequal respect for people's collective identities, is generally trickier, more subtle to identify and diagnose than unequal opportunity. What counts as respect or contempt can be highly sensitive to framing, perception, interpretation in the light of historical precedents, recent and ancient, real and imagined, and of the analogies and associations they suggest. The Bruges incident is no exception. But being relative in this way does not prevent parity of esteem from constituting an important aspect of what matters for a society to be just.[5]

Secondly, there is something about language that distinguishes it from other criteria of social categorization or collective identities, namely that it is a medium of communication. When people belonging to different genders, races, castes, or religions interact, there is no need to give a primacy to one of them. A just society can reasonably ascribe itself as an objective to stamp out any asymmetry that may involve or suggest any such primacy. Language is trickier.[6] Under conditions of linguistic diversity, people cannot interact without choosing a language. This choice will nearly always be asymmetric and very often amount to opting for the exclusive use of the native language of a subset of the participants. When this happens systematically, when it constitutes a practice rather than a succession of random events, it can easily lend itself to an interpretation analogous to situations in which it is always the members of the same caste or gender that need to bow when meeting members of the other, or to get off the pavement where it is too narrow for two people to walk past each other. When such an interpretation—

definitely present in the Bruges incident—is credible, a form of linguistic injustice arises even in the absence of any effect on the distribution of opportunities.

These two claims—parity of esteem as a requirement of justice, and asymmetric linguistic practice as prima facie evidence for injustice in this sense—will operate here as conjectural components of a reflective equilibrium to be clarified and evaluated in the light of the discussion to follow, including the proposals made to address the putative injustice involved. Even though justice as parity of esteem can be said to be essentially a matter of attitudes, our inquiry will remain, as it has been in previous chapters, about how justice requires institutions to be shaped, not about how it requires individuals to behave towards each other. It will not deal directly with the question of which language you should use when ordering your pint, but about how institutions should be shaped so as to affect appropriately the probability of using a particular language in a particular context and the interpretation this use will be given. A further claim that I am therefore making—and that will be also tested as we go along—is that, while not omnipotent, institutions do matter to this dimension of justice as they do to cooperative and distributive justice. They can help by expressing, recognizing, asserting the parity of esteem between (some of) the languages with which members of the society concerned identify. I shall argue that there are essentially two ways in which institutions can try to do that. Spelling them out will help give an operational meaning to the expression 'parity of esteem'. One of these ways is straighforward yet limited, indeed, as regards our central illustration—English in the EU—increasingly limited. It will be the subject of the remainder of this chapter. The other way is potentially far more significant but, some are bound to say, hopelessly problematic. It will be presented and discussed in the next chapter.

4.2. All languages on the same symbolic footing

When some political entity contains a multilingual population, a first and obvious way in which its institutions can express parity of esteem between the native languages with which substantial numbers of its members identify is by granting them symbolically the same public status or, if they grant them a different status, by using a criterion that can be easily understood and accepted. The message thereby conveyed to those linguistic communities most suspicious of having their language and the associated culture looked down upon by others is something like: 'No, it is not true that your language is inferior, less worthy, less noble. Just see how it is given the same space or time as the other(s), or possibly one that is different but then for reasons publicly given that could not be interpreted as demeaning.' The history of officially bilingual or multilingual countries is replete with illustrations of how painstakingly this equality between relevant languages is being asserted and of how sensitive this matter can be.

For example, it took until 1898, nearly seventy years after independence, for Belgium to recognize Dutch, by then adopted as the standard version of all Flemish dialects, as the second official language of the country, next to French. In sharp contrast to standard practice until then, it soon became unthinkable to print bank notes or postage stamps, to publish legislation or official documents of any kind, to erect national monuments or make public declarations, which did not use both languages, indeed which did not allocate to both languages equivalent amounts of space and carefully alternated the order in which they appeared.[7] Countless examples could be adduced from many places, with the offensiveness of the gesture or the inscription often looking trivial to outsiders and nearly always impossible to decipher properly. For example, protest sprang up in Kinshasa in 1997 when its Lingala-speaking population discovered that Laurent-Désiré Kabila, after ousting President Mobutu, had printed bank notes exclusively in his own native tongue, Swahili, instead of using either only French or all four of the DRC's national languages (Swahili being among them), and uproar arose in 2006 in the bilingual part of Austria's province of Carinthia when the local authorities replaced a standard Slovenian–German signpost with one in which German featured in bigger letters than Slovenian.[8]

The public assertion of equality can work well enough as long as the number of languages between which equality needs to be expressed is small. But the need for a lingua franca and for its dissemination— the central illustration throughout this book—arises precisely when there are many of them, and many among them with which parts of the populations concerned strongly identify, as both revealed and reinforced by the fact that many European and Asian countries use a form of the same word to refer to their language and to their state. How can linguistic identity be symbolically asserted by a polity, such as the European Union, that needs to operate on such a scale that many linguistically defined collective identities are involved? At first sight, the response should be the same as with a small number of languages. Simply use on an equal footing all relevant languages, here conveniently circumscribed as being the official languages of at least one member state.[9] This has been happening, in the European Union, through the extension to any newly recognized official language, of 'regulation no. 1', adopted in April 1958 by the representatives of the six member states of the European Economic Community: all the Treaty's languages (four at the time) are 'the official and working languages of the institutions of the Community'.[10] Dropping some of the languages would be considered just as offensive or humiliating as hoisting just one or a few of the national flags or as shrinking some of them to the size of a handkerchief.

As the number of officially recognized national languages gradually rose from four to twenty-three, however, this policy hit obvious limits. Consider a particularly symbolic dimension of language choice: the way in which the various EU institutions choose to identify themselves on the front of their Brussels buildings. The European Parliament is clearly the institution that takes linguistic equality most seriously. The plaques on which it identifies itself use all twenty-three languages, and room has cautiously been made for a couple of vacant slots. By contrast, the Council of Ministers took the easy route of opting for Latin: it calls itself the 'Consilium', its building is called 'Justus Lipsius' after the sixteenth-century Louvain humanist and it was inaugurated by a French 'praesidens'.[11] Its rotating presidency sometimes wants to signal that it is in charge and introduces some variation in the process. Thus, the Spanish presidency used Spanish, English, and French, whereas the French presidency used all twenty-three languages with French at the top and English at the bottom.

Present for the longest time and most massively, the European Commission is still sticking to the ever less plausible fiction that it is simply hosted in Belgium's officially bilingual capital and therefore consistently endeavours to conform to the local legislation by using Dutch and French to name itself and the relevant 'Direction Générale' on the front of each of its buildings, as if long established

Brusselers were the only people who cared to know what these buildings were used for. However, tempting room for richer messages became available in 2004, after the completion of the renovation of the Berlaymont building, which houses the offices of all twenty-seven Commissioners. The Commission then started posting gigantic slogans on the wall that towers over the busy Rond-Point Schuman. It gave up the pretence of being just a guest institution conforming to local language rules and soon opted squarely for English, usually alone, occasionally supplemented, in shortened formulations or smaller print, by a sprinkling of French and Dutch, more rarely of German. Using all twenty-three languages would no doubt be a wonderful celebration of equality, but a pathetically ineffective exercise in communication. Amidst the information overload that surrounds us, cluttered messages, written mostly in languages unintelligible to each particular reader, are at a great disadvantage and would be tantamount to saying nothing. They therefore tend to be wisely reserved for two occasions per year: the posters that wish the European population a Happy New Year and those that celebrate the European Day of Languages. Even when the European Commission undertakes to celebrate 'Equality' or 'Diversity', English-only, it turns out, is deemed to work just fine.

What is illustrated by this linguistic gymnastics, often convoluted, hesitant or embarrassed, is the growing tension, even in the case of very rudimentary and highly symbolic messages, between efficient communication in today's EU and the wish to assert parity of esteem among its official languages.[12] The larger the number of recognized languages and the more widespread the asymmetric learning of just one of these languages becomes, the stronger this tension. Attempts to dodge the issue by going for the Council's nostalgic Latin option or for the Commission's obsolete Belgian option are gradually giving way to formulas that grant English a paramount role while paying increasingly marginal lip service to other languages.

4.3. Piggy-backing on the instrumental function

Highly symbolic practices of this kind matter a great deal in plurilingual national contexts.[13] In the multilingual EU context, giving them more than a very modest role would seriously impair efficient communication. Whatever is left should not be dismissed as unimportant but does not exactly seem serious enough to secure parity of esteem. Should we care? Perhaps not. For there are after all far more massive ways in which the daily operation of the EU institutions expresses the equality of all official EU languages—or at least twenty-two of them (Gaelic being the exception)—albeit as a by-product of non-symbolic imperatives. Far more than a handful of posters and plaques, the practices I have in mind account for the fact that the EU possesses the largest and most expensive linguistic services in the history of mankind. They include the obligation to publish all EU legislation in all official languages, the right of all members of the European Parliament to express themselves in the official language(s) of their country, and the right of EU citizens to address the EU institutions in the official language(s) of their country and to receive an answer in that language.

Unfortunately, with the rising number of languages, the equal right to use any of the official languages in many contexts has become increasingly time-consuming, tedious, confusing, and costly. Moreover, as competence in the lingua franca continues to spread, the part of it that can count on a pragmatic rationale is shrinking by the day. To illustrate, let us consider two particularly central and sensitive examples.

First, European citizens are entitled to have all directly applicable EU legislation available in the official language(s) of their country. As technical legislation starts being as easy (if not easier) to understand by those concerned if read in English than in their own native language, it is becoming ever more pointless to translate it at the great expense of jurilinguistic expertise into over twenty languages, in several of which some of this legislation will not be used or read even once. The requirement of publication in all languages is often justified by appealing to a conception of fundamental liberties that demands that all citizens subjected to the law should possess the ability to understand it. However, competence in English is gradually spreading so widely that, in the younger generation of some non-Anglophone countries, English is known, on average, just about as well as national languages currently are by regional or immigrant linguistic minorities. In a foreseeable future, the principle of equality before the law and the presumption of knowledge of the law will hardly be at greater risk under a monolingual English legal regime at the European level than it currently is under monolingual regimes in some national contexts.[14] Moreover, the additional difficulty created by the use of English will become negligible compared to the difficulty inherent in the use of (sometimes needlessly intricate) legal jargon. Indeed, many mistakes unavoidably creep into translations that cannot realistically be treble-checked by experts[15] and, in case of ambiguity or discrepancy, courts will have to decide which version is the authorized one.[16] In some countries and domains, we may already have reached the stage at which equality before the law would be better served if all were expected to use directly an authoritative English version rather than a translation.

As a second example, consider the right of the members of the European Parliament to express themselves in the language of the people they represent. With the growth in the number of languages, communication in the plenary sessions and committee meetings of the European Parliament is slowed down and becomes more uncertain as a result of interpretation having to use a relay language.[17] At the same time, competence in English spreads both among the people back home to whom accountability is due and even faster among the members of the European Parliament, their immediate addressees.[18] Hence a growing pressure on Euro MPs, starting with those with less commonly known native languages and with more bilingual populations back home, to express themselves in English not only in informal encounters, but also in more formal, more symbolically laden contexts. Against the background of a rapidly spreading competence in English, the generalization of such a regime would enhance rather than reduce mutual understanding, it would hardly affect the Euro MPs' accountability to their electorate and it would not shrink the recruitment pool of qualified Euro MPs.[19]

4.4. Who should pay for costly symbols?

These two examples illustrate how symbolic equality is less and less in a position to piggy-back on pragmatic considerations of efficient communication.[20] As long as expensive translation and interpretation services are plausibly required by equality before the law or fair access to democratic participation, expecting all components of the

European Union to pay for them according to their wealth can remain a pretty uncontroversial demand. And the massive expression of equality among all official languages is then a welcome and uncontroversial by-product. But as the spreading of competence in the lingua franca depresses the communicative benefit to zero or even, in some instances, makes it negative, only the symbolic value is left to justify a costly and cumbersome practice. Much of it is therefore increasingly perceived, resented, and resisted as unnecessary waste by some of those who have to foot the bill in terms of money, time, and inconvenience.[21]

Against this background, we should not be surprised to discover a number of proposals for switching to a system that would enable member states to waive their right to avail themselves of some translation or interpreting services in exchange for cashing in the money saved as a result, typically in the form of reduced contributions to the EU budget.[22] Hardly any reflection is needed to realize that the implementation of such a proposal would amount to granting some countries a subsidy (or a lump sum discount on their contribution to the EU budget), irrespective of their sizes and wealth, simply by virtue of their having a distinct official language. Slightly more reflection leads to a generalization of this observation. Once growing competence in the lingua franca will have undermined instrumental justifications for expensive translation and interpretation services, the countries insisting on the EU budget paying for such services into their official language would be claiming something analogous: a subsidy in the in-kind shape of language services funded out of the common purse, with the function of enabling them to satisfy in this expensive way their desire for symbolic recognition.[23]

In this light, a country's insistence on the full range of EU-provided linguistic facilities will understandably start being perceived and resented by others as the reflection of an expensive taste for their language being honoured in a particularly lavish and wasteful way. If the Maltese government wants an interpreter flown specially to Strasbourg in order to spend two minutes translating what a Maltese Euro MP could have said in English, one can understand that Luxemburgers, who are demanding no such recognition for their own national language, should be reluctant to keep paying for it.[24] If a country wants such services, some will sooner or later argue, it should be expected to fund it itself. This would not be totally unprecedented. In 2005, Spain's official languages other than Spanish—Catalan, Basque, and Galician—were given some limited recognition in the EU context, on condition that the Spanish government foots the bill. What would gradually emerge, as instrumental needs wither away and only symbolic claims remain, would simply be a generalization of the idea of making countries—and ultimately linguistic communities—financially responsible for their expensive 'linguistic tastes'.

Would this be fair? To make sure we focus on the construal of this question relevant to the present discussion, let us suppose that competence in English has been acquired throughout the EU at a level approaching competence in the national language in the EU's average member state at this stage. Hence, common funding of the whole range of linguistic services cannot be justified, as it still can today to a large extent, in terms of equality before the law or democratic participation. Let us further suppose that there is cooperative and distributive injustice between the Anglophones and all the others, who had to learn as a second language the language in which they are now all able and expected to communicate directly. Linguistic injustice in the corresponding senses has been addressed in previous chapters and is here supposed to have been fixed. The question that needs answering, assuming cooperative and distributive justice to be realized, is whether expensive linguistic services, once reduced to their symbolic function, should be funded by all or only by the linguistic communities that request them.

In particular, is it fair that small and poor linguistic communities may not be able to afford these services, or are more likely to find it unreasonable to request them than large and wealthy linguistic communities? Wealth inequalities could not make this unfair. Why not? Not because we are here assuming, only for the sake of the argument, that distributive justice has been achieved. Under a lax-egalitarian interpretation, inequalities would subsist even when distributive justice is achieved. The reason is rather that, even with large inequalities across European countries, there would be no good reason to insist on this particular form of in-kind redistribution as soon as at least some countries indicate, in the way Sweden already did (see note 22), their preference for cashing in the equivalent of the language services they wish to give up once these have lost their instrumental point. If there is room for redistribution from the richer countries to the poorer ones, the latter should not take this narrowly ear-marked and poorly targeted form and it should be up to each member state to decide whether, with the resources at its disposal, it wishes to keep enjoying any particular expensive form of symbolic recognition.

What about the unfairness that may stem from differences in the sizes of the respective linguistic communities? Even if their speakers are equally wealthy, languages with less native speakers will be far more expensive (per capita) to honour in this way than languages with many speakers. No member state is responsible for its language having ten or fifty times less speakers than other national languages. Does this not make it unfair to expect each country or linguistic community, however small, to cover the full cost of the language services it requests for the sake of symbolic recognition? This is no more unfair, I submit, than expecting each of a set of religious communities—here assumed, for the sake of the argument, to have equal per capita wealth—to pay for the buildings it considers its religious activities require. As a consequence, those with more members may be able to afford a magnificent cathedral while those with less members may have to make do with a modest chapel.[25] Most likely, in the case that concerns us, there will be no cathedral or chapel, but only a cheap banner or bell that each member state will agree is required to express parity of esteem between its language and all others and that none of them will object could be funded out of a common purse.

So, imagine that the instrumental rationale is gone and that, as I have just argued must happen, the possibility of charging others for expensive services demanded for purely symbolic purposes is switched off. Then it seems that the present expensive arrangement will soon unravel, starting, as the Swedish request illustrates, with the countries with smaller languages and more widespread competence in the lingua franca.

4.5. Downsized plurilingualism

Should one conclude that, as a consequence of the number of official languages having risen steeply and of competence in one of them spreading dramatically, any significant form of affirmation of linguistic equality in the EU context is on the way out? This would be too rash. In the many contexts in which using all languages would involve a cost impossible to justify on pragmatic grounds, an alternative strategy consists of using a subset of them as a symbolic reminder of the diversity of European languages and a public denial of what would be an insulting *tout à l'anglais*. This is a delicate path to tread, as expanding the subset beyond a single language unavoidably creates the risk that those whose language is still excluded after expansion will feel belittled even more than when only one language was used.[26] If there is only one prize and you do not get it, you are less likely to be humiliated than if everyone is getting a prize except for you. If this danger is to be avoided, we need a justification for the chosen subset that is easily understandable and acceptable by all concerned.

One formula sometimes adopted—including at the weekly formal meetings of the twenty-seven European commissioners—consists of granting a special status to French and German in addition to English. One possible justification is that French and German are the two most widely spoken languages that have the majority of their native speakers inside the EU. Another is that each of them is, within Europe, the main language of one of the EU's two main language families. But the most persuasive one is probably still that the EU would never have existed had some French and German leaders not had the intelligence and found the strength, under inauspicious circumstances, to make the founding move. Stopping at these three languages is therefore arguably less arbitrary with regard to symbolic significance, than any other short list of European languages. However, as continued enlargement keeps reaching far beyond the Latin and Germanic domains and/or as the EU grows away from its founding moment and/or as the French–German partnership plays less of a driving role in its further development, the feeling of arbitrariness is bound to grow. So will also, consequently, impatience at giving French and German, at everyone's expense, a symbolic privilege that interferes with pragmatic considerations, typically by cluttering posters, boards, and screens or by occupying meeting time with speeches directly intelligible to only a minority.[27]

Another common and convenient formula consists in combining the use of English with the official language(s) of the country in which communication is taking place. However, this option is not available when communication is deterritorialized, as is the case when it is being staged inside the building of one of the European institutions or indeed, to a growing extent, anywhere in Brussels, to the extent that the city is increasingly perceived as the capital of the Union rather than as a national capital that happens to host the bulk of the EU's political institutions. More crucially, most of the information massively produced by the European institutions is now being disseminated through the web. This dissemination can be done very quickly, efficiently, and cheaply. But producing and constantly updating that information in twenty-two or more languages is very costly. Given the deterritorialized character of the web, the far cheaper alternative of combining English with the local language is, here too, unavailable.

In the long term, therefore, the symbolic assertion of the equality of the EU's official languages may well amount to very little. The multilingual plaque will remain firmly stuck on the wall of the European Parliament, and be updated whenever necessary. And surely the next time the EU organizes some event of sufficiently grand symbolic significance, the chairperson will greet the participants in twenty-two or more languages instead of the eleven used by Valéry Giscard d'Estaing to say 'Mesdames et Messieurs' when he opened the EU's 'constitutional' convention in February 2002. But ubiquitous multidirectional interpretation, translation into over twenty languages of all legislation and official documents, and daily updates of twenty-two versions of huge websites will, bit by bit, belong to a remote past.

4.6. Rhetoric and exhortation

These gloomy prospects can be to some extent compensated—or should one rather say covered up—by an ebullient rhetoric that celebrates linguistic diversity, extols the beauty of all European languages, glorifies the cultural traditions that found expression in each of them and rehearses tirelessly that none is inferior to any other.[28] On occasion, especially when some signs of arrogance can be detected, it may also help to demystify any intrinsic superiority claimed or suggested on behalf of the English language or the associated culture (see §1.8). Above all, any suitable occasion must be used to distinguish emphatically Globish from British and American, the language adopted as a handy European and worldwide lingua franca from the cultural language(s) of a small number of countries (see §1.11).

Even accompanied by this rhetorical varnish, the affirmation of equality in the face of blatantly unequal use is quite feeble, and is bound to sound hypocritical if not accompanied by some relevant action. Most straightforward is the active promotion of symmetric language learning. Crucial in the Bruges incident with which this chapter opened was the unwillingness to learn attributed to the native speakers of the dominant language. Public authorities can do something about this by making the other official language(s) of a bilingual or plurilingual country part of the compulsory curriculum, and by encouraging by other means the learning of 'the neighbour's language'. This is not easy, even when there are only two languages involved, because language acquisition and maintenance are mainly a matter of practice, and the maxi-min dynamics, as repeatedly mentioned, traps speakers of the stronger language in a vicious circle of linguistic ineptitude.

The situation is even trickier when many languages are involved, as is the case at EU level. If all Europeans are encouraged or obliged to learn just one language of their (individual or collective) choice on top of their home or main school language, it is not hard to guess (except for the Anglophones) which one this is going to be. Far from counteracting the inequality between languages, this would reinforce it. Hence the 'mother tongue plus two' objective heralded by the European Commission's Action Plan (European Commission 2004: 22) and refined in the Maalouf report (2008), commissioned and endorsed by Leonard Orban, the EU commissioner for multilingualism: each European is meant to acquire a 'personal adoptive language' chosen because of some special affinity, in addition to the unavoidable lingua franca. The (nice) idea is that for any combination of two among the EU's twenty-three official languages there should be many native speakers of one of them who will choose and manage to become proficient in the other. This would be a great way indeed of expressing parity of esteem among all the EU's official languages: from generation to generation, each of these would be learned as a second or third language by a substantial number of citizens from each of the member states in which it is no official language.

But again, the maxi-min dynamics offers a formidable obstacle. The very diversity of the adoptive languages which their advocates hope will be chosen implies that in most contexts in which several Europeans will need to interact English will be used and hence better learned. The obstacle will be all the more prohibitive if, either unavoidably (through television) or by design (on the sound assumption that children learn additional languages more easily than adults), the effective learning of English occurs early in life, before the age at which intensive interaction with foreigners starts for most people. Under such circumstances, the prospect of any language but English featuring more than marginally in maxi-min position when people from different countries meet will be pretty dim. If the 'adoptive language' is to carve out a durable slot in the linguistic repertoires of a sizeable proportion of Europeans, it will be only in those places in which a vigorous policy of prior learning of the language of a community with which there is some special link (typically, vicinity, but perhaps also migration) will have been put into place, through the mobilization of the compulsory school curriculum, the audio-visual media and sustained direct contact. Even under those particularly favourable conditions, improved competence in the lingua franca, joined with growing mobility, will maintain a constant pro-English bottom-up pressure which public authorities will find hard to resist to an extent sufficient for competence in the 'adoptive' language to flourish.[29]

In this light, it seems that the rapid emergence of a lingua franca, to be further accelerated for reasons developed in earlier chapters, should leave little room for anything like a serious pursuit of linguistic justice as parity of esteem: apart from symmetry-friendly policies which, however seriously meant, will keep bouncing against the power of the maxi-min dynamics, all we seem left with is polite but increasingly superficial symbolic lip service to the equality of all (recognized) languages. If this despondent conclusion holds at the level of the EU, it holds of course even more on a global scale. Is there really nothing else that can be done to secure linguistic justice as parity of esteem? Yes, there is, something that is to a large extent already being done, often unwittingly, and that will need to keep being done more widely, more self-consciously, and more vigorously in the future. So at least I shall argue in the next chapter.

CHAPTER 5

Linguistic territoriality

5.1. A territorially differentiated coercive regime

In order to introduce what I regard as the most important strategy for pursuing linguistic justice as parity of esteem under present conditions, I shall use another local anecdote. Some years ago, a Brussels-based British journalist was talking to an American executive living with his family in Waterloo, a suburb of Brussels located in (French-speaking) Wallonia. 'You'll never believe it,' the American told him with some irritation, 'I have been renting this villa for three years now, and the owner is still not able to speak English!'[1] There is something wrong, I submit, with this 'colonial' expectation that the locals should adjust linguistically to the newcomer—even had he been a direct descendant of the Duke of Wellington—rather than the other way around. More specifically, there is something in this attitude that clashes with linguistic justice as parity of esteem, and public institutions can and must do more to prevent this by moving beyond symbolic affirmation, rhetoric, or exhortation, namely by enforcing *linguistic territoriality* or, more precisely, a *territorially differentiated coercive regime*, in a sense to be clarified shortly.

The claim I am about to present and defend can be spelled out as an answer to the question of how public services—among them education—need to be organized in a multilingual area so as to secure parity of esteem. One obvious candidate is what I shall call an *accommodating linguistic regime*: the supply simply adjusts to the demand of the population in a way that is not fundamentally different from the way in which the market would adjust, except that the effect on demand of the ability to pay is at least partly neutralized. Public authorities realize that language cannot be disestablished, and hence that a straightforward policy of benign neglect, which is an option in the case of religion, dress code, or cuisine, is not available in the linguistic case. But they give no a priori privilege to any language and simply provide services of all types so as to best satisfy the preferences of the citizens, providing numbers and concentration make it economically reasonable. This corresponds to a sensible interpretation of liberal neutrality as 'even-handedness'. It leads naturally to an accommodating regime of 'pro-rated multilingualism', which may lead to the maintenance, expansion, or extinction of the various languages in competition. What matters is not any specific outcome, but fair background conditions that do not give an a priori privilege to any language and thereby express parity of esteem to all of them.[2]

In contrast with an accommodating linguistic regime, I shall call *coercive* a linguistic regime that does not simply respond to demand under the sole constraint of threshold levels imposed by a cost-conscious use of resources. Under a coercive regime, the law imposes an *official* language, that is stipulates which language (or which pair or small set of languages) is to be used as the medium of public education in a sense that need not be restricted to publicly organized education but can cover any form of education that qualifies for the school obligation; and as the medium of public communication: the language in which laws are published, courts operate, public media broadcast, official information is disseminated, elections are organized and proceedings are conducted in local, regional, or national assemblies, sometimes also the language of commercial messages in public spaces and of formal business in large private firms.[3]

Whether a regime is accommodating or coercive is a matter of degree. How coercive a regime is depends in the first place on how *extensive* its constraints are. For example, if it governs the medium of education—as it generally does—does it affect all schools, whether publicly organized, publicly subsidized or strictly private, or only a subset of them? If it regulates communication in public spaces, does it affect only street names and public buildings or also private shop windows and advertisements? While remaining within the limits imposed by fundamental liberties (see §3.2), there is plenty of room for a coercive regime to be more or less extensive in terms of the range of contexts on which it imposes linguistic constraints.[4] How coercive a regime is also depends on how *ambitious* it is. In most cases, a coercive regime imposes the learning or use of a single language. But in some cases, it imposes the learning or use of two or more languages disjunctively (which makes it less ambitious). In other cases it imposes the learning or use or of two or more languages disjunctively (which makes it more ambitious).[5] How coercive a regime is further depends on how *general* it is, that is on whether or not it makes exceptions for some categories of people (e.g. diplomats) and/or some places ('linguistically free zones'). Finally, how coercive a linguistic regime is depends on how *severe* the sanctions are in case of infraction: this is not simply a question of what the legislation says, but also of how strictly it is enforced: in case you were to use the wrong language on your shop window, would anyone take notice, take action, fine you, imprison you? How high would the fine be, how long the prison sentence? Would informal social sanctions—say, hostile tagging—be repressed, tolerated, approved, encouraged by the authorities?

How coercive a linguistic regime is in these four senses—extension, ambition, generality, severity—must be distinguished from how *binding* it is. If the language it forces people to learn or use is the same as the one they would choose to learn or use under an accommodating linguistic regime, the coercive regime is not binding at all. What it means for a regime to be binding is essentially that it interferes with the maxi-min dynamics: it blocks or bends either probability-sensitive learning or maxi-min choice or both (see §§ 1.3–1.5). Typically, a coercive regime will be binding by virtue of imposing public education in the local language on those who would have preferred to have their children taught in a different one, and by virtue of imposing administrative procedures in the local language even in cases where another language would better facilitate mutual understanding.[6] A binding regime leads more people to learn the local language, or to learn it more thoroughly, than if probability-driven learning had been left unconstrained, thereby increasing the frequency with which the local language will be the maxi-min language. At the same time, it makes interactions occur in the local language more frequently than if the maxi-min criterion governed public communication, thereby creating both a stronger incentive and a wider opportunity to learn the local language.[7] Consequently, even though fundamental liberties protect the language of private communication against the coercive grip of the coercive regime, private language use is far from immune to the latter's influence: the choice of the language picked as the medium of schooling and public communication can obviously be expected to have a profound impact on linguistic competence and hence on the spontaneous (maxi-min-guided) choice of language even in totally uncoerced private communication.

In a multilingual area in which people learn languages and interact linguistically with one another, a coercive regime can be either *territorially differentiated* or *categorically differentiated*: the constraints it comprises can vary according to the location of the interaction or according to the category to which the people involved belong. In the former case, linguistic borders are crucial, in the latter linguistic community membership is. The alternative to an accommodating regime I shall defend is a *territorially differentiated coercive linguistic regime* or, for short, a *territorial regime*.[8]

In a *categorically differentiated* linguistic regime, the coercive rules do not differ from place to place in the area under consideration, but they apply differently to different categories of people in the population under consideration. Typically, people with a specific mother tongue (or presumed to have a particular mother tongue by virtue of their parents' schooling or their own prior schooling) or with a specific religion are obliged to use that language in all or some contexts, wherever they happen to be inside the area in which the legislation applies. Categorically differentiated regimes are not exactly frequent, for good reasons as we shall see. The compulsory use of Latin, Arabic, or Hebrew for liturgical purposes could be interpreted as very narrowly circumscribed approximations. Somewhat more significant yet still very limited illustrations are supplied by legislation that applies differentially to linguistically defined groups. Thus, the obligation placed since the 1970s upon Québecois parents to send their children to a French-language school is restricted to people who were not themselves educated in a Canadian English-language school. Another example is a rule briefly implemented in Brussels in the 1970s that forced people educated in Dutch to send their children to a Dutch-medium school.

In a *territorially differentiated* linguistic regime, by contrast, which language is favoured by the coercive constraints varies from one place to another within the area under consideration. It is therefore essential to specify the scale regarded as relevant. For example, the Grand Duchy of Luxemburg, which imposes Luxemburgish, French, *and* German as the obligatory mediums of education at different stages of the curriculum throughout the country, does not have a territorial linguistic regime when looked at on a national scale. But it constitutes an exceptionally ambitious component of a territorially differentiated coercive regime when looked at on a European scale. In sharp contrast to the United States, the European Union taken as a whole operates with a highly coercive territorially differentiated linguistic regime, partly explicit and partly implicit, with linguistic borders coinciding mostly, though not entirely, with national borders. Often applied unwittingly by nation states, coercive linguistic regimes become salient when introduced, modified, or strengthened as part of the formation of new independent states (from Norway to Bangla Desh, from Latvia to East Timor). A territorially differentiated regime has been present from the start within the highly decentralized plurilingual Swiss Confederation and it has been introduced—under strong pressure from one of the linguistic communities—in a number of other plurilingual states such as Belgium in the 1930s (with the adoption of official monolingualism for the bulk of the areas that were later to form the Flemish and Walloon Regions) and Canada in the 1970s (with Québec's notorious 'Law 101').

5.2. Non-starters: right of the soil and national sovereignty

A territorial regime or 'linguistic territoriality principle' should not be confused, as it sometimes is by both friends and foes, with a 'right of the soil', in contrast to a 'right of the people', itself assimilated to a 'linguistic personality principle'. In the terminology introduced earlier, imposing on the soil such a 'right of the people' corresponds to a fully accommodating linguistic regime. But a territorially differentiated coercive linguistic regime cannot be interpreted as imposing on the people a 'right of the soil' in the sense that the language that was first spoken by human beings on a particular stretch of land must be known and used forever by any person who settles on it. If this were the case, introducing such a regime would obviously have no relevance whatever to the protection of French in Québec, for example. In Europe, Basque is apparently the only language that came straight from Africa rather than, much later, from Asia, as all other European languages did. It would therefore be the only language that could—cautiously—stake a claim by appealing to a 'right of the soil'. A territorial linguistic regime does not need to rely on any (pre)historical speculation on who was first to tread on a particular bit of soil, on who can claim the territory as their ancestral land. It consists in the public authorities deciding to impose specific constraints on the conduct of the inhabitants of a territory as regards the medium of education and the public use of language—instead of simply accommodating its old and new inhabitants' individually expressed preferences—just as it imposes constraints as regards the teaching of mathematics in the school curriculum or requires the payment of taxes.[9]

Nonetheless, as we shall see shortly, a territorial regime will only be able to do what it needs to do for the sake of parity of esteem if it fixes language borders and constraints in a way that is sensitive to the linguistic competence and wishes of the population currently present in the territory and does not keep adjusting them to the competence and wishes of newcomers, thereby slipping into an accommodating regime. Consequently, it can be said to give a privilege to the 'sons of the soil', in the precise sense of those residing in the territory concerned at the time the regime is put into place. This is crucially different from the 'right of the soil', but nevertheless entails in most cases that the linguistic claims of 'national minorities' that have been living in the territory for a long time need to be treated differently from those of 'ethnic minorities' the presence of which derives from recent immigration.[10] In many cases, there will be some disagreement about whether such a regime was tacitly in place, where exactly, and for how long.[11] The only way of avoiding such disputes is to make the language regime explicit as soon as possible, rather than overconfidently assume that the assimilation power of the local language is so great that its coercive protection could never be binding. But the prior question, to which we now turn, is why a coercive territorial regime is justified at all.

If there is no 'right of the soil', that is no natural right for some territory's original settlers to demand that their language should be spoken there forever, how can a territorially differentiated linguistic regime be justified? What can justify the imposition of French or

Danish as the medium of education, administration, and politics on French or Danish territory? The answer may seem obvious: national sovereignty. Suppose a state, a nation, a people has the right to keep non-members out of its territory or to admit them on any condition which it fancies imposing, including in linguistic matters, providing fundamental liberties are respected. Since there is no reason to believe that a territorial regime, as described, violates these liberties (see §4.6 above), a sovereign state is perfectly entitled, if its democratic majority so wishes, to impose such a regime. Appeal to national sovereignty, however, would be inappropriate in the present context. Nations, politically organized peoples, are not part of the ethical framework of global egalitarian justice (§1.9). They are sheer instruments to be created and dismantled, structured and absorbed, empowered and constrained, in the service of justice in a sense that far from reduces to fundamental liberties. Consequently, whether a territorial linguistic regime is legitimate is not a question that can be settled by appealing to national sovereignty, but rather one that needs to be settled in order to determine how extensive national sovereignty is allowed to be.

5.3. First argument: colonial attitude

If neither a 'right of the soil' nor national sovereignty can legitimately be appealed to, what is it then that justifies a territorial regime, whether or not it matches what existing states have democratically chosen, indeed whether or not linguistic communities are already politically structured? It is its ability to better serve justice as parity of esteem than either an accommodating regime or a categorically differentiated coercive regime. This superiority rests on three distinct grounds, which I shall spell out in this section and the next two. In presenting this parity-of-esteem-based justification, I shall initially focus on simple situations in which a territorially differentiated coercive regime is in operation in a set of neatly circumscribed territories that are each monolingual, or multilingual to such a modest degree and in such a fashion that even a fully accommodating regime would not treat them differently than it would treat monolingual areas.

In order to understand the three arguments I am about to pro-pose, it is crucial to realize that a coercive territorial regime can be binding even in situations of this sort provided there is significant real or potential immigration from areas in which different lan-guages are being spoken.[12] What makes a coercive regime binding is that it interferes with the spontaneous competition between lan-guages. When two languages are competing in a given population, I shall call *stronger* the language which native speakers of the other language in that particular population are more strongly motivated to learn than its own native speakers are to learn that other language, abstracting from any coercive measure. Conversely, I shall call *weaker* the language for which that motivation is weaker. These adjectives should therefore not be understood as referring to a sociolinguistic relationship that holds universally between two lan-guages, let alone to an intrinsic linguistic superiority of one of them over the other. A coercive regime may affect language competition by favouring either the stronger language or the weaker one so defined. In the former case, it accelerates dissemination. In the latter case, it slows down or reverses the spontaneous process of erosion. To illustrate, think of the impact of Québec's language legislation on immigrants coming from the USA and from Poland, respectively. The main illustration used throughout this book—the spreading of English as a European and universal lingua franca—is a typical instance of the former case. I shall first develop the arguments with reference to this case, and ask afterwards whether a territorial regime can also be vindicated when the immigrants are native speak-ers of a weaker language (§5.6).

The most straightforward argument that leads from parity of esteem to linguistic territoriality addresses the question of how to counteract the sort of 'colonial' attitude illustrated by my 'American in Waterloo' anecdote (§5.1). In the background, there is the recog-nition that equality between languages is impossible. Some lan-guages are more widely spread. Asymmetric bilingualism is unavoidable and, I have argued (§§1.9–1.10), indispensable. This is evident in organized international meetings of various sorts, but also in unplanned interaction with tourists and other travellers. We could not reasonably request anyone entering our territory, for however short a time, to have the will and ability to learn our language. But we can reasonably expect this from people who intend to settle among us for good, or at least for a long time. If they do not bother to learn the local language, if instead they require the locals to use their own language when interacting with them, and even to learn it if they did not know it before, the suspicion can legitimately arise that there is some arrogance involved, some lack of respect, a denial of parity of esteem, not fundamentally different from the one associated with the relationship between a colonizer and the population being colonized. This holds most clearly when the stronger language being imposed is the colonizer's native language, but it can hold more generally whenever the colonizer masters the stronger language better than the colonized. Of course, grasping the maxi-min dynamics should make both sides aware that sociolinguistic obstacles may have played a greater role than bad will in the persistence of linguistic incompetence. But a set of real or imaginary historical episodes or contemporary anecdotes often feeds the suspicion that arrogance is an important factor, if not the main one.

Now, public authorities must not and could not monitor and sanction individual attitudes and behaviour, but they can design the linguistic dimension of public institutions in such a way that one can reasonably expect allophone newcomers to muster both the courage and humility to learn the language of the local population, however more useful, more beautiful, more distinguished they believe their own language to be. The way this can be done is by deliberately and visibly failing to accommodate spontaneous preferences for the stronger language, by indicating publicly that people who intend settling in the territory will need to acquire the capacity to communicate in the local language and by requiring that their children be educated in that language. In other words, a territorially differentiated coercive linguistic regime is the best that can be done to secure parity of esteem—to avoid it always being the same group who do the linguistic 'bowing'—consistently with fundamental individual freedoms and with the unavoidably inegalitarian need for a lingua franca.

Could a categorical coercive regime not provide an equally effective way of pursuing parity of esteem? Under a territorial regime, everyone has to learn or use a particular language in certain contexts in a particular territory. Under a categorical regime, people belonging to a specific category, typically with a specific origin, have to learn or use a particular language in certain contexts wherever they happen to live. In both regimes, there is a form of protection of the weaker language. But a categorical regime does not offer an alternative common medium of communication to people who need to interact with one another by virtue of sharing the same space. Hence, it does nothing to prevent communication between people with the stronger and people with the weaker native language from continuing to operate systematically in the stronger language wherever they meet. By thickening the walls between co-habiting linguistic communities, a categorical regime may make the 'bowing' less frequent, but it does nothing to make it less unilateral. By contrast, a territorial regime creates a realistic expectation that interaction between native speakers of the stronger and of the weaker language will not always happen in the former, but also often in the latter, owing to the realistic expectation that some native speakers of the former, by virtue of where they live, will have been induced to learn the latter.

5.4. Second argument: kindness-driven agony

Thus, a territorially differentiated coercive regime can serve the ideal of parity of esteem by inhibiting 'colonial' attitudes and preventing them from pervading relationships between newcomers with a stronger language and the local population. But this is not the only way in which it can serve that ideal. An accommodating regime does nothing to resist the gradual erosion of the use of the local language, in context after context, as the maxi-min dynamics spreads competence in the stronger language. Once the process of erosion is on its way, and the various parties concerned are aware of it and aware that the others are too, parity of esteem requires that each linguistic community should be allowed, consistently with fundamental rights, to design its institutions so as to preserve a linguistic and cultural heritage in which it takes a legitimate interest. A territorially differentiated coercive regime provides them with what they need.[13]

To better see this, it is helpful to realize that there are two fundamentally distinct mechanisms, one top-down, the other bottom-up, that lead to the extinction of languages. The first one, articulated and advocated in particularly vigorous fashion in the Abbé Grégoire's

(1794) famous report on the necessity 'to annihilate the patois and to universalize the use of the French language', is typical of nation states attempting to homogenize their territories linguistically, using the tools of compulsory public schooling and military service in conjunction with the powerful processes of industrialization and urbanization which linguistic unification both facilitates and is facilitated by.[14] As the trans-national migration of individuals and families expanded, the same tool of compulsory education in the national language, routinely coupled with a stigmatization of the immigrants' original languages, was massively used over the last century or so by all countries of immigration in order to secure the assimilation of immigrants and their offspring. In the case of both regional and immigrant languages, the process can be aptly described, using Gellner's (1983: 139–40) telling metaphor, as a mechanism that gradually converts the linguistic map—and tirelessly re-reconverts it, as new stains appear—from a Kokoshka landscape into a Modigliani portrait, from a motley patchwork of coloured spots to a neat juxtaposition of smooth surfaces demarcated by firm lines.

However, this Gellner-type, top-down, state-driven, anti-accommodation mechanism does not constitute the only mechanism through which weaker mother tongues are being displaced by stronger ones in a post-agrarian, frequent-contact, high-mobility context. There is another, bottom-up, people-driven type of mechanism, a soft brand of Modiglianization as it were, which can be captured in what I shall call *Laponce's law*: the friendlier the relations across language groups, the more savage the competition between their languages. Or, more compactly: the kinder the people, the fiercer the languages.[15] Languages can cohabit for centuries when, typically for religious reasons, there is hardly any contact between the sections of the population that speak them—think of Yiddish in European ghettos, of the Mennonites' German dialect in Pennsylvania or of Aramaic in Turkey and Syria. But as soon as people begin talking, trading, working, dating, procreating across language groups, the weaker of the two languages will be slowly but inexorably driven out by the other, by the one which people have a stronger incentive and greater opportunity to learn because of its being more prestigious or more widely spread.[16] This macro-law is nothing but one macroscopic reflection of the interaction of the two micro-mechanisms of probability-driven learning and maxi-min language use (§§1.3–1.5). Even in the absence of any Gellner-type top-down assimilation, a permanent drift from Kokoshka to Modigliani can therefore be expected, at a pace that will depend on how intense trans-community interaction is and on how unequal the 'strength' of the languages concerned.[17]

Suppose we agree that in the absence of action by the relevant communities kindness-driven agony will be the fate of their languages. Is a coercive legal framework really necessary for them to halt this process? Might voluntary collective action not suffice, even with a legal framework that remains accommodating? Firm commitment to the preservation of the language on the part of a significant proportion of the linguistic community concerned can no doubt affect the pace of the decline. But it is hard to see how it could stop or reverse the decline without using social sanctions that would be no less coercive than legal rules and far worse for the quality of social life. The structure of the problem is that of a classic prisoner's dilemma. An accommodating regime will make room for schools using the stronger language if they are preferred by a sufficient number of newcomers. Some parents from the local population will send their children to these schools while being able to transmit their native language at home. However, as asymmetric bilingualism develops, more and more interaction will have the stronger language as its maxi-min choice. Of course, people could in principle resist opting for the maxi-min, and some will insist on doing so. But as a shopkeeper, for example, you will need to be very strongly committed to risk losing your customers for the sake of preventing the erosion of your language. If the others stick to their commitment, it does not really matter if you defect: the erosion will not happen. And if they do not, it does not matter either: the erosion will happen anyway.[18]

Consequently, to prevent individual rationality from defeating the attainment of an option preferred even by all members of a particular linguistic community, tireless collective mobilization and sanctioning would be required. People's kindness—their willingness to use the idiom that makes communication easiest—will need to be severely repressed, as it is precisely this kindness that equips the stronger language with its unkind claws. Implementing the will to maintain one's language through this stubborn, exclusionary and hence 'unkind' insistence on using one's language unavoidably generates a permanent climate of face-to-face tension between members of the two linguistic communities. Coercively imposed rules, even imperfectly enforced, have the advantage of reducing—without suppressing—these strains: it is less 'aggressive', 'nasty', 'sectarian', 'unwelcoming', 'petty-minded' for a public official to say 'Sorry, I know it is stupid, but the law does not allow us to provide schooling, information or other services in your language' than for a lady in the street to say 'Sorry, I refuse to listen or speak to you in the language most convenient for you, even though I am both able and allowed to do so.'

Consequently, countering the Laponce-type extinction process cannot be achieved under an accommodating regime, which simply helps it along unless accompanied by a system of informal sanctions no less oppressive and more unpleasant. It requires a territorially differentiated coercive regime. Why not a categorically differentiated one? Such a regime would seem to provide a guarantee of transmission of the linguistic heritage about as safe as the territorial regime. True, the community may get extinct, but then the territory may also run empty. However, an effective categorical regime would require people to be rigidly ascribed from an early stage to a particular category with specific lifelong obligations as regards their children's education and the public use of language. This is bound to be considered more problematic from the standpoint of fundamental liberties than being subjected to the same territory-specific duties as everyone else while retaining the right to leave the territory at any time.[19]

Suppose now that we agree that language survival requires, under the constraint of fundamental liberties, a territorially differentiated coercive linguistic regime. Are we then not forced to plead, on analogous grounds, for a coercive culinary or religious regime? Language being a means of communication, the weaker language is plagued by an intrinsic vulnerability that has no analogy in the case of other components of culture, such as religious practices or cooking habits. For these other components, an even-handed policy of accommodation is perfectly defensible: some cultural forms will disappear as a result of people's voluntary choices, but as long as background conditions are fair, no injustice occurs. In the linguistic case, it is the friendly interaction between speakers from different communities itself that is at the core of the slow killing of one of the languages. This killing need not be the explicit purpose or justification of an accommodating regime. Most often, it will be its unintended effect. However, once the linguistic communities involved become aware (and aware of everyone's awareness) that accommodation leads to the gradual elimination of one of the languages, it is legitimate for its native speakers to feel denied parity of esteem if they are not allowed to use effective means, consistent with fundamental liberties, to prevent this predictable agony.

To conclude the presentation of this second parity-of-esteem-based argument for a territorial regime, it is important to stress that it does not appeal to anything like a holistic right of each language to survive or have a fair chance of survival, nor to a right of communities (dead or alive) to have their language perpetuated forever.[20] Just as the other two parity-of-esteem-based arguments, this one is individualistic in the sense that the respect owed to the language derives from the respect owed to individuals currently alive who happen to have that language as an important component of their collective identity, and it appeals to nothing beyond the interests, rights, opportunities, etc. of the individual language users. Nor does the argument proposed here appeal to two important by-products of the regime it helps justify. One such by-product of a coercive regime, whether territorially or categorically differentiated, is that it enables some linguistic communities to preserve the societal culture associated with their language and thereby protects crucial resources required for leading an autonomous or meaningful life. Universal access to a societal culture, duly characterized, is arguably essential to justice. But the circumstances under which languages are most threatened are precisely those in which a switch to an alternative, more powerful, societal culture is easiest for people to achieve.[21] Another important by-product of any such regime is its contribution to the preservation of linguistic diversity. This by-product plays no role whatever in the parity-of-esteem-based argument proposed here. Whether it can play any role in justifying the preservation of a language will be discussed in Chapter 6.

5.5. Third argument: every tongue a queen

There is a third way in which a territorial regime can contribute to justice as parity of esteem. It constitutes an essential condition for the local language to be able to function fairly in the top function, that is as the medium of the local population *qua* political community. With a stronger language invading, an accommodating regime would soon fail to guarantee ongoing competence in the local language for all citizens. A territorially differentiated coercive regime makes it possible for each local language to be and legitimately remain a 'queen', or at least a 'princess', within the linguistic borders assigned to it by the regime. If incentives and opportunities are structured in such a way that the whole of the Catalan population learns Catalan, the Catalan parliament and other political institutions can legitimately operate in Catalan, just as the municipal councils of Switzerland's Romansch communes can function in Romansch if the bulk of the local population can reasonably be expected to know Romansch. By itself, a territorial linguistic regime requires administrative borders that define the various linguistic areas, but it does not require these borders to be political borders in any sense. However, part of their point, according to this third argument, is to enable them to function as political borders too, though not necessarily as the borders of sovereign states.[22]

It may be objected, that this third objective would be more easily and directly met if political communities were structured along categorical rather than territorial lines. Indeed, the first attempts to design political institutions for linguistically divided societies opted for this 'personal principle' against the 'territorial principle'. In the non-territorial federalism first proposed and developed by the Austrian social-democratic thinkers and statesmen Karl Renner (1902) and Otto Bauer (1907), each citizen of the Austro-Hungarian Empire was supposed to belong to one and only one of eight 'nations' linguistically and not territorially defined (Germans, Czechs, Poles, Hungarians, Slovenes, Slovaks, Croats, Italians), and each of these nations was to be given its own Parliament and granted full autonomy in matters of culture, education, and some aspects of social policy, with issues of joint concern settled through negotiation between the governments of the various nations. Such a formula would seem to have the major advantage of enabling each language to be the 'queen' of a politically organized community without confining people to the territory assigned to their native language or forcing them to 'convert' to the language of the territory in which they would like to live.

However, many policy domains have such an essential spatial dimension that devolution to these categorically defined political communities has to be restricted to competences directly linked to language like education and culture. Moreover, elaborating a coherent political project even in these areas quickly bumps against interdependencies with other policy areas, such as town planning, mobility, or employment, which can only be devolved on a territorial basis. Such a personal federalism therefore suffers from a deep structural tension. Politically organized communities live side by side in an apartheid-like set up, with separate schools, associations, and media. If they are to be given the greatest possible autonomy, they will have to fund these out of their own resources, which will generally be unequal, sometimes very unequal. And even if there are transfers from the richer communities to the poorer ones, segregation will tend to perpetuate sharp inequalities of opportunities.[23] Moreover, each of the cohabiting political communities will have great difficulty articulating a coherent political vision of its future as countless space-related interdependencies will constantly force them to negotiate with each other. If significant powers are to be devolved in a sustainable way to linguistically distinct communities, this will need to be a territorial basis. For a language to be more than a folklore queen, it needs to keep or get hold of a territory.[24]

This may or may not trigger or strengthen centrifugal forces that will lead to full independence of the linguistically defined territories. The political entities that currently exist are not sacrosanct, and in some cases full independence may be the best option, or at least the highest degree of national independence that is compatible with belonging to a European Union that provides a single market and a common currency.[25] But in other cases, there can be a decisive case for keeping a country together, politically speaking. This case may simply rest on economies of scale—for example in matters of monetary or defence policy, if not lifted to a higher level—or it may rest on strong linguistic-border-crossing interdependencies that make optimal political borders from the standpoint of efficient governance diverge sharply from those that would maximize linguistic homogeneity within the territories they separate.[26] While not enjoying national sovereignty, the linguistically distinct political entities may still live a very autonomous life in a federal framework. To prevent centrifugal tendencies creating a permanent state of tension, this framework will need to include fair and realistic institutional arrangements that secure a sufficiently smooth operation of a common federal demos, in particular as regards the linguistic ability and political incentives to communicate with the linguistically distinct parts of the federation. Multilingual democracies cannot be run in the same way as monolingual ones. Institutional inventiveness needs to be mobilized to tackle the powerful challenge of largely separate public opinions.[27] But linguistic subdivision does not need to imply full political partition.

5.6. Territorial reciprocity

This set of arguments should be sufficient to make a strong case for a territorial linguistic regime based on parity of esteem in those situations in which there is a threat of invasion by a stronger language, in particular English today in Europe and elsewhere. But what if the newcomers speak a weaker language, that is, by definition (§5.4) if they are more inclined to learn the local language than conversely. A territorial regime has an impact in this case too: it accelerates a process of linguistic integration that is happening anyway, though sometimes very slowly and laboriously. However, there is no risk of colonial attitude in this case, nor of displacement of the local language, nor any challenge to the latter's political function, and therefore no direct parity-of-esteem argument for a territorial regime.

Yet, even in this case, the coercive rules are justified on grounds of parity of esteem in so far as they are viewed as part of a global regime that incorporates an expectation of reciprocity. Parity of esteem can be served by the coercive protection of a particular language in a particular territory only if the native speakers of that language can be expected to comply symmetrically with the coercive protection of other languages in their own respective territories. No doubt, the territories claimed by the various languages will be far from equal. Some will be bigger than others, prettier, wealthier, more glamorous, more populated, more likely to draw immigrants. But the symmetry needed for parity of esteem does not require equal size or equal attractiveness. Those who expect immigrants to adjust to their own language must simply accept that, if they were ever to settle in a territory, big or small, rich or poor, in which the immigrants' language operates as the official language, they will similarly adjust.[28]

Could this reciprocity condition not be made more egalitarian? Could one not require the territories claimed by each language to be equal in terms of size, population, or wealth? It is not hard to see that this would have absurd implications. Suppose first that the linguistically protected equal shares are small—say, close to the current share of the world's smallest linguistic communities. This would leave the bulk of the planet up for linguistic grabs, thus reducing the implementation of the territorial regime to a marginal reservation-like operation. Suppose instead that the protected equal shares are big—say, close to an equal share of the total surface, population, or wealth of the world. This would require converting to a different native tongue the bulk of the population of the world. Anything in between these two extreme formulas would combine both drawbacks in varying proportions. Moreover, any egalitarian formula would involve an inbuilt perverse incentive to multiply the salience of linguistic differences so as to be able to grab a larger territory.[29]

The weaker condition of counterfactual reciprocity will therefore have to do. A particular immigrant's duty to integrate linguistically in his new home country can be said to be a demand of justice only if it is part of a general regime that satisfies the following condition. All the languages involved must enjoy a similar protection on territories that may be very dissimilar but all support, in principle, the three promises discussed above: they must provide a place where native speakers of those languages can be expected not to be treated as if they were colonized, where they can hope to secure the survival of their language and where they can legitimately give their language the top public function.

In this light, it is no objection that many immigrants with a weaker language would have been better off if linguistic integration had been expected and organized in a stronger language—say, Spanish in Catalonia or English in Sweden—rather than in the territorially protected local language. True, the linguistic skills acquired, being less territory-specific, would have been more easily exportable were the immigrants to move elsewhere. Moreover, the 'sons of the soil' would have enjoyed a lesser advantage over them.[30] This is all true, but a necessary side effect of the pursuit of parity of esteem, to be mitigated through an effective implementation of the linguistic regime itself.

This mitigating effect is a necessity because no territorial regime could be defended using the third argument above if it did not require the education system and other institutions to be organized and funded in such a way that all allophone long-term residents, whether with a stronger or weaker native language, could have easy and cheap access to an adequate level of proficiency in the local language. This is not only a matter of providing free and effective language courses, but also of organizing schools, workplaces, residential neighbourhoods, and other meeting spaces in such a way that mixing across language groups happens routinely and provides plenty of occasions for improving and maintaining competence in the local language.[31] The joint operation of this whole range of instruments should secure the linguistic conditions for any allophone who so wishes to get as full an access to effective political citizenship as any native speaker of the local official language. As an important by-product, the same set of instruments will also contribute directly and indirectly to the pursuit of distributive justice between all inhabitants of the territory: it will equalize opportunities between insiders and newcomers and it will boost 'bridging social capital' by improving communication, trust, and solidarity across groups of different origins. This whole set-up, along with the reciprocal expectation that a similar set-up will be in place wherever other languages are protected, must be regarded as part of the territorial linguistic regime which is here being justified in terms of parity of esteem. How many languages will be protected by such a regime and which ones is a question that can be tackled only after discussing how high the cost of protecting a language can be expected to be and by whom this cost should be borne (§§5.9–5.14). Before turning to these questions, however, we must consider one potential further argument in favour of a territorial regime and one strong objection to it.

5.7. Pacification through territoriality?

The justification offered in §§5.3–5.5 for a territorially differentiated coercive regime rests on a threefold link with parity of esteem. This justification is related to, yet crucially distinct from, the quite frequent claim that such a regime has a pacifying effect. In support of the latter claim, it is sometimes mentioned, for example, that the secret of Switzerland's greater linguistic peace, relative to other multilingual democracies, resides in its much earlier implementation of a territorially differentiated coercive regime as an unintended by-product of its cantonal autonomy: at least in part thanks to clear and firm language rules, there has never been a Germanization of Geneva (or Frenchification of Zurich) analogous to the Anglicization of Montréal, the Frenchification of Brussels, or the Hispanization of Barcelona, and the greater acuteness of the linguistic conflicts that have plagued Montreal, Brussels, and Barcelona have thereby been avoided.

Further support for the existence of a pacifying effect can be garnered from Fearon and Laitin's (2011) observation that many cases of civil violence in recent decades were the making of *sons of the soil*, that is of autochthonous populations that felt invaded by members of a distinct ethnic group moving in, either spontaneously or in organized fashion, from another part of the same multi-ethnic state, without any expectation that they should integrate into the local population, in particular by bothering to learn the local language. In a more or less acute form and with a more or less pronounced time lag, many of the inter-ethnic conflicts most familiar to us—from Ulster and Latvia to Israel and Kosovo—illustrate the same basic pattern. In circumstances of this sort, a firm and unambiguous territorial regime could have been expected to have a pacifying impact for reasons closely linked to the expression of parity of esteem. By creating a realistic expectation that the newcomers will adjust linguistically to the local population rather than demand the opposite, the coercive framework will make the 'sons of the soil' feel more respected, more secure, and hence less inclined to resort to possibly violent social sanctions against 'invaders' and 'traitors' alike.

This suggests a close link between parity-of-esteem-based and pacification-based arguments for linguistic territoriality. The two arguments must be firmly dissociated, however, because of two considerations that pull them apart. First, underlying the pacification effect, there is bound to be a second mechanism that has nothing to do with parity of esteem. As pointed out by Jean Laponce (2004), any geographically concentrated linguistic community suffers a negative externality when native speakers of the local language are replaced by non-natives who are unable to speak it. This negative externality is particularly onerous for local people poorly equipped for communication with aliens culturally quite different from themselves. All sorts of mutual informal services on which one routinely relies—from keeping an eye on each other's property to sharing child care or petitioning the local administration—are made significantly more difficult, if not impossible, when communication and trust are blocked by the lack of a common language. An effective territorial regime addresses such concerns by accelerating convergence towards competence in the same language and thereby reducing the occurrence of mutual ignorance, distrust, fear, and hostility between native speakers of different languages sharing the same spaces, the same streets, the same apartment buildings.[32] This mechanism is part of what lends plausibility to the pacification-based argument for a coercive territorial regime. It applies to the case of immigrants with a weaker language even more than to the case of immigrants with a stronger language, but it has nothing to do with parity of esteem.[33]

Secondly, there is no guarantee that the regime that is optimal for the sake of parity of esteem will systematically be the best one for the sake of peace. Indeed, there turns out to be a significant *positive* correlation between the institutionalization of language rights—at least some of which can be assumed to take the form of territorial regimes—and the occurrence of inter-ethnic violence. This need not contradict the existence of a pacifying effect. David Laitin's (2004) own interpretation of this correlation is not that the institutionalization of language rights causes inter-ethnic violence, but rather that both are the consequence of the weakness of states. Hence, his analysis is consistent with the view that the concession of (the right sort of) linguistic rights is a way of taming inter-ethnic conflict, just as the strong correlation between the occurrence of flu and the absorption of flu medicine is consistent with a favourable healing impact of (the right sort of) flu medicine.[34] Nonetheless, it suggests that there is often a surer way of stamping out ethnic conflict than linguistic concessions in the form of a territorially differentiated regime: a strong state that imposes a single national or colonial language on powerless, unorganized, or intimidated linguistically diverse populations.[35] Hence, what is best for the sake of peace need not systematically coincide with what best

expresses parity of esteem. Justice, one may hope, generally contributes to a durable peace, and some welcome pacifying effects can
often be expected from a clear specification of which language is
supposed to be known or learned by people who settle in a particular territory. Yet, if pacification is all that matters, a parity-of-
esteem-guided territorial regime may not be part of the optimal
strategy. It is linguistic justice as parity of esteem, not linguistic
pacification, that provides the arguments I am offering with their
normative foundation.

5.8. Territoriality versus homogeneity

So far our defence of a territorially differentiated coercive linguistic
regime has been operating explicitly against the simplified background of a set of neatly circumscribed monolingual territories
(§5.3). From Renner and Bauer onwards, however, the critics of
the territorial approach to language issues have emphasized, as a
decisive objection, that linguistic heterogeneity is ubiquitous and
that territorial linguistic regimes, therefore, are unfeasible or undesirable or both, indeed that attempting to introduce them in such a
context, far from bringing peace, would trigger never-ending
strife.[36] It is now time to bring this heterogeneity into the picture.
I shall argue that it provides no strong argument against the feasibility of a territorial regime, nor against my parity-of-esteem argument
in its favour. However, it does affect the fair cost to be borne by the
linguistic communities that may wish to claim territorial protection
for their language (§§5.9–5.11), and therefore also how many languages will end up enjoying coercive protection, and it requires a
sensitive treatment if endless conflict is to be avoided (§§5.12–5.13).
   Before anything else, it is worth stressing that a territorial linguistic regime is not to be confused with the imposition of linguistic
homogeneity.[37] It does not require the resident population to know
one language and only one language within the territory concerned.
One reason is that, as it has been defined (§5.1), such a regime is
consistent with the coercive rules favouring simultaneously more
than one language in the same entity, either conjunctively (as in
Luxemburg or Catalonia) or disjunctively (as in the Region of
Brussels-Capital). The main reason, however, is that, even in the

standard case in which a single language enjoys official status, a territorial regime is perfectly consistent with the persistence and even the promotion of multilingualism. Nothing in the concept of a territorial regime prevents native speakers of the official language from being allowed, indeed strongly encouraged to learn the lingua franca and other foreign languages. Nor is there anything in that concept that should prevent the cherishing and inter-generational transmission of local dialects distinct from the official language or of foreign languages spoken by immigrants.

What a territorial regime is meant to achieve is not that the official language should be the only language known and spoken by most or all of the permanent inhabitants of a territory, but that it should be sustainably shared by them. This is what will enable that language to claim parity of esteem, by functioning as the residents' lingua franca, by having its survival secured and by being the medium of the political community. What matters, therefore, is that the coercive measures should be powerful enough to keep promoting the official language into maxi-min position often enough for all permanent residents to have both the desire and the opportunity to become proficient in it. Using Gellner's metaphor, the lines of the Modigliani painting entailed by the regime must be firm and the contrasts can be sharp, but none of the coloured surfaces needs to be pure, and a close look can reveal complex mixtures at every point.

Thus, permanent linguistic heterogeneity within a territory is by no means incompatible with a territorial regime. Nevertheless, it can legitimately be viewed as problematic for the territorial approach proposed here, for two reasons, which I shall consider in turn. First, heterogeneity can increase the cost of the territorial protection of a language to the point of making it prohibitive (§§5.9–5.11). Secondly, heterogeneity can sometimes take such a form that conflict arises about which (if any) of the languages already present should be coercively protected in a particular territory (§§5.12–5.13).

5.9. The cost of universal proficiency

Imposing a coercive regime that protects a weaker language in a particular territory can be expected to involve a cost, relative to accepting the rule of a stronger language, whether through a regime

that imposes the latter as the official language or through an accommodating regime that allows it to prevail as the unintended outcome
of individual choices. Think of the protection of Europe's national
languages against the invasion of English, or of Slovenian versus
Serbo-Croat in the Republic of Slovenia, or of Basque versus Spanish
in the three Basque provinces, or of Romansch versus German in
parts of the Swiss canton of Graubünden, or of Ciluba versus French
in the two Kasai Provinces of the Democratic Republic of the Congo.
In all these very diverse situations, the cost of introducing and enforcing a coercive regime on behalf of a weaker language has two main
potential components. The more obvious one relates to the resources
needed to secure universal proficiency in the protected language
throughout the population concerned (§5.9). The other component
is somewhat less obvious. It relates to the impact of the regime on the
territory's attractiveness (§§5.10–5.11).[38]

As mentioned before (§§5.5–5.6), whatever linguistic regime applies to a territory must ensure that all permanent residents are given
easy access to an adequate level of proficiency in the local official
language, sufficient to give them fair access to political participation
once this language is made a 'queen'. The formulation of this constraint is somewhat vague. Obviously, the more ambitious the interpretations of 'easy access' and 'adequate level', the higher the
expected cost of the territorial regime to the linguistic community
concerned. Not only will the resources required to secure the
learning be greater. In addition, owing to quicker effective competition by newcomers, the economic rent captured by the locals will be
less than under less ambitious interpretations, and—assuming the
illegitimacy or unfeasibility of closed borders—the territory's
attraction to outsiders will be greater. Whether the interpretation
is modest or ambitious, the relevant cost is comparative. How much
more—or possibly less—will it cost to provide everyone with easy
access to adequate proficiency if the weaker language is made the
official one than if one opted for the stronger one?

Opting for the weaker language entails forgoing the economies of
scale—and also in part the exploitation of the big by the small—that
is associated with the use of material of all sorts, written and audio-
visual, that is available in the stronger language. Children's stories,
school and university textbooks, films, and TV programmes will
need to be produced and distributed in sufficient quantity and

quality to provide a sufficiently rich and effective language learning environment. The size of the cost involved obviously depends on the relative sizes of the two linguistic communities involved. There should be a significant difference in this respect, for example, between opting for French rather than English in France and opting for Basque rather than Castilian in Euskadi, and an even greater difference, given the paucity of didactic and other material available, between both these cases and opting for one of the four national languages rather than French in the Democratic Republic of the Congo.

However, this cost needs to be matched against the advantage of being able to rely on the local children's prior widespread competence in the language used as the medium of education and on the dynamics of spontaneous use and spontaneous learning powerfully fostered by this widespread competence. This easily turns the option for French into a massive saving in the case of France, and may well do the same as regards the option for the national languages in the case of the Congo. As long as resources remain so scarce that for most Congolese primary school pupils the only French that is heard or read is the French spoken or written on the blackboard by a non-native speaker who never learned French properly, the gains from economies of scale remain rather virtual and are easily offset by the possibility of using an African language that is the native language of many of the pupils.[39] Under less dire material circumstances, Finland and Flanders opted for Finnish and Dutch, respectively, rather than the once dominant Swedish and French. One may conjecture that this linguistic choice greatly contributed to the effectiveness of their education system. Would Finnish and Flemish pupils now feature at the top of the OECD's PISA rankings of average educational performance had a different choice been made?

In this light, it would seem that the territorial protection of a weaker language, far from being a burden—owing to the sacrifice of some economies of scale—should provide in many cases a less expensive way of spreading proficiency in the territory's population. But taking the linguistic heterogeneity of many territories into account forces us to qualify this suggestion immediately. First, the advantage of the local language over the stronger one is reduced if the native language of the local population consists of a wide variety of dialects rather than a single standard that matches exactly the official language picked by the coercive regime. The greater the linguistic distance between the dialects and this language and the more numerous and concentrated the speakers of each of them, the costlier it will be to achieve universal proficiency in the chosen language, and the smaller, therefore, the cost advantage of choosing it.

Secondly, the advantage of choosing the local language also shrinks as a result of linguistic heterogeneity generated by immigration, again especially if the languages spoken by immigrants are very different from the official local one and if immigrants with the same native language come in large numbers and settle in the same neighbourhoods. Under contemporary conditions, this second form of heterogeneity makes for a greater challenge than the first one because the language spoken by immigrants, unlike local dialects, is often a language used in audiovisual media. Thanks to the spreading of satellite dishes, cable TV, and the internet, these can now easily and cheaply reach the immigrants themselves and their offspring. Exposure to the local official language is thereby considerably reduced. This trend is reinforced and its effects are amplified by various sorting mechanisms: if the café's TV broadcasts nothing but Turkish programmes, what is the chance of it attracting or retaining non-Turkish customers? This makes it considerably more difficult for linguistic competence in the local language to spread among the immigrant population, including through the school system, as children are far more likely to keep speaking the immigrant language to each other than used to be the case when only local TV channels were accessible.

Heterogeneity of this sort increases the cost of achieving universal proficiency everywhere.[40] It does so even when the language in which it is supposed to be achieved is English, as it is in Bradford or Los Angeles. In continental Europe, it reduces the otherwise huge cost advantage of opting for the local language rather than the lingua franca: achieving universal proficiency in Italian among Prato's Chinese or in German among Kreuzberg's Turks is no longer that much easier than making them all proficient in English.[41] Moreover, there is a growing number of situations in which the linguistic heterogeneity generated by immigration is of such a nature that the cost advantage in favour of the weaker local language is not only reduced but starts being reversed. This is the case when immigrants, whether native speakers or not, are already competent to some extent in the stronger language—say, Ecuadorians or Moroccans speaking at least some Spanish in Catalonia, or Pakistanis or Kosovars speaking at least some English in Sweden—and can count on many locals understanding it. Immigrants will soon find out that they can get away with hardly any knowledge of the local language. Especially when the local language is not widely spread and when the immigrants are not sure how long they will stay, probability-driven learning will never be sufficient for competence in the local language to overtake competence in the lingua franca and hence become the maxi-min language often enough to trigger the virtuous circle of linguistic integration.

When the cost of universal proficiency is boosted by home-grown and/or imported linguistic heterogeneity, now made more recalcitrant by the availability of modern media, a linguistic community may discover that it has become much cheaper to forgo the (now reduced) advantage of pursuing universal proficiency in a language closer to the mother tongue of its members and take full advantage of the economies of scale offered by surrender to a stronger, more widely spread language. It may then start asking whether the coercive protection of its language is worth the emerging net cost. This question is even more likely to arise once the community becomes aware of the second main dimension of the cost of a coercive territorial regime: its impact on the attractiveness of the territory concerned.

5.10. The ground floor of the world

This second dimension of the cost of a territorial regime shows most strikingly in the growing asymmetric flow of human capital towards what I shall call the *ground floor of the world*, that is those parts of the world in which English, the worldwide lingua franca, is the dominant language, essentially the greater part of North America, the British Isles, Australia, and New Zealand. Estimates by the World Bank indicate that three of the ground floor countries (the USA, Canada, and Australia), totalling hardly more than 5 per cent of the world's population, house nearly 75 per cent of the world's 'expatriate brains', defined as those graduates of tertiary education who are not currently domiciled in their country of birth. In 2000, the OECD as a whole had an aggregate net surplus of about 12 million brains, that is there were about 12 million more graduates born outside the OECD and currently living in the OECD than there were graduates born in the OECD currently living elsewhere. However, the six Anglophone OECD countries alone enjoyed a surplus of about 14 million brains, about 10 million of them in the USA, while the non-Anglophone part of the OECD suffered a net brain loss of about 2 million. More compactly (and paradoxically): out of the 12 million brains gained (in net terms) by the rich portion of the planet, 14 million flocked to its ground floor compartment.[42]

This strong asymmetry has more than one cause. But it would be hard to deny the importance of the linguistic factor. Just imagine that you are thinking of moving abroad. Which country you will seriously consider moving to will no doubt be affected by many factors, and above all by job opportunities. However, which job opportunities you are likely to be best informed about and which you feel you would be (or could quickly become) suitable for will be significantly affected by whether or not you know the country's language. Moreover, if you have a family, which country you would find it sensible to move to is bound to be influenced by which languages your spouse and children already understand and speak, or could easily learn, or which you believe it would be useful for them to learn wherever they settle later in their lives.[43]

These considerations have some weight for all categories of migrants,[44] but they can be expected to be particularly weighty for the migration of the highly skilled.[45] First, the highly skilled are more likely to have acceptable job opportunities at home and can therefore afford the luxury (relative to the needs of sheer survival) of not inflicting too much of a linguistic adjustment cost on themselves and their families. Secondly, the jobs for which they would qualify have, on average, far greater linguistic requirements than unskilled jobs. Thirdly, the probability that highly skilled workers and their families already have, before migration, a good knowledge of at least one foreign language is far higher than for other workers. Finally, the highly skilled have a greater probability of having studied abroad, with a preference for countries whose language they knew best or particularly wanted to know better, and where they have studied is bound to affect where they may stay or return to in order to work.[46]

In a world in which a number of mother tongues have developed into regional lingua francas, the asymmetry just described can be expected to generate a number of regional attractor basins into which the highly skilled will tend to descend from the linguistic hills formed by countries whose languages are hardly known abroad. In a world in which English is being snowballed, through the mechanism sketched at the start (§§1.3–1.5), into the single global lingua franca, we can expect the formation of a huge ground floor towards which the highly skilled of India and China, Finland and Hungary, Germany and France, will tend to converge more and more, without anything like a matching tendency for the highly skilled of the United States or Britain to climb up to the Mandarin plateau, let alone to the Hungarian peak. In an increasingly knowledge-based economy, it is not difficult to understand how heavy a cost this systematic net loss of highly selected, expensively trained people may mean in terms of economic dynamism.[47] As the lingua franca spreads further, one can expect a constant swelling of the pool of potential recruits for highly skilled jobs on the ground floor. With such a large pool, the countries concerned can allow themselves to be selective.[48] The more economic dynamism is boosted as a result, the more attractive these places become, language aside, and hence the greater the scope for more creaming off from the highly skilled population of the rest of the world.[49] For upper-floor territories, this chronic net outflow of human capital, in so far as its causation has a linguistic dimension, looks like a cost inherent in their linguistic regime far more significant, under present conditions, than the loss of economies of scale.

5.11. Diaspora buffers and regime relaxation

As always, however, it is important to mind the limits of partial equilibrium reasoning and to reflect on likely general equilibrium effects. In this case, we should explore the possibility that convergence to the ground floor may systematically induce processes that buffer, perhaps even reverse, the impact on the cost for the upper floors. First, as for all types of migration in today's world, there are the remittances sent back home by migrant workers to their close or more remote relatives. For various reasons, including the enhanced safety of trans-national bank transfers and the dwindling cost of keeping in touch, the volume of these remittances has been growing steadily.[50] Secondly and presumably far more significantly as regards the highly skilled, there is the transfer of knowledge by those returning to their countries of origin, whether by virtue of what they learned when studying, training and working in a foreign country, or by virtue of the network of trusted contacts they established during their stay abroad.[51] Thirdly, the presence on the ground floor of bright brains from all over the world makes the ground floor particularly vulnerable to the cheap worldwide spreading of whatever knowledge it possesses and produces. The presence of highly trained non-Anglophones on Anglophone soil greatly helps in making this information quickly detectable, understandable, and usable in the rest of the world.[52] Fourthly and more speculatively, one by-product of the ground floor intelligentsia being swollen and intimately infiltrated by people arriving, permanently or temporarily, from all over the world may have the effect of making the international and development policies favoured by the ground floor countries more favourable to the rest of the world than they would otherwise be.[53]

Awareness of these four buffering mechanisms should make upper floor countries somewhat less nervous about the haemorrhage of human capital that is beginning to take on worrying proportions. But even when these diaspora mechanisms work best, they cannot be assumed to drive the cost of the brain drain to zero. Can upper floor countries do more to reduce this cost, short of dropping their territory to the ground floor, that is abandoning the territorial protection of their language by making it as comfortable linguistically for the highly skilled of the world to settle in their territory as to settle on the ground floor, whether in terms of schools, administrative procedures, or participation in political life? Perhaps they can cautiously relax the coerciveness of the regime without letting it unravel altogether.

The most common way of doing this is by making the coercive regime less extensive, more specifically by exempting from it the whole or parts of the daily operation of institutions of higher education and scientific research.[54] In the absence of such a relaxation of the territorial regime, the spreading of competence in the lingua franca (and of the desire to improve it) would keep swelling the pool of students wanting to study in the higher education institutions of the ground floor. The latter's ability to attract and select the best students would keep being enhanced and the relative quality of its higher education system would keep rising, both because the quality of one's peers is a chief determinant of what one gets (including network-wise) out of one's years in higher education and because institutions with better students are better positioned to attract and retain better teachers. In a knowledge-based economy, being home to dynamic institutions of higher learning and research is a major asset. For upper floor countries, having the quality of their higher education eroded by the ground floor effect is a major handicap which they can and do try to minimize in various ways. The rapid weakening of the resistance to the use of English in higher education is a central part of this strategy, at the expense of the universities' ability to keep irrigating the national cultures of non-Anglophone countries.[55]

Rather than making the regime less extensive by exempting some institutions, one could also make it less general by making exceptions for some some people, typically by lengthening the period or broadening the spectrum of toleration for the linguistic adjustment of highly skilled people immigrating for good. Or, if this is hard or expensive to implement for people scattered throughout the territory, one could instead opt to lower a small but crucial part of the territory to ground floor level, that is to create duly circumscribed 'linguistically free zones' in which the constraints of the territorial linguistic regime are lifted, at least as regards the lingua franca. The highly skilled and their families who settle in these zones, typically selected because of their high-tech vocation, would be relieved of the heavy 'tax' of having to learn the local language. Owing to the maxi-min dynamics, the lingua franca can be expected to gradually impose its imperial rule on these zones, but the rest of the territory would remain protected.[56]

Automatic diaspora-linked buffers and carefully circumscribed relaxations may reduce significantly the economic disadvantage—relative to the ground floor, the part of the planet in which English is the only language one needs to know—that is inflicted on a territory by the adoption of a coercive linguistic regime, but they are unlikely, in most cases, to reduce it to insignificance.[57] Note that the advantages and disadvantages that accrue to a territory associated with a linguistic community must be clearly distinguished from those that accrue to the members of that community. If the conclusion of the previous section remains correct despite the qualifications just made, the conjunction of lingua franca spreading and territorially differentiated linguistic coercion already confers a major advantage to Anglophone *territories* and will do so even more in the future. But if the conclusion of Chapter 3 is correct, this same conjunction will inflict a long-term disadvantage to Anglophone *populations*.[58] At the root of this paradox is the fact that the maxi-min dynamics will make it increasingly difficult for Anglophones to learn any language other than their own, whereas the multiplication of opportunities to hear, read, speak, and write English makes it ever easier for native speakers of other languages to learn it (§3.9). Consequently, as long as coercive territorial differentiation prevails, Anglophones will tend to be confined to the ground floor, while non-Anglophones will have access to both the ground floor and their own upper-floor niche, big or small.[59]

This discussion of the ground floor argument shows how domestic linguistic heterogeneity of a very specific sort increases the cost of implementing a territorial regime. It is not just that home-grown or imported linguistic heterogeneity makes it harder to secure universal proficiency in the official language (§5.9). In addition, the population's highly skilled becoming fluent in the lingua franca makes them footloose, and insistence on the territorial regime keeps feeding a net brain drain (§§5.10–5.11). Consequently, relative to letting the lingua franca rule, the coercive protection of a weaker language faces a potential net cost far higher than would have been the case in the context of a perfectly homogeneous monolingual population. We shall turn shortly to the question of whether this cost is worth paying and of who should pay the bill. Before doing so, however, we need to consider the most serious challenge that arises from linguistic heterogeneity.

5.12. Deep heterogeneity

The hardest problem that a territory's linguistic heterogeneity creates for a territorial regime is not that it makes universal proficiency in the official language costlier to achieve, nor that it induces a permanent leakage of human capital. The hardest problem arises when a subset of the territory's population resists subjection to the coercive regime because it has its own language and wants to protect it in a similar way. How should we handle *deep linguistic hetero-geneity* of this sort, that is the presence in the territory of substantial communities of permanent residents that not only speak a distinct language, but perceive it as distinct and identify sufficiently with this distinctiveness for them to wish it to enjoy the parity of esteem territorial regimes are meant to pursue? To simply subject them to the coercive rules that apply to the territory would seem to blatantly contradict parity of esteem and to be far worse from this standpoint than an accommodating regime. But two other options are available, consistent with the concept of a territorial regime (§5.1): the joint protection of two or more official languages and linguistic subdivision.

Extending coercive protection in the same territory to more than one language can be done in two ways: disjunctively, that is by offering the choice in public communication and in education between two or more languages, and conjunctively, by requiring and securing competence in these languages in the whole popula-tion. The disjunctive formula, however, does nothing to protect a weaker language against gradual eviction by a stronger one, as illustrated by the cases of bilingual Canada and bilingual Belgium before the introduction of the territorial regime (see §5.4). It would therefore fail to achieve what is expected for the sake of parity of esteem.[60]

The conjunctive formula is more promising, but very demanding. It requires a determined and persistent effort in order to prevent the maxi-min dynamics from perpetuating a massively asymmetric bilingualism, against the background of general awareness that one shared language is sufficient for effective inter-communication. The size of this effort is such that, in the conjunctive interpretation of bilingualism, the dream of a bilingual Canada never materialized, that the project of a bilingual Belgium was dismissed and that the idea of a bilingual or trilingual Spain is envisaged by no one.[61] The only situations in which a conjunctive regime is a real option are close to monolingual territorial regimes protecting an official language widely spread locally in combination with universal learning of the same lingua franca.[62] Think of Catalan combined with Spanish within Catalonia and, more ambitiously, Luxemburgish combined with (closely related) German and French in the Grand Duchy of Luxemburg.[63] Compulsory schooling in the weaker local language as the exclusive medium at the early stage is a necessary condition for this to work.[64]

Thus, a plural official language regime does not really provide a solution to deep linguistic heterogeneity within a territory. Its disjunctive version misses the point altogether. And its conjunctive formula cannot dispense with giving a firm priority to the universal early learning of the weaker local language, with the stronger language being learned both in immersion mode at later stages of schooling and above all outside school, in roughly the same way as a lingua franca can and should be. This is not that different from a monolingual coercive regime. It may nonetheless remain sufficiently distinct from it to be regarded as securing parity of esteem, especially when competence in the second school language is achieved to the same or a greater extent than competence in the first one. But in other cases the primacy given to one language, albeit a weaker one, is precisely what is being challenged in a situation of deep linguistic heterogeneity. If there is a solution, therefore, it can only come from subdivision: the creation of new borders around a new territory with its own protected language, or possibly the redrawing of linguistic borders so that part of the territory can join an adjacent one with a shared language.

If the deep linguistic heterogeneity is spatially structured, that is if the various languages are fairly neatly concentrated in some parts of a country, and if the areas so defined are sufficiently large and continuous, it should be possible to draw linguistic borders, give a privileged status to a different language in each area, and allow each of these languages to be a 'queen' or at least a 'princess' in the area concerned, once given a certain degree of political autonomy (see § 5.5). Even in this favourable case, there is likely to remain a fair amount of deep linguistic heterogeneity within the newly drawn borders. Linguistic cleansing of the hard, fundamental-liberties-violating sort illustrated by the Greek-Turkish population swaps in the 1920s is not the only way of dealing with this.[65] In some circumstances, there can be an effective soft form of linguistic cleansing that does not resort to the forced relocation of residents with a particular native tongue, but to the forced relocation of enterprises that work as attractors for residents with that mother tongue.[66]

Under far more general circumstances, the remaining conflict can be appropriately alleviated by the concession of temporary 'linguistic facilities'. Residents taken by surprise when new linguistic borders are being established or when a new legal interpretation is being given to existing linguistic borders can legitimately ask, consistent with the requirement of parity of esteem, that they should keep enjoying the linguistic rights they enjoyed before the change, at least under some reasonable cost constraint: a whole school will not be kept open for the one remaining pupil. They can make use of this possibility until they die or move away, without this possibility being extended to any newly born or newly arriving resident.[67] These transitional measures will be automatically phased out as the original victims of the new regime leave the scene. Their offspring will be subjected to the new regime, consistent with respect of their fundamental rights, such as the right to transmit their native language to their children or to run voluntary associations in their language.

The purpose of such transitional measures is to make the pursuit of parity of esteem through a territorial regime feasible in a way that is respectful of people whose linguistic preferences need to be overruled. It is definitely not to ensure that no one loses as a result of the new linguistic regime. For example, the coercive protection of a language, when introduced, will make access to the territory less convenient for some allophones who were considering entering the territory. Some will decide not to come because of the new linguistic constraints, and some will come but, however generously and effectively linguistic integration is being organized, will have to incur an adjustment cost which they would have preferred to do without. This is not a problem. It cannot be expected that the introduction of a new linguistic regime, just as that of a new tax-and-transfer system, should be a Pareto improvement, that is, that it should compensate those who suffer from it as much as is needed to make them at least as well off as beforehand. On the contrary, it is inherent in the justification of territorial coercion on grounds of parity of esteem that there should be this costly 'bowing' through language learning. Even assuming a right of free movement across borders, linguistic communities that have laid a successful claim on a territory can legitimately place a hurdle in the way of those wanting to come and share the territory's opportunities, albeit one that needs to be lowered through the provision of cheap and effective language learning opportunities (§5.9).

So far so good. Unfortunately, there are other situations of deep linguistic heterogeneity that are not easily amenable to a territorial solution through subdivision, owing to the small size, scattering and/or intertwining of the linguistic minorities concerned. But the guiding principle should remain the same. For the three reasons presented above (§§5.3–5.5), justice as parity of esteem allows these communities to claim a territory for their language. However, they must be aware of the cost involved: chiefly the resources required to secure universal proficiency in the chosen language among the people, possibly many of them allophones, choosing to stay living or to settle in the territory (§5.9), and the loss of human capital and economic activities induced by the dissuasive obligation to learn a language with what is, generally, a relatively small spread (§§5.10–5.11). Moreover, they must also be aware of some qualifications in the benefits to be expected: allophones whom the new regime would deprive of some of their linguistic rights should be allowed to retain them until they leave or die, and if the territory is small, or discontinuous, or strongly interdependent with territories with a different official language, the extent to which the chosen language will enjoy a 'queen' status may have to remain very limited.

Once a realistic assessment is made of both costs and benefits, many, indeed most linguistic communities will not even think of claiming a territory for their ancestral way of speaking. They will resign themselves to letting their dialect melt away, and reserve it for private celebration. Shaping a territorial regime in a way inspired by parity of esteem does not require that each existing language should be territorially protected. From this standpoint, the preservation of a language is not a fetish to be imposed on its native speakers on the ground that loyalty to their ancestors requires it, or that it would enable them to lead a more authentic life, or that linguistic diversity is an invaluable part of the human heritage that should not be squandered. As Helder De Schutter (2008: 116) puts it, there is nothing wrong with linguistic suicide. Or at least there is nothing that makes it wrong in the justification of territorial regimes on the basis of parity of esteem. If against the background of a realistic anticipation of the costs and benefits involved (the geographically concentrated part of) the community of native speakers of a particular language does not want to claim territorial protection for it, then parity of esteem does not demand that it should be protected.

5.13. Democratic settlement

As a consequence of assessing the relative sizes of costs and benefits, both enthusiasm for and resistance to alterations of the existing linguistic regime should be tempered, and territorial claims should become more modest than would otherwise be the case. In particular, borders proposed by all sides will get closer to those that maximize the inclusion of native speakers *and* minimize the inclusion of non-native speakers, whose proficiency in the chosen language will have to be secured and paid for. In many cases, however, conflict will persist, for example concerning border areas that are resource-rich but sparsely populated, or areas in which the respective proportions of native speakers are changing fast as a consequence of economic development and urbanization. How should persistent disagreements be settled?

Ultimately, no doubt, by some sort of democratic process.[68] But this answer is far too short. It leaves open a number of questions, crucial in this case, about the contours of this democratic consultation. What is the scale at which the latter is to be organized? Should it be organized in several entities and obtain a majority in each? Are the existing administrative borders of the chosen entities the appropriate ones? And should such a consultation happen once and for all, or be organized at regular intervals?[69] As usual, the role of political philosophy is not to usurp the prerogatives of democratic politics but to guide it, including in the shaping of the relevant democratic consultations.

In the spirit of parity of esteem, the consultation should be structured so as to be most favourable to the weaker language that is meant to be given territorial protection. This means a territory that includes as many native speakers of that language as possible, so as to benefit as much as possible from economies of scale, and as few residents as possible with no or little knowledge of the language and little socio-linguistic propensity to learn it, so as to minimize the likely cost of achieving universal proficiency in the chosen language. In the spirit of parity of esteem, it is also essential that the democratic consultation that creates or endorses a territorial regime should establish stable expectations. If the borders or their meaning can be easily revised at any time, the regime cannot effectively foster the respectful attitude of linguistic adjustment it is meant to help generalize. On the contrary, it will stimulate an uncompromising attitude of conquest on one side and a hostile resistance to invasion on the other.[70] At the same time, one cannot and should not prevent politically organized linguistic communities from changing their minds in the light of new trends and democratic debate about whether or not territorial protection is worth the trouble. But the purpose of the regime is likely to be better served if subsequent debates and the uncertainties unavoidably associated with them did not focus on abolishing, creating, or shifting some linguistic borders, but rather on relaxing or stiffening the coercive rules for the territory concerned (see pp.134–5).

Once properly framed both space-wise and time-wise, it is important that the democratic consultation should ask the right sort of question. The consultation needed is not a linguistic census. It is not about which language one was brought up in, speaks best, speaks most often, or is most attached to. It is about whether or not, in the light of the many positive and negative consequences one can reasonably anticipate, one wants firm territorial protection to be granted to a language to which one has a privileged relation by virtue of where one lives. Some people may not care about such protection, or be opposed to it, even though the language concerned is both their native language and their best language. This language may form no central part of their subjective identity and they may not feel insulted in the least if it were deliberately left to die. More generally their emotional attachment to the language may not be worth the cost its territorial protection would involve, once realistically assessed. For a given level of identification or emotional attachment, the answer will differ according to the socio-linguistic factors that affect the cost—how large is the community of native speakers, how linguistically heterogeneous is the territory it claims—but also on the economic prosperity of that territory. This is the case not only because parity of esteem is a 'superior commodity', one for which the demand increases as a population rises above poverty, but also because linguistic coercion on behalf of the local language can be expected to have a less disastrous effect on the net outflow of human capital when the territory is thriving. The impact of the economic cost, and hence also the answer to the question, will also differ within the population of a given territory, between those who would benefit from facing less competition from outsiders at home and those who would suffer from the loss of their contribution to the local economy.

For these various reasons, opinions may differ widely, and however the voting body is territorially circumscribed, unanimity is out of reach. If those against protection are the losers, they may try to exempt part of the territory though a consultation on a smaller scale. Or they will have to resign themselves to taking advantage of transitional facilities they may be granted (§5.12) or to moving out if this is not sufficient. If, instead, those in favour of protection are a minority, they too may try again a lower level, where the native speakers of the language are more densely concentrated. If that fails too, they should simply come to terms with the fact that their linguistic community is not willing to shoulder the fair cost associated with the coercive protection of their language under contemporary conditions.

5.14. Fair resignation

This is how—and how far—the requirement of justice as parity of esteem can justify and guide the coercive territorial protection of languages. What matters is not that each language should be so protected, but that each linguistic community should have the right to opt for such a protection providing it is willing to shoulder the fair net cost (if any) of doing so, the various facets of which have been explored above. Clearly, poor, small, or scattered communities will more frequently find that the territorial protection of their language is not worth the cost they would need to pay for it, and for many of them the price will simply be prohibitive. The right each of them has to elicit parity of esteem by imposing coercive rules that protect its language can be described as a sheer formal freedom, unmatched by a corresponding real freedom for some of them, owing to circumstances beyond their control.

Let us abstract, for the moment, from the inequality in real freedom or opportunities that arises from unequal wealth. Even with equal per capita wealth, territorial protection will tend to be prohibitively costly for linguistic communities that are small or scattered. This is, I submit, as it should be. If the justification given for a territorial regime were that it is needed to give every person access to a societal culture, or to a normal range of opportunities, or more generally to the conditions of personal autonomy,[71] then redistribution could be justified from the bigger to the smaller communities, so that each can afford the cost of an appropriate linguistic regime. But this is not the approach adopted here. What should guarantee opportunities and autonomy to all is the efficient acquisition of whatever language is allowed to rule the territory. It does not need to be the weaker language for which territorial protection could be claimed on grounds of parity of esteem.

Small linguistic communities that would like to give territorial protection to their language can appropriately be described as entertaining a taste for a particular way of honouring their language that happens to be expensive because of their small size. They did not choose to have that native language, and they wish that the price they have to pay for protecting it were lower, just as they may wish that the per capita cost of TV series originally produced in their language were not much higher than average as a result of the sheer fact that their language happens to have less native speakers. This is bad luck of a sort that requires no compensation. It is analogous to the bad luck experienced by those attached to a family house that turns out to be expensive to maintain. And because the option of shifting to a competing language is less tricky than the option of shifting to another religion, failing to compensate on this ground those whose language is more expensive to protect is, if anything, less problematic than failing to compensate those whose religion happens to be more expensive to practise.[72] If given a realistic estimate of the costs it will have to bear, a linguistic community finds the expense excessive, it is not for others to chip in. The vanishing of a language must be accepted. This may be sad, but not unjust.[73]

The position adopted here is strictly parallel to the one adopted with regard to the first strategy for pursuing linguistic justice as parity of esteem (§4.4). In contrast to the linguistic services required for equality before the law or political participation, expensive ways of asserting the equal dignity of a particular language have to be funded—at a per capita cost that will vary greatly—by those linguistic communities that insist on it, or the countries with which they are associated. Similarly, the possibly expensive implementation of a territorial regime has to be funded—at a level that can vary greatly per capita—by the linguistic communities that want it, without expecting the burden to be shared by others. In the case of the symbolic assertion of equal dignity, some minimal—cheap and salient—provision can even be made mandatory and its funding is not an issue. Think about the way in which Gaelic now features on the EU buildings' multilingual plaques, but hardly anywhere else. An analogous inexpensive minimal service in the territorial dimension might take the form of the preservation of place names and the name of some institutions—say, calling the Parliament the *Oireachtas* or the Prime Minister the *Taoiseach*. Beyond this, what is required by parity of esteem is only that every linguistic community should have the right to protect its language through the enforcement of a territorial linguistic regime, not that it should have the real capacity to exercise it.

It is conceivable that only a few linguistic communities will be able or choose to exercise this right—at the limit none at all, which would give the lingua franca free rein. In that case, the reciprocity clause essential to parity of esteem will start sounding hollow (§5.6). To most newcomers, it will then be impossible to say: 'Adjust to our language exactly as we would adjust to yours if we moved to the territory in which yours has been made the official language.' We would then need to resort to a rather far-fetched counterfactual reciprocity twice over: 'Adjust to the language we are paying the price of protecting, just as we would adjust to yours if we moved to a territory in which your linguistic community had chosen to pay the cost of protecting its language.' But it is unlikely that we shall be driven that far. It is precisely the likelihood that many linguistic communities will be able to exercise their right to territorial protection and will choose to do so that gives the second strategy far more substance than the first one under contemporary conditions.

Moreover, as we move closer to greater global distributive justice, wealth inequalities will decrease and more linguistic communities will be enabled to exercise their right to protect their language. As their budget set is expanded and the threat of crippling emigration is reduced, the protection of more relatively small languages will become affordable. Resignation to the disappearance of one's language is only really fair if it operates against the background of a just distribution of global wealth. The quicker we move to global distributive justice, therefore, the less unfair resignation will occur and the more numerous the languages that will be territorially protected before it is too late.[74] However, both because of differences in size and concentration and because of the possibly large discrepancy between a lax-egalitarian conception of global justice and strict equality, global distributive justice will not make territorial protection equally affordable to all communities, nor so affordable that all will opt for it. Nonetheless, in this ideal world even more than under contemporary conditions, one may expect many languages to be preserved by virtue of the territorial regime parity of esteem justifies.

If we now turn, against this background, to today's European context, justice understood as parity of esteem gives us unambiguous guidance: it is perfectly fine to allow and even accelerate the spreading of competence in English, but at the same time we must introduce or reaffirm a territorially differentiated coercive linguistic regime that makes it realistic to expect immigrants to learn weaker local languages, makes it possible to counteract or reverse the latter's slow agony, and makes it legitimate to make them the political languages of the territories concerned. By following and reinforcing the powerful maxi-min dynamics, an apparently even-handed accommodating regime would just play into the hands of the lingua franca's ubiquitous supremacy. With a well-entrenched territorial regime, by contrast, Europe can observe and foster with equanimity the democratization of the lingua franca and its adoption as the medium of a Europe-wide demos. Parity of esteem will be secured by something far more significant than the increasingly marginal symbolic assertion of the equal dignity of all languages in supranational contexts. Universal supremacy being blocked, the arrogance of lingua franca native speakers will be kept in check, they will have to bow before the local 'queens', and Europe's many official languages will be safe.

CHAPTER 6

———

Linguistic diversity

6.1. What is diversity?

When addressing the normative side of language issues, lawyers and philosophers tend to focus on linguistic rights. Linguists and social scientists tend to focus instead on linguistic diversity. And they are not alone. Diversity is, for example, the angle under which language appears in the European Union's Charter of Fundamental Rights (2000: art. 22): 'the Union shall respect cultural, religious and linguistic diversity'. And that the European Union regards diversity as a value it cherishes is further emphasized by the fact that, in May 2004, it chose as its motto 'Unity in Diversity' ('In varietate concordia'), as did the Indian Union before, but in sharp contrast to the United States' 'E pluribus Unum'.[1]

In a normative inquiry about language-related institutions and policies, it is therefore impossible to ignore linguistic diversity. Does it matter if linguistic diversity expands or shrinks, and if so why? Is linguistic diversity valuable in itself or as an important means for something else we value? How does it relate to linguistic justice as characterized in the previous chapters? Does it run the risk of being excessively eroded by the dissemination of the lingua franca? Is it sufficiently protected, or excessively constrained, by the enforcement of a territorially differentiated coercive linguistic regime? If linguistic diversity clashes with linguistic justice, which of the two should yield? Could the extent of linguistic diversity condoned by linguistic justice clash with other demands of justice? And if so, which should be given priority? These are questions that I cannot afford to ignore. But before addressing them, it is important to scrutinize the concepts of diversity in general and of linguistic diversity in particular, as their routine rhetorical use hides confusions and ambiguities that are worth debunking from the start.

Our intuitive notion of diversity contains three dimensions. These I shall label, borrowing from the discussion on biodiversity: richness, evenness, and distance. Take a population A consisting of individuals belonging to three distinct types (or categories), and another population B whose members belong to five distinct types, each of them also speaking only one language. The *richness* of population B is then said to be greater than that of population A, in the sense that the number of distinct *types*—whether species, races, religions, or, in the case that will interest us, native languages—is larger in B than in A. It may therefore be tempting to infer that population B is more diverse than population A. But this would be premature. Why?

Suppose that the three types of our population A are about equally represented in it, whereas 99 per cent of our population B belong to a single type. In the light of this additional information, we shall have no difficulty agreeing that our population A is, after all, more diverse than our nearly homogeneous population B. Diversity, we can conclude from this, is not only a matter of richness, that is of number of types, but also a matter of *evenness*, that is of how equally the population is distributed between those types, or, to put it the other way around, a matter of how little the members of the population are concentrated in one or few types. Thus, richness does not capture diversity adequately without being combined with evenness. Conversely, evenness will not do without richness. To see this, imagine that our population A is joined by one individual belonging to a fourth type. Surely diversity, as we understand it intuitively, can only have increased. Yet evenness unambiguously declines, since the initial distribution of individuals between types was perfectly even (one third for each type) whereas the new one is not. Hence evenness cannot be all there is to diversity. Richness matters independently.

How should these two dimensions be combined? Several indices of 'fragmentation' (or 'fractionalization') have been proposed for this purpose. The most widely used among them is the very intuitive Simpson index:

$$F = 1 - \sum s_i^2$$

that is, 1 minus the sum of the squares of the shares (s_i) of the various types in the population, that is to say of the squares of the numbers of individuals belonging to each type each divided by the number of individuals in the population ($s_i = n_i/N$).[2] The Simpson index increases monotonically with both richness and evenness. It can be interpreted as the probability that any particular member of the population concerned meets someone belonging to a type different from hers in random encounters within the population.[3]

Richness may be enough to capture our intuitive notion of diversity *qua* 'variety' or 'plurality'. Richness and evenness together may be enough to capture our intuitive notion of diversity *qua* 'fragmentation' or 'segmentation'. But they do not exhaust the whole of our intuitive notion of diversity. If island A houses three species of mosquitoes and island B, in the same proportion, one species of mosquitoes, one species of parrots, and one of crocodiles, we shall have no difficulty agreeing that there is more diversity in B than in A. Making such a judgement presupposes some notion of distance. In the case of biodiversity, the extent to which the genetic equipments characteristic of two species differ from one another (genomic distance) and the number of nodes that separate them in the most plausible conjectural genealogical tree (taxonomic distance), have been used for this purpose.[4] This third dimension of diversity can be added to richness and evenness, not just in the area of biodiversity, but whenever some sensible measure of distance can be devised, including, as we shall see shortly, between languages.

Diversity can increase in terms of Simpson-style fragmentation while decreasing in terms of distance, and the other way around. However, the partial ordering produced by the intersection of the three dimensions just discussed (number of types, spreading among types, distance between types) should be sufficient to enable us to assess, in most cases, whether diversity is increasing or decreasing in a particular population, and in many relevant cases whether diversity is greater in one population than in another. On the other hand, if some sufficiently robust and relevant notion of distance is available, one might be tempted to side-step types altogether. Rather than proposing a compound out of the number of types, the spreading of individuals among types and the distances between types, one might wish to go straight for the average distance between individuals.[5] However, what could be considered a rougher index, based on discrete categories, may be more appropriate for some purposes even when a generalized index based on a precise measurement of inter-individual distance is available. Take race, for example, as defined by skin colour. Degrees of darkness may matter for some purposes, but the most useful index of racial diversity is most likely to remain an index of fragmentation defined in terms of that small set of discrete types to which people perceive themselves as belonging and to which others ascribe them.[6]

6.2. What is linguistic diversity?

As regards specifically linguistic diversity, the definition and use of Simpson-style indices of fragmentation is straightforward enough as soon and as long as two conditions are met. First, one must be able to draw a sensible list of distinct languages: there is no continuum of dialects. Secondly, one must be able to ascribe each individual to one and only one of these languages: there are no multilingual individuals. The Simpson index of linguistic fragmentation is then given by the probability that two randomly paired members of the population do not have the same language. The two conditions stated, however, are seldom or never met. How can linguistic diversity be defined when they are not?

Dialectal continuity can only been addressed without arbitrariness by appealing to a notion of linguistic distance. To capture linguistic distance, three families of indices have been proposed. The first family is an analogue of taxonomic distance in the field of biodiversity. Thus, Laitin (2000) and Fearon (2003) use an index based on the number of branches two languages share in a hypothetical family tree of languages, while Pinelli (2005) uses estimates of the length of time since the linguistic communities involved were separated. One problem with such indices is that they need to rely on risky historical speculation for all but the most closely related languages. Another is that they overlook proximity generated through lexical borrowing and other linguistic influences after separation.

This defect could in principle be remedied by using a second family of indices, this time analogous to the biological notion of genomic distance, as suggested by Greenberg's (1956: 109–10) 'resemblance factor'. An index belonging to this family is applied by Kruskal, Black, and Dyen (1992). It is based on the proportion of words with a common origin in a small sample of basic words. The smaller this proportion, the greater the lexical distance between two languages. The limits are obvious: this measure can only rise above zero among languages that belong to the same linguistic family (Indo-European, for example) and, at least in this particular version, it is again insensitive to lexical borrowings and other influences that do not affect the stock of basic roots.[7]

A third family of indices could not possibly have an equivalent in the area of biodiversity. It is based on the assumption that the distance between two languages is reflected in how difficult it is for native speakers of one language to learn the other one. The longer it takes, starting from scratch, to reach a given level of proficiency in one language for an average monolingual speaker of another language, the greater the distance between the two languages. The great advantage of this method is that it can apply to any combination of languages. Its great limitation is that the data it needs are generally very hard to collect. Systematic data with random samples and many language combinations would be prohibitively expensive to collect, and any data set casually constituted will tend to be based on small and biased samples of multilingual people who already had some knowledge of the language to be learned or of related languages before starting the measurement. Nonetheless, in the case of the distance between (American) English and a subset of other national languages, an interesting dataset exists and has been used.[8]

Thus, there are at least these three ways of operationalizing the notion of linguistic distance. The advantage of indices of diversity that incorporate distance is that they can handle situations in which there is a continuity of dialects. In particular, they are far less sensitive to the fairly arbitrary choice between regarding two dialects (say, Neapolitan and standard Italian) as two variants of the same language and regarding them as two distinct languages. Simpson-type indices of fragmentation can take very different values depending on which of these two options is chosen, whereas distance-based indices behave far more smoothly. Furthermore, some empirical studies indicate that indices of linguistic diversity that take linguistic distance into account can be better predictors of important other variables than are indices of fragmentation.[9]

Let us now turn to the question of how to conceptualize linguistic diversity when the second condition is violated: this time, languages are neatly distinct, but individuals can know several of them. Even when discussing the possibility of measuring linguistic distance by learning difficulty, we have taken it for granted so far that linguistic diversity in a population is to be assessed with each of its members assigned to one and only one language, just as biodiversity is to be assessed with every organism assigned to one and only one species. Like other organisms, human beings are stuck with the single species into which they were born, but they have the capacity to become multilingual. This fact has two important consequences for the conceptualization of linguistic diversity.

First, it makes room for a distinct notion of linguistic distance as the lack of overlap between linguistic repertoires rather than as the degree to which two languages differ. Take the case of a population consisting initially of two monolingual communities A and B, and suppose that half of B's members learn the language of A. This learning generates a new mixed type AB, and diversity, as measured by Simpson-type fragmentation indices, would unambiguously rise. But surely, it makes at least as much sense to assert that diversity has thereby been reduced: by being turned into ABs, some of the As have come linguistically much closer to the Bs, and have thereby reduced the average distance between the linguistic repertoires of the members of the population. As soon as some degree of multilingualism is present, in other words, it is natural to define linguistic distance between two individuals as the lack of overlap or degree of non-coincidence between their respective linguistic repertoires, and to define the linguistic diversity of the population as a whole as average linguistic distance so defined. The more languages two people have in common, and the better they know these languages, the smaller the linguistic distance between them. And the smaller this distance, on average, between members of a population taken two by two, the less diverse the population.[10]

Secondly, the possibility of multilingualism forces us to make a further distinction that has no analogue in biodiversity: between the diversity of linguistic competences and the diversity of linguistic performances. Linguistic competence is the knowledge of the rules and vocabulary that constitute a language, while linguistic performance is the actual use of that language in spoken or written utterances. Native speakers of one language can end up speaking most of the time another language learned later in life. Diversity among performances may therefore diverge significantly, typically downward, from diversity among competences. Even in the case of ethology, there is no parallel distinction in the biological realm: the distribution of individuals between species in genetic terms and in behavioural terms will be exactly the same, and hence the degree of diversity will be identical. If you are born a chimpanzee, you will not behave like a mosquito, nor conversely.

The upshot of this conceptual discussion is that it is possible and fruitful to mobilize and transpose the notions of richness, evenness, and distance used to capture biodiversity. But a straightforward transposition is only possible on the assumption that people can each be assigned to one and only one language, say their (single) mother tongue. Once the reality of multilingualism is taken into account, linguistic diversity must also be understood in terms of non-coincidence between linguistic repertoires and at the level of performances, not only of competences. The importance of identifying and distinguishing these various senses of linguistic diversity will now be illustrated by exploring the relationship between linguistic diversity and the spreading of a lingua franca.

6.3. Multilingualism against linguistic diversity?

For this exploration, a handy point of departure is provided by the two chief official goals of the European Union's language policy: the protection of linguistic diversity and the promotion of multilingualism.[11] At first sight, there is a natural complementarity between these two objectives: multilingualism is logically impossible without linguistic diversity, and linguistic diversity is pointless in the absence of multilingual individuals capable of enjoying it. There would indeed be no tension whatever between the two objectives if the EU's multilingualism took the form of the Germans learning Cantonese and Quechua, the French Afrikaans and Telugu, the British

Javanese and Lingala, and so on. But this is not the form it takes, for two main reasons. First, there is an officially declared bias favouring the learning of other EU languages rather than, say, Arabic or Chinese. Secondly, there is an officially unintended bias towards the learning of English, powerfully driven by the maxi-min dynamics.[12] It is this convergent nature of the 'multilingualization' of the European population that generates a strong tension between multilingualism and linguistic diversity in four distinct senses.[13]

First, as the European population is growing more multilingual (or at least bilingual) as a result of EU citizens developing their competence in at least one foreign language, linguistic diversity might be said to increase in terms of richness and evenness, owing to the appearance and gradual expansion of mixed types. However, it can also be said to decrease, if defined by a lack of overlap between the linguistic repertoires of its members. The reduction of linguistic diversity in the latter sense is simply a logical correlate of the reduction of the inability to communicate with one another. It is a direct, unavoidable, and intended consequence of the spreading of a lingua franca or any policy of language learning for the sake of mutual understanding, such as the European Commission's 'mother tongue plus two' programme. And it is presumably no more regrettable as such than the very existence of any language as a link between human beings. Hence, this is definitely not the sense in which the European Union or any other sensible institution would want to promote or protect linguistic diversity.

By virtue of a causal mechanism rather than a logical implication, widening competence in a shared language can be expected to reduce linguistic diversity in a second sense. Whenever native speakers of a language learn another language, this expands the possibility of lexical borrowing and other forms of linguistic influence. If many native speakers of a given language become competent in *the same* non-native language, this possibility becomes a strong probability, and the language they all learned will tend to exert a lasting influence on their native tongue—most obviously through the import of vocabulary, sometimes also through morphological and syntactic changes.[14] Moreover, as the native speakers of *several* languages all become competent in the same lingua franca, such influences bring their languages closer not only to this lingua franca but also to one another. For example, there must be few languages today in which it has not become 'cool' to 'google' 'blogs' and 'tweets' on the 'web'. Owing to this process, it is not just the distance between linguistic repertoires that shrinks—trivially—as a result of the emergence of a lingua franca. It is also the distance between the native languages themselves. Persecution of borrowings and other impurities could attempt to maintain the level of linguistic diversity in this sense. But one may doubt the effectiveness of such a policy, and even more whether preserving or enhancing the distinctiveness of the various languages will matter to more than a handful of purists. This cannot be the main sense in which the EU proclaims its attachment to linguistic diversity.

Thirdly, the spread of the lingua franca can be said to reduce linguistic diversity even in a sense that takes no account of distance between repertoires or between languages and takes only richness and evenness into account, though applied to performances rather than to competences. To illustrate, consider jointly the following two mutually reinforcing trends, both very tangible in Europe today. One is the spreading of competence in English through the explosive maxi-min dynamics to which reference has been made throughout. The other is the growth of the share of linguistic communication that is taking place between people with different mother tongues, or, put differently, the fact that we are moving away from a world of essentially monolingual communities whose members talk only to each other—their village was their world—to one in which people move and communicate across the world—the world is becoming their village. One must then stop taking for granted that the proportion of conversations held in a particular language is roughly equal to the proportion of native speakers of that language.

Once the gap between these two proportions becomes significant, it makes sense to redefine richness and evenness in terms of whether and how much the various languages are being used in conversations, rather than just in terms of their presence and distribution in people's competences. Now add the first trend. As people add competence in English to competence in their native language and interact with people who lack the latter competence, they substitute English for their mother tongue in a growing proportion of their conversations.[15] Hence, while diversity, defined by richness and evenness, need not decline and may even increase as regards EU citizens' competences, it will exhibit a strong tendency to decrease as regards their performances.[16] We are of course very far from a situation of random mixing, but trans-national mobility and trans-national communication are sharply on the increase, and further facilitated by the very spreading of the lingua franca, the use of which they keep favouring. Some people concerned about linguistic diversity may be inclined to dismiss the loss of diversity in this third sense as being no more worrying than the first two, but not when viewed as paving the way to loss of diversity in a fourth sense, to which we now turn.

When the process just described reaches a stage at which people with the same native language start talking to each other in the lingua franca even in the absence of anyone with a different mother tongue, one must be prepared for a decline in diversity in yet another, fourth sense, which concerns competence, not just performance (as did the shrinking of diversity in the third sense) and affects richness, not just distance between repertoires or between languages (as did the shrinking of diversity in the first two senses). The generalization of bilingualism in a linguistic community through the learning by all its members of the same more widely spread language is commonly regarded by sociolinguists as the last stage before the local language starts withering away.[17] Even in Sweden, Denmark, or the Netherlands, we are still quite some way from universal perfect bilingualism. Yet, as English-language courses spread downward from postgraduate to undergraduate levels, there will be a number of domains in which native speakers of a particular language will find it easier to communicate with one another in English than in their own common mother tongue—the alternative being a variant of their mother tongue perforated by strings of lexical borrowings and occasional full sentences in English. This looks like a path to language loss analogous to the standard path to dialect loss, and hence to a loss of linguistic diversity that would be, unlike the first three, a genuine impoverishment.

Throughout the linguistic history of the world, the development of convergent plurilingualism and the associated decline in diversity in the first sense—the lack of overlap between linguistic repertoires—has typically put pressure on diversity in the other three senses. In many cases, oppression and shame accelerated the process. But in today's high-mobility context, the explosive maxi-min dynamics may be powerful enough to complete the job unassisted. Can, and must, loss of linguistic diversity in the last of our four senses be prevented? In Chapter 5, it has been argued both that it can and that it must. Not by resisting the maxi-min dynamics in supranational contexts and international contacts, nor by introducing a categorically differentiated coercive framework that would force people to speak and transmit their native languages, but by implementing a territorially differentiated coercive regime. Part of the parity-of-esteem-based argument in favour of such a regime is precisely related to the need to prevent the 'colonial' dominance of stronger languages at the level of performances (§5.3) and the associated kindness-driven agony of weaker languages at the level of competences (§5.4).

The preservation of some degree of linguistic diversity in at least these two senses is therefore a necessary consequence of the requirements of linguistic justice, as specified in the previous chapter. But the parity-of-esteem-based argument does not justify the preservation of all existing linguistic diversity. Moreover, whatever preservation of linguistic diversity it justifies is simply a by-product of what justice requires, not an aim in itself. We shall turn shortly to the question of whether linguistic diversity should be given independent normative weight. But we need first to make another distinction.

6.4. Local diversity versus inter-local diversity

Just as important as the distinction between three dimensions of diversity—richness, evenness, and distance—is the distinction between what could be called its two levels. Here again, it is helpful to glance at the literature on biodiversity, where a distinction is commonly made between *alpha-diversity*, or the number of species within a particular habitat, and *gamma-diversity* or the number of species within a particular landscape consisting of a set of habitats. Alpha-diversity and gamma-diversity both express richness—or 'variety' or 'inventory diversity'—respectively at the local level of each habitat and at the global level of the landscape. By contrast, *beta-diversity* is meant to express differentiation—or 'distinctiveness' or 'specialization' or 'segregation'—that is the extent to which habitats differ from one another within a given landscape.

Beta-diversity has been defined in the biodiversity literature either as the ratio or as the difference between gamma-diversity (the total number of species in the landscape) and average alpha-diversity (the average number of species in the habitats that make up the landscape). Under either definition, beta-diversity reaches its minimum when all species present in the landscape are present in each habitat, or in as many habitats as the (possibly small) number of their members allows, and its maximum is reached when each species is gathered in a single habitat, or in as few habitats as the (possibly large) number of its members allows.[18]

Beyond the case of biodiversity, we can make a more general distinction between alpha-diversity (or variety) *within* some unit (habitat, neighbourhood, region, country, etc.) of a broader entity (landscape, city, country, world, etc.) and beta-diversity (or differentiation) *across* such units. These units are usually defined in spatial terms, but they need not be. They could correspond, for example, to the various sections of a school or to the various regiments that make up an army. To the extent that the units are defined in spatial terms, I shall speak of *local diversity* to refer to alpha-diversity within one of the smaller units—for example, the number of native languages among the inhabitants of a particular neighbourhood—and of *inter-local diversity* to refer to beta-diversity across these units—for example, the difference (or the ratio) between the total number of nationalities in the population of a city and the average number of nationalities in the population of each of its neighbourhoods.

To capture the notion of inter-local diversity properly, however, it is essential not to confine it, as I have done so far, to the richness dimension, that is to the number of types (species, languages, races, etc.) present in each local unit or in the set of all units. Richness must be supplemented by evenness. Consider the case of an island consisting of two regions. At an early stage, each of the two regions has native Greek speakers and native Turkish speakers in equal proportions, say 50/50. At a later stage, one region has a 90/10 majority of Greeks and the other one a 90/10 majority of Turks. Despite the dramatic shift, the island's inter-local diversity, using the measure specified above, has remained unchanged at its minimum level, since the average number of native languages per region has remained equal to the total number of native languages on the island (beta-diversity = $2 - (2 + 2)/2 = 0$). This obvious defect can be addressed by taking the evenness dimension into account. Various indices which do precisely this have been developed for quite different purposes by sociologists and economists.[19] For example, one could use as an index of inter-local diversity the difference between the Simpson index of fragmentation for the whole entity—the probability of meeting at random someone belonging to a different type from oneself in the population as whole—and the converse of the isolation index used in the sociological literature on segregation—the probability of meeting at random someone belonging to a different type from oneself in one's own local unit. The larger the gap, the more differentiation there is between local units.[20] In our island example, the probability of meeting at random someone belonging to the other ethnic group in one's own region falls from 0.5 to less than 0.2 as one moves from the 50/50 distribution to the 90/10 distribution.[21] Since the Simpson index (for Greeks and Turks in the whole population) is 0.5, the index of inter-local diversity accordingly rises from 0 (= 0.5 − 0.5) to over 0.3 (= 0.5 − 0.2). If each part of the island became completely homogeneous, it would rise to 0.5.[22]

Suppose then that we have some sensible notion of both local diversity—how heterogeneous each place is—and inter-local diversity—how distinctive places are. It does not take much reflection to perceive a potentially strong tension between the two. Maximum local diversity means that every type can be found in every place, whereas maximum inter-local diversity requires that each place hosts only types that cannot be found anywhere else. This holds, in particular, for linguistic diversity.[23] Hence, those wishing to promote local linguistic diversity must realize that this will come at the cost of reduced inter-local diversity. By contrast, if preserving inter-local diversity is a meaningful objective, the development of local diversity will need to be counteracted. Thus, typical 'multiculturalism policies' will tend to foster local diversity at the expense of inter-local diversity, whereas the imposition of a territorially differentiated linguistic regime necessarily favours inter-local diversity at the expense of local diversity. As to the spreading of a lingua franca, it will tend to systematically reduce distance between linguistic repertoires both across local units, as multiculturalism policies do, and within each of them, as a territorial regime does, and will therefore put pressure on the diversity of both performances and competences (as argued in §6.3), unless kept in check through some other means.

In the normative framework proposed so far, a territorially differentiated coercive linguistic regime is the only justified way of containing these diversity-reducing pressures. Should linguistic diversity be protected more than this or indeed resolutely promoted, whether for its own sake or because of its contribution to some valuable objective irreducible to linguistic justice as characterized so far? This is the question to which we now turn.

6.5. Curse or treasure?

Let us start by recognizing that many people find linguistic diversity a plain nuisance. Among them are those who care for nothing as much as for the smooth working of an efficient Europe-wide or global market, with information about what is being supplied anywhere directly understood by all in a single language and with goods and services flowing across all borders without being subjected to cumbersome linguistic constraints.[24] Among them are also those sensitive to the analogue of the economic case for linguistic unification in the national context: as Ernest Gellner and others have emphasized, a labour force rendered more mobile by the sharing of a single language is a major asset for the industrialization of a country.[25] Those who emphasize the drawbacks of linguistic diversity even include some of those who make a living out of it, such as the French linguist Antoine Meillet (1928: 244): 'The small national languages are a stage through which poorly cultured peoples pass on their way to universal civilization. But the multiplicity of the languages currently used in Europe, already inconvenient today, prepares crises which will be hard to resolve, as it goes against the general trends of civilization. The unity of the common language is an immense strength for those who possess it.'[26]

Linguistic diversity, after all, is conceptually tied to mutual unintelligibility, and what is so great about not being able to understand each other?[27] The more languages there are, the more evenly spread these languages, the more distance there is between them, the less overlap between multilingual repertoires, the more difficult, indeed often impossible it will be for people to communicate directly with one another. If a powerful language were to drive all others into gradual extinction, not only would we all enjoy the convenience of being able to use our mother tongue in all the conference rooms and hotel lobbies of the world, but incomparably more would become possible: even in the most remote bazaars, farmyards, and play-grounds, we would be able to understand directly what the locals are telling each other. Once this universal mother tongue is in place, the global reach of diverse yet worldwide media and the massively enhanced trans-national mobility could be relied on to prevent the stable development of mutually unintelligible dialects. Once again, all human beings would 'speak the same language and form a single people', and hence conceivably 'no goal will be unachievable for them' (Genesis 11:6). Is there anything to prevent us from looking forward to this new stage in the progress of mankind, apart from the irrational fear that a jealous Yahweh may strike once more and cruelly thwart our neo-Babelian hubris?[28]

Unlike Meillet, most professional linguists are understandably not keen to see the bulk of the world's languages wither away, many of them only poorly documented, thereby irreversibly ampu-tating the subject matter of their discipline. But most of them are probably also reasonable enough to admit, when pressed, that it would be unfair to attempt to induce some people to keep learning, talking, and teaching a language they would otherwise abandon, for the sole purpose of enabling a small bunch of inquisitive scholars to indulge their intellectual curiosity or to advance their careers by writing erudite pieces in academic journals. To broaden their coali-tion, linguists should have no trouble enlisting translators and inter-preters, who may fear being downgraded to the less lucrative job of philologists, were linguistic diversity to disappear. But this would hardly make the argument less suspiciously corporatist. Nor would their case be much strengthened by the support of the aesthetes who love steeping themselves in delightfully varied linguistic environ-ments. One can sympathize with those who believe (as I do) that the attraction of Tuscan villages would be diminished if Italian had gone into disuse, and that the charm of Rio would suffer if the locals had all switched from Brazilian to American. But all this seems of precious little weight in regard to the great collective benefits of easy universal communication. No doubt those who want to make a persuasive case for the value of linguistic diversity do realize that they need arguments that appeal to less factional interests.[29]

One such argument emphasizes that each language is a unique repository of human knowledge. It comes in two main variants. The more subtle variant rests on the interesting observation that the syntax of a language, its phonological system, its morphology, and its lexicon contain information about the history of the peoples who have been speaking that language for centuries, most obviously about where they came from and which other peoples they are related to or interacted with. With any language that goes extinct without having been adequately recorded, knowledge of this sort is lost forever. A great pity, admittedly, for anyone interested in the relevant fragments of human history. But as an argument for discouraging people from giving up their ancestral language, the irreversible loss of such potential historical knowledge is no more persuasive than the shrinking of the subject matter of professional linguists.

The second variant is less subtle but incomparably broader in scope, and hence more promising as a non-corporatist argument. It rests on the plausible assumption that some things have been known only to people of a particular language, uniquely equipped with the terminology needed to formulate them. It is strikingly illustrated by the attempt to seal a strong alliance between advocates of biodiversity and of linguistic diversity.[30] There is an undeniable positive cross-regional correlation between biodiversity and linguistic diversity, with both species and languages particularly numerous (relative to the sizes of the local human populations) in tropical areas. What explains the correlation, according to at least some supporters of the alliance, is a causal link from linguistic diversity to biodiversity: in the absence of the nature-respecting knowledge incorporated in the many local languages, species diversity would soon be reduced. The correlation, however, is bound to have far more to do with the relative attractiveness of certain climatic conditions for nature- and culture-destroying colonization and industrialization. The relationship between biodiversity and linguistic diversity, as we saw above (§§6.1–6.2), can be instructive, but appeal to a spurious correlation is an unpromising way of harnessing interest in the former in order to generate support for the latter. Consequently, the impact that language conservation may have on species conservation must be, if at all real, very modest, and is likely to be offset by the potential of knowledge dissemination which a switch to a more widespread language would create. This last remark would seem to apply more generally to any instance of this second variant of the argument: people who possess some knowledge encapsulated in their native language can express it in the more widely spread language they have learned, even if this means enriching the latter with some useful lexical imports from their ancestral language. By doing so, they will not only preserve the knowledge in question, but also make it more widely available.

However, the knowledge encapsulated in a language may not consist in a set of discrete information items of this sort, but rather, more vaguely and more profoundly, in a 'mental universe' that is intimately associated with a language and would vanish if the language were to go extinct. The idea here, commonly associated in quite different versions with Johann Gottfried von Herder, Wilhelm von Humboldt, Edward Sapir, and Benjamin Whorf, is that some features of the language help determine some features of a 'worldview', of a 'way of thinking', and that a reduction in the diversity of the mental universes so determined would be a regrettable loss of knowledge to mankind. This is an intriguing argument. But to make it stick, one would need, first, to identify a number of features of the 'worldview' or 'way of thinking' shared by all or most native speakers of a language and not too commonly found among native speakers of other languages. Secondly, one would need to be able to ascribe these features to the language itself—rather than to the boundaries with the rest of the world that a shared and distinctive language creates.[31] And thirdly, one would need to motivate the belief that a variation in mental universes induced by haphazard, unintentional linguistic change, is a promising way of acquiring more knowledge—as distinct from providing a fascinating object of study for linguists and cognitive scientists.[32]

Despite these problematic assumptions, the previous argument can sound plausible because it is often confused with a different one, which cannot be so easily dismissed. This distinct argument also appeals to a connection between linguistic diversity and cultural diversity, but one that is not based on the determination of (part of a) culture by features of the language spoken by the relevant community, but rather on the role played by languages in structuring the patterns of interaction and hence the flows of information, education, persuasion, or imitation that relentlessly shape and reshape all aspects of culture. Culture can be roughly defined as a set of ways of thinking and behaving that is durably shared by, and distinctive of, a multi-generational community. Given the nature and reach of present and future media, so this line of argument goes, linguistic diversity is the firmest and increasingly the only serious protection of the diversity of cultures so defined. In the absence of the niches created by language barriers, the culture(s) of the most powerful part(s) of the world would trample on all others. Whether in Europe or in the world, therefore, linguistic diversity preserves more options for individual human beings to choose from—it breeds more 'cultural freedom'—and it leaves more room for collective experimentation, from which mankind as a whole may benefit in the long run.[33]

Though unavoidably speculative, this line of argument must be taken seriously. Cultural diversity is far from being the whole of diversity, but it is a significant part of it, and one can make a case for its being valuable along the path just sketched without being driven to the absurd conclusion that adding obnoxious cultural options makes our world a better world. However, there is a specific negative side inherent in protecting cultural diversity using the tool of linguistic diversity. The more diversity there is—that is, the more linguistically fragmented the population, the more distant the languages involved, the less overlap between linguistic repertoires—the more difficult it is to have access easily, reliably, and rapidly to whatever exists or is invented in any particular culture. True, the dissemination of a lingua franca reduces this obstacle—while at the same time putting downward pressure on the distinctiveness of cultures. But it does not provide as quick and easy access to what is being thought, imagined, discussed, written within any particular culture as would be the case in a linguistically homogeneous world, except for what is expressed directly in the lingua franca or is instantly translated into it. Hence, while we can safely conjecture that linguistic diversity has a positive impact on cultural diversity, we cannot infer from this that it also has a net positive impact on the achievement of the two effects of cultural diversity that most contribute to making the latter valuable: the real freedom of choice among ways of life and the learning potential generated by the greater diversity of cultural experiments. For the greater cultural diversity made possible by linguistic diversity will be partly offset, and in some cases probably far more than offset, by the lesser availability of whatever cultural diversity there is, owing to the linguistic barriers intrinsic to linguistic diversity.

Thus, the case for linguistic diversity as a shield for cultural diversity is definitely stronger than the defence of a plurality of languages as receptacles of knowledge that would be lost if they died. Yet the support to be found from this corner for the preservation, let alone the expansion or maximization of linguistic diversity remains very fragile, and it is certainly insufficient for us to be able to assert with any confidence that we would be better off worldwide, all things considered, with a level of linguistic diversity in excess of what parity of esteem ends up justifying.

6.6. Economic solidarity, identification, and communication

In this light, let us adopt the (albeit provisional) conclusion that no more and no less linguistic diversity is justified than what would be preserved by the territorial regime required on grounds of parity of esteem. But rather than being insufficient, might the linguistic diversity thus justified not be excessive by the standards of the conception of justice adopted in this book? The reason for believing that this may be the case is that linguistic diversity seems to form a powerful obstacle to the effective pursuit of an egalitarian conception of distributive justice.

A useful point of departure for the formulation of this challenge is provided by a set of econometric studies showing a robust negative correlation between linguistic diversity and a number of variables that can be regarded as more or less plausible proxies for the achievement of distributive justice so conceived, or of the extent of economic solidarity understood as institutionalized redistribution from the better off to the worse off within particular societies.[34] For example, an analysis based on a sample of over two hundred countries showed that, after controlling for many variables, there remains a significant negative correlation between, on the one hand, ethnic diversity (using the Simpson index), especially when defined exclusively in linguistic terms, and, on the other, the share of transfers in the country's GDP.[35] Owing to other relevant differences, some linguistically more diverse countries may of course achieve greater economic solidarity than others that are far more homogeneous.[36] But the robust correlations do provide strong evidence for the existence of a genuine *ceteris paribus* relationship.

To make sense of this negative relationship between linguistic diversity and economic solidarity, several mechanisms have been suggested. How generous an economic solidarity system manages to become and remain can schematically be conjectured to be affected by two factors: the willingness of the better-off to share with the worse-off and the ability of the worse-off to mobilize so as to force the better-off to share.[37] Each of these factors can in turn be affected by the degree of linguistic diversity through two mechanisms. On the one hand, linguistic diversity makes *identification* more difficult: a different language makes one part of the population perceive another as alien, as not belonging to the same kind, and hence as less trustworthy, less likely to reciprocate, and less likely to have reciprocated had the roles been reversed. Lesser identification makes both the better-off more reluctant to accept economic solidarity and the worse-off less capable of organizing collectively to press for it.[38] On the other hand, linguistic diversity can also be expected to affect solidarity by making *communication* more laborious: in the absence of an effective medium, it is more difficult for the better-off to be persuasively exposed to arguments of fairness in favour of the worse-off, for the worse-off to coordinate effectively their struggle against the better-off, and for all to settle on the fine grain of the organization of solidarity.[39]

6.7. Local diversity and solidarity

The tension thus highlighted can be expected to hold for both local and inter-local diversity. That local linguistic diversity should weaken the potential for economic solidarity is not a problem for supporters of a territorial regime who care about distributive justice. For a territorial regime, as justified by parity of esteem, is not exactly friendly towards local linguistic diversity. The local language, it was stipulated, cannot legitimately be made a queen without enabling all the territory's permanent residents to acquire proficiency in it (§5.5). For this reason, one constraint imposed on any linguistic community wishing to make use of its right to protect its language is that it should be willing to bear the net cost (if any) of meeting this condition (§5.9). One effect of spreading proficiency in the official language is a major direct contribution to the equalization of economic opportunities. Another is that having a language in common enables all members of the local community to form a common *demos*, and thereby to satisfy an important precondition for a more effective pursuit of economic solidarity at the local level. On the one hand, people from all layers of society are thereby enabled to explain their standpoint to each other, to listen to each other, to take decisions that can seriously claim to reflect an equal concern for the interests of everyone affected. On the other hand, having a language in common enables those who stand to gain from greater economic solidarity to communicate and mobilize far more effectively.

At the same time, a territorial regime will unavoidably tend to reduce local linguistic diversity in each of the four senses listed when discussing the impact of the emergence of a lingua franca and for strictly analogous reasons (§6.3). The intensification of contact may threaten the local survival of languages other than the one that is granted territorial protection, and local cultural diversity will tend to be eroded, possibly even squeezed out altogether, as a result of every local resident becoming exposed to the information and ideas available to every other local resident. No unfairness, no infringement of parity of esteem, is thereby being inflicted on anyone, providing the background assumption is one of reciprocity, however counterfactual (§5.6). Had the roles been reversed, had the (current) autochthonous population been migrating into a territory in which the (current) immigrants' linguistic community had its language fairly protected, they could not have claimed or expected more by way of preservation of the local linguistic and cultural diversity which they would have been causing by moving there. Against the background of this condition, the likely reduction or containment of local linguistic diversity induced by the learning of a common language is perfectly consistent with linguistic justice as parity of esteem, while being a side effect of the pursuit of linguistic justice as the local equalization of opportunities.

Note, however, that the joint pursuit of parity of esteem and equality of opportunities does not dictate that one should aim to eradicate local linguistic and cultural diversity. Indeed, attempts to impose full assimilation are likely be counterproductive. Competence in a shared language is essential to facilitate dialogue, discussion, argumentation, understanding between all components of the political community, but there is no need to turn the community into a linguistic and cultural monolith. Belonging to a common *demos* is essential. Belonging to a common *ethnos* is not. A plurality of languages and associated cultures can be transmitted from generation to generation in addition to the language known in common. Stronger identification with a subset of the political community may persist as a result and compete to some extent with a more inclusive identity. However the sustainability of a high level of local economic solidarity need not be affected if the discourse, institutions, and policies manage to promote and nurture a strong and inclusive territorially defined political identity that not only respects local diversity but gives it pride of place.[40]

Hence, while promoting the equalization of opportunities among all members of the local population, a territorial regime may make room for some *multiculturalism policies*, understood as policies aimed at preserving or respecting local cultural and linguistic diversity. Whether they do must be assessed on a case-by-case basis. There cannot be either a blanket endorsement or a blanket condemnation.[41] To illustrate, take the teaching of, or in, the immigrants' mother tongues. This is a typical multiculturalism policy that can plausibly be defended, in some cases, as a way of formalizing and strengthening the children's valuable competence in a major world language such as Spanish, Arabic, Turkish, or Bengali, but also possibly, far more generally, in the spirit of parity of esteem: especially when the reciprocity condition is particularly virtual—there is little chance of any local ever settling in the territory in which the language concerned is protected, or worse still, there is little chance of the linguistic community concerned ever being able to claim territorial protection for its language (§5.14)—this can be a significant way of symbolically asserting the equal dignity of all languages and the associated identities.

The most straightforward way of providing such language teaching consists in offering this possibility in those schools in which there is sufficient demand for a particular language, owing to a high proportion of pupils with the corresponding origin. In countries in which school choice is not constrained by districting, the provision of such courses will create an incentive for parents of the relevant origin to send their children to those schools. As a result, whatever degree of ethnic mixing has been achieved in the school system will be reduced, and bearing in mind that children's acquisition of the local language depends more on interaction with their peers than on formal teaching, the long-term threat posed to social cohesion (through the causal chain of poor linguistic competence, low productive skills generally, low probability of landing a good job, low chance of social and geographical mobility) is quite considerable. In countries in which school choice is strongly constrained by districting, the threat will be slower to show but deeper, as the provision of immigrant language courses will not only create an incentive to change schools, but also to move, thus fostering segregation not just in schooling but also in housing.

Much of this effect can be switched off, however, if instead of being organized as part of the curriculum of a particular school, the courses are open to pupils from different schools, which, in an urban context, can be a realistic possibility.[42] A small organizational difference between two 'multiculturalism policies', in this case two ways of accommodating local linguistic diversity, is here of crucial importance. One formula, by fostering the separation of linguistic communities, can be expected to have a negative impact on the equalization of opportunities, both directly through peer group effects in schooling and indirectly through hindering the bridging mechanisms required for competent participation in a common public forum and effective trans-ethnic mobilization of the worse-off. The second formula is far more innocuous in both respects and can therefore be accepted with equanimity by those determined to secure favourable conditions for the pursuit of distributive justice at the local level.

Underlying the discussion of this illustration is the general presumption that bridging mechanisms between linguistically distinct communities are crucial, directly and/or indirectly, to the equalization of opportunities in linguistically diverse localities. This presumption holds on the assumption that the equalization of opportunities is more deeply affected by formal institutions to be created and reformed at the level of the political community as a whole than by the informal interaction constitutive of local social capital, apparently more abundant in ethnically homogeneous communities (Putnam 2005). It should motivate the search for institutions and policies that inhibit the development of segregated education and health care, discourage the formation of ethnically exclusive associations and neighbourhoods,[43] foster political participation outside of ethnic parties and movements, and above all favour economic participation beyond ethnic niches.[44] Such institutions and policies are distinct from and reach far beyond the achievement of universal proficiency in a shared official language, but they should all be facilitated by it and facilitate it in turn.[45] The contact they foster is also likely to add its own distinct contribution to the tendency for local linguistic and cultural diversity to grow (owing to continuous immigration) less than it would otherwise have done, or to wither away altogether. This erosion is not only the outcome of the communication potential created by a common language, but also of intensive interaction, including as a consequence of inter-ethnic marriage, and of exposure to common circumstances, information and other influences.[46] This loss of local diversity may be experienced as a sad loss by some, but again there is no reason to be disturbed for anyone committed to both egalitarian distributive justice and parity of esteem.

6.8. Inter-local diversity and solidarity: an unexpected alliance?

As we shall see, no such comfortable conclusion is available as regards inter-local linguistic diversity. For whereas at the local level, that is within the territory concerned, the territorial regime justified on grounds of parity of esteem tends to reduce linguistic diversity, it tends to preserve or even to strengthen it at the inter-local level, that is across territories. Hence, whereas it helps promote the conditions for egalitarian distributive justice on a local level, it seems to undermine those conditions on a global scale. If the segregation of linguistic communities at the local level is a bad thing for the sake of distributive justice, fortunately counteracted by the constraints of the territorial regime, how can it fail to be a bad thing on a larger scale too? By hindering both identification and communication, as explained above, linguistic diversity can be expected to weaken the prospects for economic solidarity at the inter-local no less than at the local level.

Before addressing this challenge, we need to consider a puzzling argument to the effect that there is no challenge to be faced, that there are on the contrary good reasons to expect inter-local linguistic diversity to go hand in hand with a developed redistributive system. The point of departure of this argument—and part of what it is meant to explain—is the contrast between the United States and the European Union taken as a whole. At present, the level of economic solidarity can still safely be said to be higher in the latter than in the former. Yet it is uncontroversially also the European Union that exhibits the higher level of inter-local linguistic diversity, firmly preserved by political boundaries that coincide by and large with linguistic boundaries.

Economic reasoning suggests that this positive correlation between solidarity and diversity is no coincidence. Here is the argument. Industrial development relies crucially on specialized skills. But heavy investment in these skills will happen only if enough insurance is provided in case local demand for them disappears or never materializes. One way of providing such insurance is by unifying linguistically a large area within which one can then move at comparatively low cost in search of another employment for the same skills. If this first route cannot be taken, another one can, albeit at the cost of the deadweight loss inherent in income redistribution: the development of a welfare state. As the European space is cut up into smaller linguistic areas and therefore imposes on its workers a higher average cost of moving in search of another use for their skills, the optimal welfare state is bound to be, on average, considerably bulkier in the European Union than in the United States. This argument has been used to explain the development of Europe's social insurance systems and it can plausibly be stretched to explain why the level of public funding of higher education must be and actually is higher in Europe than in the USA, or in Francophone than in Anglophone Canada, or to explain why rigid pay scales linked to educational credentials are far more common in Europe than in the USA. These are just different ways of collectivizing part of the risk involved in the expensive acquisition of potentially remunerative skills.[47]

Can we happily conclude that, far from being antagonistic, inter-local linguistic diversity and generous economic solidarity are complementary? We cannot. To start with, what is shown to be optimal, under conditions of greater linguistic diversity, is greater social insurance, not greater genuine (*ex ante*) solidarity. That Europe should have a larger genuinely redistributive welfare state can therefore be explained by this argument only to the extent that it forms an unavoidable by-product of a strong social insurance system, as administrative simplification and political dynamics push the transfer systems of each nation state beyond what fits under the umbrella of the insurance principle.[48]

This is a major qualification. But there is an even more serious objection to drawing complacent conclusions from this argument. Suppose that national solidarity systems become immersed in a common market in which capital and commodities move freely, while people remain essentially stuck within national borders as a result of language differences. Considerations of competitiveness will put the truly redistributive, 'compassionate' aspects of the welfare state under growing pressure, as mobile capital and consumer demand will tend, other things being equal, to move to those places where redistributive taxation weighs less heavily on the efficient remuneration of factors of production. The pressure is further exacerbated as the upper layers of the skilled labour force become more mobile trans-nationally—precisely by virtue of having become competent enough in a global lingua franca—thereby increasing considerably the (redistributive) tax elasticity of the domestic supply of human capital, that is the propensity of the highly skilled to leave or stay depending on how much they are being taxed in favour of the worse off.

In this context, even if we accept without qualification that a country's optimal human capital formation requires a developed welfare state, there is no reason to expect the latter to emerge and subsist. Instead, the country may need to lower the effective taxation of high incomes, for example by substituting regressive consumption taxes for progressive income taxes, by expanding lax and generous 'expatriate' or 'non-resident' statuses, by deliberately tolerating tax loopholes that primarily benefit affluent taxpayers, and by shifting government expenditures to the advantage of high earners. Put differently, it will need to shift resources towards subsidized opera performances, public golf courses, and convenient airports, and away from subsidies to low-paid jobs, cheap public housing, and benefits for the unemployed; towards the cleaning or policing of the better neighbourhoods at the expense of education or public transport in the poorer ones. Immersion in a competitive transnational market turns states into firm-like entities, under constant pressure to downsize their redistributive ambitions, to shrink those aspects of their welfare systems that go beyond insurance, to reduce public expenditures that effect genuine transfers from the high earners to the low earners, from the more talented, the more skilled, the more mobile, towards the less qualified, the less able, the less mobile.[49]

Of course, as solidarity becomes more difficult to organize, for the reasons just sketched, at the level of individual nation states immersed in a common market, one might hope that a larger political entity, pitched at a level closer to the one at which the market is operating, say the European Union, could take over the task. Indeed, in the USA, the bulk of the net redistribution accomplished by the tax-and-transfer system is the work of federal, not of state programmes.[50] But by switching to this higher level, the EU's advantage over the USA in terms of prospects for sustainable economic solidarity would be turned into a handicap, since its far greater inter-local linguistic diversity, as entrenched by the territorially differentiated linguistic regime currently in place, tends to make both identification and communication at the relevant level more difficult than in the USA.

6.9. Inter-local diversity and solidarity: an undeniable tension

Consequently, no comfort whatever can be found from the side of this intriguing economic argument. What is economically desirable is not *ipso facto* economically sustainable. And we are left at this inter-local level too with the general challenge posed to sustainable solidarity as a result of both identification and communication being made harder by linguistic diversity. Indeed, the challenge is made even more serious at the inter-local than at the local level because of an additional factor: the natural association between inter-local linguistic diversity and political decentralization along linguistic borders.

To see this, let us remember that part of the point of adopting a territorial regime—and thereby preserving some inter-local linguistic diversity—is to show respect for linguistic communities by allowing them to make their language the 'queen' of their territory, that is to make it the medium of political discourse for the political community that rules over that territory (§5.5). I mentioned that there may often be good reasons to make the protected language a 'princess' rather than a 'queen', that is to make it the official language of a territorially defined political community that is not fully sovereign. But a specific variant of the so-called subsidiarity principle entails a presumption in favour of granting more political autonomy to territories that are linguistically distinct than to others similarly situated. What the principle of subsidiarity says is, roughly, that one should systematically allocate competences to the lowest level of political authority, unless there are strong reasons to do otherwise. This principle can be motivated by appealing to distributive justice as real freedom for all by recognizing that some possibilities people may want to use can only be realized by politically structured communities. The more decentralized the political community in charge of a policy domain, the closer its collective choices can be to the wishes of its current members (both because they can weigh more on the choices and because they can better check their implementation) and the easier it is for its current members to move to another political community whose collective choices may better satisfy their wishes.

The principle of subsidiarity can meaningfully apply to any system of multi-level governance, whether or not all levels function in the same language. But it applies with particular force to those cases in which not all levels function in the same language. The presumption in favour of political decentralization to lower and therefore linguistically more homogeneous political communities then gets additional support. This support can stem, along Herderian lines, from the idea that, if decisions that affect us need to be taken by others, it is better for each of us if these decisions are taken by people who are like us because they belong to the same multi-generational linguistic community and hence share the culture that developed in it.[51] It may also stem, along Millian lines, from the idea that it is better for collective decisions to be taken by communities of citizens who have access to the same set of positions and arguments, and hence for democratic life to operate, unless there are strong reasons to do otherwise, in the language with which the bulk of the citizenry is most familiar.[52] Consequently, once a territorially differentiated regime is in place, there is a particularly strong case for devolving competences to levels no higher than the linguistically distinct territories.

Now, locating most policy domains at such levels is in principle compatible with letting the bulk of economic solidarity be organized by a more centralized authority. But a tension unavoidably arises between the centralized organization of solidarity and the decentralization of competences in such fields as education or public health, town planning or environmental policy, labour market or transport and practically any other. The reason is straightforward: owing to the centralized character of taxes and transfers, some of the benefits and costs of sound or sloppy policy in decentralized matters are exported, via the transfer system, to other decentralized units that bear no responsibility for them. This creates an efficiency-driven case for allocating to decentralized authorities at least some financial responsibility for the policy domains under their control. A necessary consequence of doing this is that the extent of economic solidarity organized at the more central level will need to be less ambitious than could be the case with a more centralized distribution of competences.[53] Added to the obstacle it creates for strong identification and fluid communication, this is a third, more specific reason why inter-local linguistic diversity forms an obstacle to the pursuit of economic solidarity which has no equivalent in the case of local linguistic diversity.[54]

6.10. Real freedom for all versus parity of esteem

In this light, a serious clash between justice as parity of esteem and global distributive justice as real freedom for all seems unavoidable. A first possible clash between the demands of parity of esteem and the equalization of opportunities at the local level was circumvented earlier, or at least softened, by making it part of a territorial regime that access to proficiency in the official language should be secured to all permanent residents (§5.6). However, the less ambitious the interpretation of the degree of proficiency required for fair political participation in the 'queen' language and the harder it is to secure proficiency in that language relative to the stronger language against which it is being protected, the more significant the residual tension between parity of esteem and the local equalization of opportunities.

The clash between entrenched inter-local linguistic diversity and trans-local economic solidarity we now have to face on the global level is more serious, even though it should not be exaggerated. First, the appropriate baseline for assessing the cost of a parity-of-esteem-motivated territorial regime by the standards of lax-egalitarian global justice is not an imaginary 'pre-Babelian' world. It is one in which there are distinct linguistic communities, though all denied the right to protect their language in the ways and for the reasons developed in Chapter 5. The pacification argument (§5.7) alone may then be sufficient to transform the loss into a gain: more and not less global distributive justice is achievable when parity of esteem is taken care of than when it is ignored.[55] Secondly, what the spreading and democratization of competence in the lingua franca is meant to achieve is precisely an attenuation of the tension between the preservation of linguistic distinctiveness and the pursuit of global distributive justice. By gradually making communication just about as easy and reliable among native speakers of different languages as it is among natives of the same one, it generates a trans-national demos—a trans-national arena for deliberation and mobilization—that does not substitute but supplements national ones. This will not get rid of the tension altogether, because of the specific subsidiarity-based case (stronger than in a monolingual setting) for decentralizing policy making to the level of the linguistically and culturally distinct political communities, and because of political identification operating and needing to operate to some extent at least at the level of these communities.

Consequently, one can certainly not rule out the possibility of a trade-off between how much justice we can achieve in terms of parity of esteem and in terms of lax opportunity egalitarian distributive justice or real freedom for all. But in the light of what has just been said, this trade-off should not be that sharp. I shall venture no conjecture about exactly how sharp it is, nor make any proposal about how to arbitrate it if it turns out not to be negligible. What I want to do instead, in closing this chapter, is speculate about how much or how little diversity will subsist in a world reckoned to be just, or as just as possible, by the standards of both real freedom for all and parity of esteem.

A world that is just in terms of real freedom for all would certainly be a world in which borders are open, or at least far more open than they currently are. This will unavoidably raise the cost of the territorial protection of weaker languages. This higher cost will in part be the reflection of the ground floor effect, further amplified by the worldwide spreading of the lingua franca and no longer contained by sturdy obstacles to free movement. Moreover, in many places, the cost of territorial protection will also rise sharply as a result of the obligation to secure access to proficiency for anyone wishing to settle for good in the territory.

This impact of greater real freedom for all on the cost and hence the likelihood of territorial protection should be partly offset by another feature of a distributively just world, namely a stable flow of systematic transfers that will structurally reduce the inequalities between richer and poorer territories. Part of these transfers will take the implicit form of quick, steady, and cheap worldwide flows of technologies and other types of valuable knowledge.[56] Another part will take the form of an explicit trans-national redistributive system of some sort, regional and global, aimed at granting the greatest sustainable real freedom to those with least of it world-wide.[57] These transfers will contribute to stabilizing the world population, thereby inhibiting an overcrowding of the ground floor but also a massive migration towards relatively affluent territories with weaker languages, and thereby preventing the cost of securing proficiency in the local official language to all newcomers from being prohibitively expensive. Thus emerges a picture of a just world in which everyone has the freedom to move and settle anywhere, but where comparatively few make use of this freedom for two reasons. One is that a worldwide system of transfers enables them to stay where they are. The other is that the territorial linguistic regime, even when adequate learning facilities are in place, unavoidably imposes a cost to immigrants with a different language.

Would this pattern be stable? Perhaps not. For in the longer term, the spread of the lingua franca may not only affect communication, but also identification. The generalization of the asymmetric bilingualism it implies can be expected to gradually reduce the extent to which the identity of the dwellers of a territory is linked to the local language. We may then be approaching a situation analogous to the terminal stage of many 'dialects', whose native speakers were led to identify with a more or less distant national language.[58] As identification with their ancestral language declines and the cost of protecting it rises—owing to the ground floor effect, to migration pressure, and also to the fact that immigrants can increasingly get away with knowing nothing but the lingua franca—more communities may judge that the preservation of their linguistic distinctiveness is no longer worth the cost and the coercion it requires and may decide to waive in turn their right to protect it. Under such hypothetical circumstances, linguistic diversity in all the senses considered in this chapter would wither away without offending parity of esteem, and it would *ipso facto* stop hindering—to the extent that it still does at that stage—the pursuit of global distributive justice as real freedom for all.

For the time being, however, justice as parity of esteem justifies the maintenance and development of a territorially differentiated coercive regime. It will therefore keep lending normative meaning to the endless quibbles to which its implementation is bound to keep giving rise. It will also keep legitimizing the entrenchment of a considerable degree of inter-local linguistic diversity. The celebrators of linguistic diversity will be relieved to read this. But they must realize that they are just being lucky. The reason why linguistic diversity must be preserved is not that it is intrinsically valuable, nor that a persuasive case has been made for its having, all things considered, beneficial consequences. The reason why linguistic diversity must and will be preserved is simply that it constitutes, for the foreseeable future, a by-product of the pursuit of linguistic justice as parity of esteem.

Conclusion

This book has attempted to address systematically the normative question of how our institutions should treat our languages. Its core idea is emphatically not that we should celebrate linguistic diversity as a value in itself which it would be our duty to preserve or promote. Nor that we should endeavour to stretch the category of fundamental human rights so as to encompass some substantive linguistic rights. Instead, this book's source of inspiration has been the widespread feeling that formal and informal linguistic regimes are sometimes very unjust in a number of distinct senses. And its main task has been to spell out the conceptions of justice that such feelings presuppose and to outline their practical implications. This has led to a distinction between three interpretations of linguistic justice: as fair cooperation in the production of a shared language, as the equalization of opportunities linked to linguistic competence, and as parity of esteem between linguistically defined collective identities.

Throughout the book, I took the growing dominance of English in trans-national communication as the primary illustration. I did so for two reasons. First, mankind has never experienced a linguistic phenomenon of a comparable magnitude. Secondly, many of its aspects can safely be assumed to be familiar to most of my readers. This spreading of English as a lingua franca has been happening at unequal speeds worldwide. It has been particularly rapid within the European Union, and particularly contentious within its core political institutions, as these are formally committed to linguistic equality. In addition to convenient access to statistical and anecdotal evidence, this is why the focus throughout has been on the European situation. However, as illustrated by a number of more exotic references, the main claims articulated and defended in this book are meant to apply far more widely. It will be for others to say how much these claims will need to be amended or qualified in order for them to apply universally.

As regards the three types of injustice generated by the spreading of the lingua franca, my main conclusions can be summed up as follows.

1 Yes, it is unfair that non-Anglophones should shoulder the whole burden of learning the lingua franca. But the extent of this unfairness will shrink as a consequence of the very spreading of the lingua franca, and free riding on Anglophone intellectual production should provide at least rough justice in the immediate future.

2 Yes, it is also unfair that the growing currency acquired by their language should give Anglophones a multi-dimensional advantage, in particular as regards competition for jobs in an increasingly trans-national labour market. But the extent of this advantage is bound to shrink, indeed even be reversed, as the lingua franca keeps spreading more widely and more deeply. Distributive justice will not be best served by protective or compensatory measures in favour of non-Anglophones, but instead by democratizing proficiency in the lingua franca throughout the world as quickly and thoroughly as possible, using for this purpose the modern media's powerful and cheap learning tools at least as much as formal schooling.

3 Yes, it is unfair that (what is perceived as) the native language of a subset of the European or world population should, in an ever increasing number of informal and formal contexts, be given manifest precedence over all other languages, many of them closely associated with the collective identities of other subsets of that same population. The most effective way of pursuing linguistic justice thus understood as parity of esteem consists in granting each linguistic community the right to impose its language as the medium of instruction and public communication in some territory, providing it is willing to bear the fair cost of doing so. One major effect of the resulting territorially differentiated regime is to secure the survival of a significant level of inter-local linguistic diversity. But this must not be its purpose, and cannot be its justification.

Provided fairness is vigorously pursued along each of these three dimensions, it is possible to accept without indignation or resentment the increasing reliance on English in Europe and in the world. We need a lingua franca, and only one, if we are to be able to work out and implement efficient and fair solutions for our common problems on a European and on a global scale, and indeed if we are to be able to discuss, characterize, and achieve linguistic justice itself. But the sheer existence of a lingua franca is not sufficient. We must urgently use it to argue, mobilize, innovate, reform, and revolutionize the way our countries, our Union, our world are run. We must urgently use it to empower a vigorous, passionate struggle against some of the trends its spreading helps strengthen. By boosting mobility, the emergence of a European and global lingua franca helps undermine the existing redistributive systems. By disseminating more than proportionally what is currently written and said using that lingua franca, it may help legitimize both local and global injustices. To resist and move forward, determined and effective trans-national action is urgently needed, and the lingua franca itself is an essential weapon if this action is to succeed.

Universal proficiency in a common language and the intense flow of trans-national interaction thereby activated are bound to have many major side effects. In particular, they can be expected both to increase the cost of protecting weaker languages through a territorial regime and to reduce the place occupied by these languages in people's collective identities. A peculiar yet intelligible English accent might one day become just as good a marker of the linguistic dimension of one's collective identity as one's ancestral language, and the curse of Babel will then at long last be undone. This day may never be reached, if only because the most destructive species the Earth ever carried did not manage in time to adopt a common language in which it could debate and mobilize in search of fair and efficient global institutions. But whether or not that day will ever be reached, this possible future world is not what this book has been about. It has been about linguistic justice for today's Europe and, more tentatively, today's world. Not more. Nor less.

NOTES

Chapter 1

1. Subjective data based on self-assessment have the obvious advantage of being cheap to collect, compared to objective data based on samples of spoken and written performance. But they have the no less obvious disadvantage of being sensitive to systematic understatements or over-statements of linguistic competence. However, unless older and younger people systematically diverge in their standards of self-assessment, this does not prevent comparisons across cohorts from providing very robust evidence of powerful trends.

2. Among the over 65s, only three countries out of 22 non-Anglophone countries (Sweden, Denmark, and the Netherlands) boast more than 50% of respondents who declare they know English well or very well. Among the 15–24 age group, this proportion remains lower than 50% in two countries only (Eurobarometer 2006 database).

3. The expression 'lingua franca' or 'language of the Franks' was initially used to refer to a language or set of dialects based mainly on Provençal and other romance languages that served as a medium of communication between linguistically diverse Christian and Muslim populations around the Mediterranean from the time of the Crusades to the nineteenth century, without ever being the native tongue of any group, the idiom of any culture, let alone the centrally controlled language of any capital city (see Dakhlia 2008 for a detailed historical account). In these various respects, imperial languages such as Latin, Castillan, Mandarin, French, English, or Russian (in the Roman, Spanish, Chinese, French, British, or Soviet empires) differ significantly from the original lingua franca, but they qualify nonetheless as lingua francas under the broad definition adopted here.

4. These are rough estimates based on censuses or surveys that stretch from 1984 to 2000 and subject to serious comparability problems, as provided by *Ethnologue* in 2006. The more recent sixteenth edition (2009) includes updated (and corrected) estimates for first-language speakers (in brackets in Table 1.1), but no estimates for secondary speakers. For the sake of minimizing inconsistency, the older estimates for first-language speakers are being used in the calculation of the ratios.

5. Edwards (1995: 32) proposes the figures of 1,400 millions for English, 1,000 for Chinese, 700 for Hindi, and close to 300 for Spanish and

Russian, while Edwards (2010: ch. 8) argues that the gap between English and other languages has further increased. As regards the spreading of English, the estimates in Table 1.1 should certainly be regarded as leaning towards the conservative side.

6. Figures quoted by Graddol (2005, 2006: 95). Moreover, when South Koreans send their children to language courses in China, these are apparently less likely to be Chinese courses than English courses, which the Chinese are believed to organize far more effectively than Koreans and more cheaply than Americans (Stevens et al. 2006: 177); in order to attract Indians, some of the advanced science courses offered by Chinese universities are organized in English (Graddol 2005); and while some signs in Chinese and in Korean started appearing in Tokyo's subway in 2005, it is in English, and not in Chinese, that the essential information is systematically duplicated in public spaces throughout Japanese cities.

7. More sophisticated measures of the communicative value of a language have been offered. For example, what Abram de Swaan (2001: 33–40) calls the *Q-value* of a language is defined as its *prevalence*, i.e. the proportion of the population that can speak it, multiplied by its *centrality*, i.e. the proportion of the multilingual individuals in that population who can speak it. However, as argued in detail elsewhere (Van Parijs 2004a: appendix 1), there is no good reason to believe that this Q-value could better capture the incentive to acquire a language than the straightforward notion of prevalence. I am aware of no other measure of communicative value that holds the promise of improving much, if at all, upon the simple probability of interaction in that language, as a predictor of differential learning and retention.

8. Physicists have started constructing potentially instructive models of language competition (see Castellino et al. 2009, §V, for an overview). In the first model of this type, the probability of 'conversion' from one language to another was simply a function of the number of speakers and of a status index, and universal adoption of one language combined with extinction of its competitor(s) was then the only stable equilibrium (Abrams and Strogatz 2003). Later developments made the essential step of introducing bilingual speakers (see Castelló et al. 2006, etc.). They suggested for example that, unlike distant languages, closely related ones may have a chance of subsisting side by side (Mira and Paredes 2005). They started studying the impact of 'social structures' that are less than 'fully connected' (Minett and Wang 2008), and offered conjectures, against this background, about when attempts to halt or slow down language decay have some chance of succeeding, and about how to proceed when this is the case (typically through raising the 'status index'). A crucial

refinement that is still missing at this stage is the modelling of the choice of the language to be used by bi- or multilingual speakers when interacting, i.e. the micro-mechanism to which the remainder of this section is devoted. But this lacuna seems to have been noticed and could in principle be remedied in more sophisticated versions of these models (see Castelló et al. 2008: 65: 'We are also currently analyzing a model we have proposed, where language is taken as a property of the social interaction instead of a feature of the agent').

9. Here is a simple illustration. Jane is a native English speaker with an excellent knowledge of Spanish and a rudimentary knowledge of French. François is a native speaker of French with an excellent knowledge of English and no knowledge of Spanish. And Blanca is a native speaker of Spanish with a good knowledge of both English and French. Jane is the speech partner who speaks French least well (rudimentary), François is the one who speaks Spanish least well (none), and Blanca is the one who speaks English least well (good). Since Blanca knows English better (good) than Jane knows French (rudimentary) and than François knows Spanish (none), English is the language best known by the speech partner who knows it least well. The prediction is therefore that English will be spontaneously picked as the medium of conversation if Jane, François, and Blanca, and only them, are involved.

10. The 'maxi-min' language should not be misunderstood as the language whose choice would make the worst off as well off as possible, and hence satisfy the normative criterion of sustainable maximin frequently proposed as part of the characterization of what justice requires (see §3.1 below). On the contrary the maxi-min language tends to be the language spoken by the dominant group. Nor should any connection be suggested with the maximin criterion of rational behaviour under uncertainty. On the contrary, it is when certainty is greatest about the linguistic competence of the audience that maxi-min language choice works most accurately. As a safeguard against these misleading associations, I shall systematically use the hyphenated form ('maxi-min') to refer to the criterion of language choice, and drop the hyphen ('maximin') in the other cases.

11. Here is a typical anecdote, perceptively narrated by a French journalist: 'True, Eurocrats and other diplomats, among whom mixed marriages are frequent and who are open to other European cultures, are very often admirable polyglots. However, with the enlargement of the European Union, they have hardly more than English in common. Thus, during a dinner offered by the Irish presidency, the French, British, and German people who are sharing a table all speak French,

German, and English, which should enable them to express themselves in their own language or, out of courtesy, in the language of the person they are talking to. But Macedonians are invited to join, and the conversation switches to English at once' (Leparmentier 2004).

12. The maxi-min language use criterion, like any other use of a maximin criterion, amounts to giving lexical priority to the lowest score in the various feasible options. It may be more realistic to soften somewhat this lexical priority. For example, if by speaking French rather than English you would prevent one person from understanding the little bit she would otherwise have understood, while enabling all the others to understand far better (and yourself to speak with less effort), you may nonetheless go for French. The most realistic conjecture for communication-driven interaction may therefore not be the extreme lexical case. But it will remain very distant from the maximization of unweighted average competence. Some strongly concave function of competence in each language may be a better bet than a strict maxi-min. But given the imperfection of the information generally accessible to the speakers, this is unlikely to make much of a difference.

13. See de Swaan (2001: 27–33) on shared languages as hyper-collective goods and Grewal (2008: 70–81) on the network power associated with shared languages.

14. Convergence to a single common language is in both respects analogous to convergence to a single capital city. Each new lobby (in the widest sense) which settles in a particular city increases each other lobby's expected utility of being located in that same city (externality of agglomeration). And the concentration of lobbying already reached in a particular place confers 'agglomeration power' to the 'owners' of that place. In the prehistory and history of the European Union, neither the choice of English nor the choice of Brussels were nor could have been the object of a deliberate decision. Both are the unchosen outcome of an irreversible process. In both cases, irreversibility is due to network power—which hinders endogenous reversal—combined with two distinct formidable obstacles to a deliberate reversal: (1) Most parties involved have invested significant sunk costs in learning the currently chosen idiom and settling in the currently chosen location; and (2) if no broad consensus, let alone strict unanimity, could ever be found for the choice of a single official language or the choice of a single political capital when there were 5, or 9, or 15 member states, how could one expect such consensus ever to emerge with 27 member states or more? (See Van Parijs and Van Parys 2010: 10–12.)

15. See e.g. Crystal (2000: 85–6); Patten (2009). There is hardly a more effective way of learning a language than to speak it with one's playmates. Speaking the language one is supposed to learn will happen spontaneously when the class group is linguistically mixed, but will need enforcing when it is not. However, chatting in the playground is hard to monitor. At an age where the long-term interest has little motivational force, instilling shame about one's mother tongue is likely to prove as powerful an instrument as any for this specific pedagogical purpose—though possibly with damaging side effects of a sort that will be central to Chapter 4.

16. See Stevens et al. (2006: 170)

17. Thus, a *vade mecum* dispatched by the French foreign ministry insistently instructed France's representatives in all European institutions that, even at informal meetings or after the interpreters had gone home, 'les Français parlent leur langue' (Ministère des affaires étrangères 2002). This instruction may also in part be inspired by more strategic considerations, based on a correct analysis of the maxi-min dynamics sketched above: to prevent French from being less and less often the maxi-min language (often chosen even when no one French was around), one must voluntaristically preserve the incentive and opportunity for the non-French to learn it by using French even when it is not the maxi-min choice. This stance is not exactly appreciated by those (French) who have to make long speeches which their supposed addressees fail to understand nor by those (non-French) who have to listen to them, and therefore quickly reaches its limits (see §4.2 below). But it can no doubt be effective, if rigorously implemented, in slowing down the convergence process in which the maxi-min criterion plays a key role.

18. A more extreme illustration is the regime 'Each speaks one of the others' languages' common for a time, I am told by a participant, at regular meetings of the European Commissioners' chiefs of cabinet: supreme expression of respect for the language of the others—or proud display of one's linguistic competence? A similar structure is to be found in a proposal made in the mid-1970s, no doubt tongue in cheek, by some Danes well aware that their joining the EU would not make other Europeans rush to learn Danish: all members of the European Parliament, they proposed, should express themselves in English, except for the British, who should speak French (Ammon 2001b: 73).

19. As Humphrey Tonkin (2003: 152) puts it (too?) forcefully: 'We have all met the phenomenon of the American who, when foreigners do not understand him, simply resorts to shouting.... When my dog fails to obey me, I do not enunciate more clearly: I shout louder. And it

works—not always of course, but more often than if I improve my diction.... It is relative power that determines language choice: all other factors are negligible in comparison. So shouting, in one's own language, can help—and we have America to prove it.'

20. One must be careful not to misinterpret in this way situations that conform perfectly with the maxi-min logic once it is realized that the audience is segmented. When an ambassador invites a colleague for a working lunch, they will not go out of their way to be understood by the waiter. Does this show that power is what matters? Not at all, as will be shown by the language shift if the ambassador happens to spill her coffee on her trousers. Maxi-min is the rule, but it applies to split audiences. Similarly, if a reception is organized in honour of some dignitary, those making the speeches will pick a language the dignitary can understand, even if many of the lesser people in the room do not. Triumph of the powerful? Again, not at all. The same would happen if the party's star were a frail elderly person whose birthday, recovery, departure, or return is being celebrated. Once the bulk of the audience needs to be told to sit down, get out, or start eating, whoever is in charge will make sure to convey this in a language they can all understand. It is not the case here that power trumps the maxi-min logic, but simply that the maxi-min language may differ depending on whether one is addressing all the people within hearing distance or only a subset of them.

21. For some modelling, at different levels of formal and sociolinguistic sophistication, see Laitin (1988, 1993), Selten and Pool (1991), de Swaan (1993, 2001), Choi (2002), and the physicists' models mentioned earlier (note 8).

22. Conspiracy theories (e.g. Durand 2001) may not be groundless: some British and American individuals and institutions did have an interest in propagating English (though arguably not, as we shall see in Chapter 3, in the long term) and it would be surprising if none of them acted to further this interest. Appeal to conspiracies is not needed, however, and is at most only marginally useful, to understand the massive trends currently under way.

23. This must be true when assuming a somewhat less demanding criterion of competence than the one used in the *Ethnologue* figures of §1.2 (see Graddol 2006), but it may even be true when applying that criterion to an updated dataset. Note that it would not be the first time that a language has more secondary than primary speakers. Using some appropriate standard of secondary competence, Hebrew and French were probably at some point but are no longer in that situation. Urdu and Bahasa still are. But for all these other languages, the proposition holds only if one

includes secondary speakers within the country or countries in which the language concerned enjoys official status.

24. Might Mandarin not have a chance? Using a sufficiently demanding criterion of competence, it can still be regarded as the most widespread language, even though, for any specific level of competence, English is catching up fast, not least, as we saw (§1.2) because of the massive efforts made by the Chinese themselves. Supposing that environmental, social, demographic, or ethnic problems do not end up stopping or reversing China's growth, might a time not come when it will be China's turn to impose its language to the world? This is most unlikely, for two reasons. One is that the very spread of English throughout the world, including in China, will make it far more difficult for non-Chinese to learn Chinese than it is for non-Anglophones to learn English: in international interaction, English will constantly pop up in maxi-min position, and it will be prohibitively difficult to generate appropriate levels of motivation and opportunity, except for those who choose (and are allowed) to migrate to China. Secondly, the experience with English will by then have made clear that having one's native language as a universal lingua franca eventually turns from a significant advantage into a significant handicap (as will be explained in §3.9). The Chinese will have discovered that the greatest worldwide linguistic advantage accrues to the natives of the most widespread of the languages which are *not* the universal lingua franca. Why should we expect them to destroy this advantage by using their economic power to impose Chinese in international contacts?

25. Even when comparing the languages of developed industrial societies to those of traditional agrarian societies, there seems to be little to back the suggestion that some evolutionary process led to the survival of the (linguistically) fittest. See e.g. Skutnabb-Kangas's (2003: §3.3) critique of Weinstock's (2003: 257) claim that 'languages might disappear simply because they are ill-equipped to deal with the requirements that modernity places on them'. *A fortiori*, when applied to a set of closely related languages spoken by similarly developed societies, no such suggestion can make sense. Even the least well-equipped language should have the phonological, morphological, and syntactic wherewithal it needs, and be just as able to plunder the lexicon of other languages as English proved to be.

26. For example, among all 6,000 languages in today's world, where could Belgium have found a more miraculously balanced compromise between Dutch and French?

27. The first developed prediction of the 'definitive triumph' of the English language seems to have been made by the Swiss biologist

Alphonse de Candolle (1873). He regarded it an advantage that English was made of both Germanic and Latin words, and that it possessed 'qualities of grammatical simplicity, brevity and clarity'. But the fundamental reason, he said, has nothing to do with the properties of the language itself: 'The future prevalence of the Anglo-American language is self-evident: it will be imposed by the movements of populations in both hemispheres.' (The original French text is quoted at length in Fidrmuc, Ginsburgh, and Weber 2005: §1.) In the same vein, the German Chancellor Otto von Bismarck is often quoted (by North Americans) as having said a couple of decades later that the adoption of English in North America was the most important event of his time.

28. See e.g. Wedgwood (1944) on William of Nassau; and Shorto (2004) on the Dutch origins of New York.
29. For quite different in-depth treatments of the question of what the European Union's linguistic regime should be, see especially Phillipson (2003), Kantner (2004), Ammon (2006), Kraus (2008) and Kjaer and Adamo (2011).
30. See e.g. Milanovic's (2005: ch. 11) striking statistical data.
31. This very vague characterization of justice as 'egalitarian' is sufficient for the purposes of this chapter. A more precise specification will be proposed in due course (§3.1).
32. This notion of 'justificatory community' is articulated by G. A. Cohen (1992: 282–3; 2000: chs 9–10).
33. The 'global-Rawlsian' (or 'global-Habermasian') position thus outlined and adopted here without further argument is by no means uncontroversial. See e.g. Walzer (1995), Rawls (1999), Nagel (2005), Miller (2007) for interesting alternative views. See also Rawls and Van Parijs (2003) for a debate with special relevance to the European Union, and Van Parijs (2007) for a critical survey of the contemporary debate on global justice and a sketchy defence of the position that will be taken for granted here.
34. I shall return later (§6.9) and at greater length to the question of the level at which redistribution should be organized.
35. The strong connection between social justice and deliberative democracy asserted here is discussed at length in Van Parijs (2011).
36. In his very despondent account of the prospects of 'social Europe', Jean-Claude Barbier (2008: esp. 257–8) rightly places great emphasis on the way in which linguistic diversity and the associated cultural diversity hinders progress towards a more ambitious redistributive programme at EU level. By blocking off the only way in which one can reasonably hope to overcome this obstacle, however, his allergy to

'international English' makes his account far gloomier than it needs to be.

37. He perceptively adds: 'The influences which form opinions and decide political acts are different in the different sections of the country. An altogether different set of leaders have the confidence of one part of the country and of another. The same books, newspapers, pamphlets, speeches, do not reach them. One section does not know what opinions, or what instigations, are circulating in another' (Mill 1861: 291–2).

38. See van Heerikhuizen's (2004) instructive presentation of Novikow's views.

39. Similarly and ultimately for the same reason, there are two crucially distinct arguments in support of the claim that linguistic diversity forms an obstacle to economic solidarity (see §6.6).

40. Fichte (1808: 190) continues: 'Such a whole, if it wishes to absorb and mingle with itself any other people of different descent and language, cannot do so without itself becoming confused, in the beginning at any rate, and violently disturbing the even progress of its culture.'

41. In the same spirit, Carl Schmitt (e.g. 1926: 14) argues that a democracy is only viable for a 'homogeneous' people, one which needs to possess, not racial purity, but a shared culture and identity, of which language is a central component.

42. This view is defended by the German supreme court judge Dieter Grimm (1995: 295–6) in a famous exchange with Jürgen Habermas.

43. Jürgen Habermas (1995: 307; 2001: 18), who holds this second interpretation, is therefore far more optimistic about the compatibility of EU democracy with Europe's linguistic diversity, providing English is learned as a second language throughout the European continent. A similar position is defended, within an explicitly Millian perspective, by Nick (2006: 17): 'No common language = no common understanding in the public sphere = no democracy'. In the absence of a common language, the European 'public sphere' is obviously bound to remain very limited (see e.g. van de Steeg 2002).

44. See Doerr (2008) on the linguistic obstacles to effective debate and mobilization on the European and the global level.

45. Analogously, those committed to egalitarian social justice at the level of a particular country will welcome the adoption of a single national language as a way of favouring the emergence of both a 'democratic society' of free and equal persons and a 'democratic polity' of fairly deliberating and mobilizing citizens.

46. For a typical formulation of this argument, see the *Appel internationaliste et progressiste à la résistance linguistique et culturelle* (COURRIEL

2010), directed against 'the extremely serious imperialist enterprise aimed at imposing to all peoples a single global language'.

47. To overcome inappropriate inhibition, it may help to remember St Augustine's justification for his unorthodox deviation from the norms of classic Latin: 'It is better to be criticized by the grammarians than not understood by the peoples' (*Melius est ut reprehendant nos grammatici quam non intelligant populi*, quoted by Deproost 2003: 73).

48. To illustrate: At many EU meetings, interpretation is provided for at least some combinations of languages, but more and more speakers choose to speak in English rather than in their own language (for reasons to which I return in §4.3). When they speak, no one or hardly anyone in the audience listens to the interpreters. But when a British or Irish participant takes the floor, you can often notice that some participants suddenly grab their earphones and start fiddling with the channel selector. Ironically, the people whose language has been learned by everyone are becoming those who most need the expensive and stiffening intermediation of interpreters in order to be understood. In the same vein, Lorenzo Consoli, president of the International Press Association, argued 'that the communication policy of the European Commission itself would be in danger if it is carried out almost exclusively by English mother-tongue officials': 'Paradoxically mother-tongue English spokespersons risk communicating less well in English than colleagues of other nationalities' (www.euractiv.com, 22 January 2010).

49. Non-Anglophone intellectuals are often forced to specialize in the same way as late medieval clerics: some of these chose to write in Latin 'scholarly, erudite works capable of attracting glory and consideration by their peers beyond all borders', while others chose to write in a vernacular language in order to reach 'a wider audience, more regional than universal, a popular, profane or lordly audience' (Deproost 2003: 86). Anglophone intellectuals can happily avoid such a choice.

50. Hence the disproportionate global resonance of minor reforms and debates happening in Anglophone countries. A typical example is the intellectual impact outside Britain of the tiny 'baby bond' programme introduced by Tony Blair's government, to be contrasted with the total absence of international discussion of far more generous birth grant or child benefit schemes that exist in countries whose language is less widely known.

51. Which, as I shall argue in Chapter 4, must not (and therefore will not) happen. In plurilingual countries, a partial shift may sometimes be possible and desirable (see, for example, the Re-Bel initiative: www.

rethinkingbelgium.eu), even if it understandably triggers some protest on the ground that it creates a damaging gulf between the debating elite and the ordinary citizens.

52. In the language of the *Appel internationaliste et progressiste* (COUR-RIEL 2010) quoted in note 46, instead of 'making everywhere linguistic resistance an essential component of popular and progressive struggle', we should instead make everywhere linguistic democratization an essential component of that struggle.

53. A typical example is Barbier (2008: esp. 186, 251–3, 256), who seems to believe in an (unspecified) version of the third proposal as a credible alternative to the dominance of 'international English'.

54. This is not everyone's opinion: 'What will you have to propose as a supranational language? ... The answer is obvious: French.—What! This language so ill suited to express the depth of the human being, this eminently rational language, this is the language you want to make the language of Europe, the language you claim Europe will accept?—I say that if you want to make Europe you have to get her to accept it, indeed to accept it precisely because of its rationality.' For the task of today's Europe is to 'reinstate among its members the supreme esteem for the rational part of man, for the Socratic spirit, for the French genius' (Benda 1933: 78, 81).

55. For an enthusiastic discussion of the potential of SATS ('synchronous automated translation systems'), see e.g. Lehman-Wilzig (2000).

56. See Crystal (1997: 22) and Maurais (2003: 19) for insightful discussions of this race.

57. As de Swaan (2001: 191) puts it: 'If only people would speak and write more like machines, machines would succeed better at translating their words.'

58. See, for example, Grin (2005a: 98–102).

59. See Okrent (2006) for a vivid illustration.

60. See Martinet's (1960: ch. 6) classic analysis.

61. See Selten and Pool (1991) for a game-theoretical modelling of this problem.

62. See Dieckhoff (2002) for a detailed account.

63. Esperanto, it is sometimes argued, is useful for other purposes, for example as a first step towards learning other languages, or as a relay language in interpreting. This is quite possible, but would not significantly affect the case for or against making Esperanto the lingua franca. I shall suggest below (§4.2) another (modest) role it might be usefully given.

64. The assumptions made are specified in Box A.1. The probabilities (with n = size of the groups) can be shown to be given by the following

formulae. Regime 1 Case A: $(2^n - 1)/3^{n-1}$; Case B: $2/3^{n-1} - 1/15^{n-1}$; Regime 2 Case A: $2(5^n - 1)/6^n - (2^n - 1)/3^n$; Case B: $(2 \times 2^n - 1)/3^n + 4/6^n - 8/12^n$.

65. Partly for this reason, a regime according to which 'each speaks her own language' is commonly practised when only two native languages are involved, as is commonly the case in Canada, Belgium, or Switzerland. It may then compete not too badly, in terms of cost-effectiveness, with the adoption of one of the two languages as the lingua franca, especially when the languages are linguistically close. However, in the context of persistent asymmetric bilingualism, this regime is often difficult to maintain, and the maxi-min logic often drives bilingual native speakers of the weaker language to switch to the stronger one and ditch the 'each speaks her own language' in order to be understood and not just politely listened to. When the regime sticks, it is seldom because of its cost-effectiveness, but rather because of the symbolic advantage of allowing each party to assert the value of its language (as mentioned in §1.6 among the deviations from maxi-min use and as further discussed in §4.2 in connection with linguistic justice as parity of esteem).

66. See for example the English–French–German proposal by the French deputy Michel Herbillon (2003) and the even more demanding four-language variant (Spanish included) proposed by the Belgian linguist Marc Wilmet (2003).

Chapter 2

1. It is nonetheless with this interpretation in mind that I first started scrutinizing what linguistic justice may mean (in the 1998 All Souls presentation mentioned in the acknowledgements, a later version of which was published as Van Parijs 2002a). From my present standpoint, the argument of this chapter is best understood as an *ad hominem* exercise addressed to those who do not share my own global egalitarian conception of justice (sketched in Chapter 1 and further spelled out in Chapters 3 and 4), but who may nonetheless be persuaded to move in what I believe to be the right direction by a type of argument which I do not regard as unsound but which makes little difference for those who share my conception. (See my discussion of cooperative justice as one of three peripheral interpretations of justice in Van Parijs 2007.) Those who share this conception may wish to skip this chapter altogether and move straight to linguistic justice as distributive justice (Chapter 3).

2. I am here concerned exclusively with the unfairness that may arise from the learning of the lingua franca producing a positive externality (for those with whom communication is thereby made possible), not from its producing a negative externality, for example by lowering the relative prestige or damaging the dignity of languages other than the lingua franca (a possibility brought to my attention by Aurélien Portuese). The issues raised by the possibility of such negative externalities I found more convenient to discuss in the context of the interpretation of linguistic justice as parity of esteem (Chapter 4) rather than in terms of fair cooperation.

3. I used this story in Van Parijs (1996) to illustrate and motivate one potential application of David Gauthier's principle of maximin relative benefit, to which I return shortly.

4. The plausibility of assuming that the cost of achieving competence in a foreign language is the same for all is problematic even if it is only meant to refer to the cost of the goods and services required (typically, teachers' working time). It becomes really tricky if, as one should, one also takes the learner's learning time into account, and hence the opportunity cost that stems from her not doing other things, including earning (unequal amounts of) money. I shall return below to some complications related to this. At this stage, however, the strong and unrealistic assumption of equal costs measurable in the same metric as benefits is important and legitimate. It makes it possible to present the competing criteria of fair cooperation and their respective advantages and disadvantages in the simplest and clearest way.

5. Those inclined to find an answer in the adoption of an artificial language are invited to (re)read section 2 of the Appendix to Chapter 1.

6. What Gauthier (1986) proposes is a maximin (as opposed to strict egalitarian) version of this criterion. This is not motivated by incentive considerations but by the possibility of indivisibilities in the range of contributions to the cost of producing the public good. This complication is unnecessary here, as cash taxes and subsidies (divisible at will) are the most straightforward way of implementing a fair allocation of the cost of learning. More importantly, unlike Gauthier himself and consistently with the normative premise that free riding is unjust (§2.1), I shall here interpret this criterion as applying beyond the range of cases in which an explicit deal is required to prompt efficient cooperation.

7. The overall benefit is then $4 - 3 = 1$, compared to $4 - 2 \times 3 = 2$ if the F-speakers learned P and to $4 - 3 \times 3 = -5$ if all learned a second language.

8. To see this, suppose, for example, that the cost of learning increases from 3 to 3.7. Learning is still efficient, as its cost falls short of its total gross benefit ($= 4$). With a surplus now shrunk to 0.3, Gauthier's criterion

entails a shrinking of each cooperator's net benefit from 1/3 to 0.3/3 = 1/10 (one third of the surplus for each). This is achieved through a subsidy of 1.8 to Petra (which grants her a net benefit of $2 \times 1 - 3.7 + 1.8 = 0.1$) funded equally by Frank and Frances (which shrinks the net benefit of each of them to $1 - 0.9 = 0.1$). But the very fact that transfers are calibrated to equalize (positive) net benefits obviously prevents this upward adjustment of the Fs' contribution from overshooting into inflicting them a net loss, as it did under Pool's regime.

9. If the number of F-speakers increases from 4 to 9, the total gross benefit becomes 18 (= 9×2), the total net benefit 15 (= $18 - 3$) and its per-capita equal share 1.5 (= 15/10). Since Petra's pre-transfer net benefit (given by the number of speakers she gets access to minus the learning cost) far exceeds this level ($9 - 3 = 6$), she must now not only pick up the full bill of the learning, but in addition finance an aggregate subsidy larger than this cost ($6 - 1.5 = 4.5$) to the nine (non-learning) F-speakers, so that each of these can enjoy, in addition to costless access to a new speech partner (1), a transfer of 0.5 (= 4.5/9), thereby achieving the same net benefit as Petra's ($1 + 0.5 = 6 - 4.5$).

10. As mentioned in an earlier footnote, David Gauthier (1986) himself would certainly subscribe to such a stipulation, as he meant his criterion to apply exclusively to the sharing of the benefits that flow from a cooperative improvement upon the laissez-faire outcome.

11. Here is Homans' (1961: 75) formulation: 'A man in an exchange relation with another will expect that the rewards of each man be proportional to his costs—the greater the rewards, the greater the costs—and that the net rewards, or profits, of each man, be proportional to his investments—the greater the investments, the greater the profit.' Many interpretations of 'investment' allowed by Homans (such as age or gender) are too morally arbitrary to make ethical sense. Moreover, even when these are filtered out in such a way that only something like 'effort' is left to convey the meaning of 'investment', Homans' rule does not provide us—contrary to what he suggests—with an acceptable criterion of *distributive* justice (see the discussion of Homans-like principles of distributive justice in Van Parijs 1995: 166–9). But this need not prevent it from playing the role it is being given here as a plausible criterion of cooperative justice, with basic entitlements taken as a given background (see Van Parijs 1995: 281 n. 87).

12. Define b_1 and b_2, respectively, as the gross benefit for individuals 1 and 2; c_1 and c_2, respectively, as the costs to individuals 1 and 2; and hence $b_1 - c_1$ and $b_2 - c_2$ as the net benefits for individuals 1 and 2. $(b_1 - c_1)/c_1 =$

$(b_2 - c_2)/c_2$ if and only if $b_1/c_1 - c_1/c_1 = b_2/c_2 - c_2/c_2$, i.e. $b_1/c_1 - 1 = b_2/c_2 - 1$, i.e. $b_1/c_1 = b_2/c_2$.

13. As mentioned earlier (§2.3), these assumptions of equal gross cost and equal gross benefit are very unrealistic. Some members of a community may hardly derive any benefit from learning the additional language, for example because they hardly interact with outsiders. Or they may face a very high cost of learning because of the high earnings they would forgo by spending time on it, or because they could spend that time learning a different language for some reason more useful to them. Taking these variable opportunity costs into account—instead of bluntly assuming roughly equal learning costs—would make the application of the criterion of equal cost–benefit ratios more favourable to wealthier communities (as well as reduce the likelihood of surplus-producing cooperative deals involving them). This need not be a problem, as long as one bears clearly in mind that we are here talking of cooperative justice, not of distributive justice (see §2.8).

14. In our example with two F-speakers, the ratio of overall cost to overall benefit is 3/4. The equal cost–benefit ratio therefore requires that each of the F-speakers (with a gross benefit of 1 and a gross cost of 0) should each transfer 3/4 to Petra. For the individual cost–benefit ratio is then given by $(3/4)/1 = 3/4$ for each of Frank and Frances, and by $(3 - 2 \times 3/4)/2 = 3/4$ for Petra. In the variant with four F-speakers, the cost–benefit ratio falls to 3/8, and the transfer to Petra from each of the F-speakers falls from 3/4 to 3/8. The cost–benefit ratio is then given by $(3/8)/1 = 3/8$ for each of the four of them, and by $(3 - 4 \times 3/8)/4 = 3/8$ for Petra.

15. See Appendix 1 to this chapter for an analytic formulation of the four criteria and a discussion of their formal relations.

16. In our example with two F-speakers, Petra is left to bear a cost of $3 - (2 \times 3/4) = 1.5$, while the cost jointly born by Frank and Frances is $2 \times 3/4 = 1.5$. With double the number of F-speakers, the per-capita transfer from the F-speaking community is required to drop to 3/8, in such a way that the total cost borne by the F-speaking community $(4 \times 3/8 = 3/2)$ remains equal to the part of the cost of learning left to Petra $3 - (4 \times 3/8) = 3/2$.

17. In the case of just two linguistic communities (as opposed to the general case, to be considered shortly), the same sharing of costs is mandated by a very different criterion, which consists in applying Gauthier's criterion of equal net benefit to each linguistic community taken as a whole rather than to each individual speaker (see de Briey and Van Parijs 2002). However, in the general case of any number of linguistic communities, this equal-aggregate-net-benefit criterion

generates wildly counterintuitive implications. In particular, what counts as a fair distribution of costs according to this criterion is absurdly sensitive to how finely linguistic groups are subdivided. The proposed equal-ratios criterion is not similarly vulnerable.

18. See Appendix 2 for a formal discussion.

19. This may seem a generous assumption after the discussion in section 2 of the Appendix to Chapter 1.

20. With a transfer of 1/4 to each of Frank and Frances, the cost–benefit ratio becomes $(1 - 1/4)/1 = 3/4$ for each of them, and $(1 + 2 \times 1/4)/2 = 3/4$ for Petra.

21. Take the case where our two F-speakers and our single P-speaker are joined by 10 Q-speakers (say, the Mandarinophones join the Anglophones and the Francophones). The overall ratio of cost to benefit is then $33/64 = 0.52$, while the ratios are $3/12 = 0.25$ for the P-speaker and $30/30 = 1$ for the Q-speakers. Most of the subsidy needed to lower the Q-speakers' ratio from 1 to 0.52 will come from the F-speakers, but some will need to come from a tax on the F-learning P-speaker, which will lift their cost–benefit ratio from 0.25 to 0.52.

22. Remember that equal ratios of gross benefit to cost entail equal ratios of net benefits to cost.

23. Another potentially embarrassing implication was pointed out to me by Andreas Cassee. It arises when the ease with which different languages are learned varies considerably. Suppose the cost of learning English is very low for all Europeans relative to learning Chinese. If they learn English first, the benefit to them of learning Chinese as a lingua franca will be much lower, and the subsidy they can claim from the Chinese in case Chinese becomes the lingua franca will be much higher than would otherwise be the case. This is fine. But what if they have not yet made use of the option of learning English? Could they explain to the Chinese that they could have done so and are therefore entitled to a larger subsidy? The answer that follows from my criterion is no: the benefit of linguistic cooperation is measured using as a baseline the situation that *would* obtain, other things being equal, in the absence of this cooperation, not a situation that *could have* obtained but did not. However, some communities may then be inclined to engage strategically in wasteful language learning (as far as communication is concerned), by unnecessarily learning a regional lingua franca in order to cheapen (through larger subsidies) their learning of the global one. This is indeed a theoretical possibility, but one that should not worry us unduly. First, learning the regional lingua franca (in this example, English) could yield benefits that would not be superseded by the learning of the global one (in this example, Chinese).

Secondly, for the cost of learning the regional lingua franca to be very low, there must be close to mutual intelligibility between that language and the learners' native language. Even in the absence of any strategic investment in the learning of this regional lingua franca, the benefit from learning the global lingua franca must accordingly be lower, and consequently the subsidy that can legitimately be claimed from its native speakers must be higher, thereby making the strategic learning option unprofitable. Finallly, for this option to make sense, there must be a huge difference in learning costs between the regional and the global lingua francas, and this difference can be shrunk dramatically through the use of appropriate early learning methods.

24. In our simple example with two languages, if Petra is the sole P-speaker and there are two F-speakers, the four criteria ('Church and King', 'Pool', 'Gauthier', and 'Homans' in that order) entitle Petra to a subsidy of 1, 2, 1.3, and 1.5, respectively. With four F-speakers, the corresponding levels of subsidy for Petra's learning become 0, 2.4, 0, and 1.5, and with nine F-speakers, 0, 2.7, −4.5, and 1.5. As the number of native speakers of the lingua franca increases relative to those who learn it, 'Church and King' stops subsidizing as soon as Petra's learning gives her a net benefit; 'Pool' keeps expanding the subsidy until it covers nearly all the cost; 'Gauthier' turns the subsidy into a tax at an ever rising level; and 'Homans' keeps the subsidy constant at half the cost.

25. Piron (2001: 95).

26. A thorough study by François Grin (2005a: 88–91) concludes that the annual per capita cost of foreign language teaching in state schools is about €36 in 2002–3 in the United Kingdom, compared to about €138 in 2003–4 in France (about 10% of the total annual education budget). In the United States, the per capita cost of foreign language learning has been estimated to be about forty times less than in Switzerland (Maurais 2003: 24, 32).

27. As mentioned before (note 13), the opportunity cost implied by the production of the public good is part of the cost to be taken into account when characterizing cooperative fairness, but its evaluation generally raises tricky questions.

28. Korean families send their children to English courses in China (Stevens et al. 2006), and Chinese institutions use Belgian teachers for English courses in their management schools (Graddol 2005).

29. This process can be expected to be far slower in bigger linguistic communities, which provide less opportunity (and hence also motivation) for interacting in the lingua franca. More than linguistic distance, this is a reason why the learning cost of the Chinese is likely to remain

particularly high, and hence justify a higher share of the subsidies than what is justified by the sheer arithmetic effect of the size of the Chinese linguistic community.

30. How this could come about is discussed in §3.7. The possibility contemplated here is crucially different from the substitution of one mother tongue for another briefly discussed above (§2.2). The cost to be shared fairly remains the cost of recurrent 'commuting', not of one-off 'conversion'. However, I am here conjecturing that as a matter of fact convergence to a lingua franca in a high-communication world will gradually make it about as cheap to acquire the lingua franca as one's mother tongue, precisely because early exposure to the lingua franca will approximate the intensity of early exposure to one's mother tongue.

31. According to Eurobarometer (2006), 36% of the French aged 15 or more say they can 'speak well enough to be able to have a conversation' (§1.22, Table D48T), and among them, 10% say that their English is very good, and 47% that it is good (§1.3, Table D48f). It follows that about 20% of the French (declare they) speak English well or very well. Given that most languages in the world are linguistically far more remote from English than French is, a 10% proficiency rate for an expenditure of €100 may not be too far off the mark.

32. To see this, note that the benefit conferred by competence in English to each of the six million speakers of each language who have learned it is given by the number of Anglophones (300 mn) plus the six million English learners in each of the other non-Anglophone communities (99 × 6 mn). The aggregate benefit to the Anglophone population (100 × 300 mn × 6 mn) is then no longer 50% of the overall benefit (itself twice the number of pairs connected by the acquisition of the lingua franca) but about 25%. With a learning cost of €100 per capita in all non-Anglophone communities, the total learning bill is €600 billion (100 × 60 mn × 100), but only a quarter of it, not a half, needs to be funded out of Anglophone pockets. This amounts to €500 (=(60 bn/300 mn) × 0.25) per capita for the 300 million Anglophones, rather than the €1,000 conjectured above, and hence to a per capita subsidy to the non-Anglophone communities of €25 (= €500 × 300 mn/6 bn), i.e. one quarter of their estimated per capita cost.

33. Under the assumptions made about the number and sizes of the linguistic communities (100 communities of 60 million speakers), the Anglophone community can be shown to be liable—if cost–benefit ratios are to be equalized—to only about 5% of the cost if everyone became proficient in English (instead of about 25% if only 10% of the non-Anglophones became proficient). But at the same time, providing the effectiveness of the learning process is unchanged, the total cost of

learning would also increase tenfold. Hence, as a rough estimate of the long-term prospect of the fair sharing by the Anglophones of the cost of their language having become universal, we are back to a contribution of €1000 = (€100 × 10 × 60 mn × 100/300 mn) × 0.05. The per capita subsidy received by each non-Anglophone community can then be calculated by dividing the total Anglophone contribution by the non-Anglophone population. This yields €50 (= €1000 × 300/6000), equal to the amount received by the French in our initial two-country scenario, but now covering 5% of the total learning cost (now ten times higher), instead of 50%.

34. Suppose there are 300 mn Anglophones, 1,000 mn Mandarinophones, 50 linguistic communities of 60 mn speakers (say, the French, etc.) and 500 linguistic communities of 4 mn speakers (say, the Lithuanians, etc.). With a level of learning that makes 10% of the non-Anglophone communities proficient in English and costs them €100 per capita, the subsidy can be shown to amount to €32 per capita for the Mandarinophones (leaving them with a net cost of €680 = (100 – 32) × 10 per proficient speaker), and to slightly over and slightly under €24 per capita, respectively, for the French and the Lithuanians (leaving them with a net cost of €760 = (100 – 24) × 10 per proficient speaker), respectively, while the tax on the Anglophone population amounts to €508 per capita. With a level of learning that reaches 100% of the population and costs €1,000 per capita, the per capita tax on the Anglophones would rise to €937, while the subsidy would leap to over €170 per capita for the Chinese (net cost per proficient speaker of €830 instead of €680), rise slightly to around €25 for the French (net cost of €975 instead of €760) and fall to below €17 yet remain positive for the Lithuanians (net cost of €983 instead of €760). In this new situation of universal spreading, the Anglophones pay a far smaller percentage (4.7%) of the total learning cost than under a modest 10% spreading (25.4%) because the part of the total benefit that consists in interaction with them shrinks dramatically (the bulk of the benefit now consists in interaction between non-Anglophones). By contrast, the Anglophone's per capita contribution to the total cost rises (from €508 to €937) above that of the Mandarinophones (which rises from €680 to €830 per proficient speaker). Why? Given the population sizes postulated above, modest (10%) spreading gives each Anglophone the benefit of 600 mn more speech partners, and each proficient Mandarinophone 800 mn, whereas universal spreading gives each Anglophone 6,000 mn more speech partners and each proficient Mandarinophone 'only' 5,300 mn. The equalization of cost–benefit

ratios requires that this change in relative levels of benefit should be reflected in relative levels of contribution.

35. This is more to pay for the UK and less to receive for France than the €50 per capita they would have had to pay and receive, respectively, if there had just been the two of them sharing half of the French learning costs (see §2.10), even though both are much better off in the former situation than they would have been in the latter because of the (now much larger) benefit of lingua-franca-mediated worldwide communication.

36. As suggested by François Grin (2005b).

37. Rough guesses based on the exercise above (§2.10) lead to a subsidy covering one quarter of the English learning costs of the non-Anglophone member states of the EU, or €25 per inhabitant and over €10 billion in total, to be funded by Anglophones worldwide. On the other hand, the 60 mn UK citizens would owe a total of about €500 per capita, or €30 billion in total, to non-Anglophones around the world.

38. Consider the blogosphere. According to an estimate made by www.technorati.com in July 2006, 39% of the blogs are posted in English, 31% in Japanese, and 12% in Chinese, 3% or less in any other language. A majority of the readers of the blogs in any language, including the three main blog languages, most probably consists of natives of that language. But the minority of non-natives is bound to be insignificant for Japanese and Chinese, whereas it is likely to be considerable for English, with the difference further boosted by the impact on search engine activity of the far wider use of the Latin alphabet.

39. Nunberg (2002: 322–4) provides persuasive evidence to the effect that the proportion of web contents in languages other than English keeps increasing and will keep doing so. It is crucial to understand that the asymmetry essential to the compensatory free riding discussed here has nothing to do with English content being more than proportionally present on the web, and everything to do with English content being far more than proportionally usable by allophones than content in any other language.

40. My (admittedly stretched) notion of poaching is meant to cover clear cases of (not for profit) pirating, but also cases in which the information is voluntarily and gladly made available free of charge and above all cases in which producers would have liked to receive some compensation from consumers but do not find it worth the trouble and therefore make no attempt to make poaching illegal or to enforce the law if it is illegal.

41. As the lingua franca and its learning become less hard, the learning of other languages by lingua franca natives becomes harder, as a direct

corollary of the maxi-min mechanism delineated above (§1.5). This means that there is ever less free riding of the learning type on the part of lingua franca speakers—i.e. taking advantage of patient speech partners in order to learn the latter's language (§1.2)—but no less free riding of this type on the part of native speakers of peripheral languages—which could already be viewed as some sort of compensatory free riding. As English spreads, however, an ever-growing majority of the people with whom non-Anglophones will be talking (and hence learning) English will be other non-Anglophones. This is no longer systematic free riding: by both learning the language and teaching it (in the same act of communication), non-Anglophones who communicate in the lingua franca provide benefits to each other.

Chapter 3

1. Beyond that, I shall simply state my conviction that philosophers can, must, and will keep entertaining themselves and teasing each other by imagining, elaborating, recycling, revamping, rehabilitating all sorts of theories of justice—libertarian and utilitarian, Aristotelian and Thomistic, Lockean and Marxist, communitarian and republican, environmentalist and feminist, multiculturalist and post-modernist, etc.—which do not look like liberal-egalitarian theories of distributive justice in the sense to be spelled out shortly; but that any such theory, once duly clarified, will either turn out to be a particular (and sometimes particularly interesting) version of the liberal-egalitarian conception or generate implications too unpalatable for us to swallow. See Van Parijs (1995) and Arnsperger and Van Parijs (2000) for some arguments in support of this bold claim.

2. The expression 'lax' is not used here in the sense in which G. A. Cohen (1992: §III) introduced it when distinguishing a strict and a lax interpretation of Rawls's difference principle. By virtue of requiring us to maximize the absolute level secured to the worst off, rather than to minimize the gap between the better off and the worse off, the difference principle in all its interpretations illustrates a lax-egalitarian conception of justice. But by requiring economic behaviour to be guided by the difference principle rather than by self-interest (as allowed by Rawls's 'lax' interpretation), Cohen's 'strict' interpretation of the (lax-egalitarian) Difference Principle, if implemented, would equalize resources to an extent closer to what would follow from strict egalitarianism than to what would follow from the (lax-egalitarian) Difference Principle in Rawls's own 'lax' interpretation.

3. The egalitarian and liberal aspects of this conception are closely related, respectively, to the ideals of 'solidarity' and 'toleration', and the liberal-egalitarian project can be understood as an attempt to combine these two ideals into a coherent conception of distributive justice. Needless to say, the content of each of these features has been the object of considerable discussion and refinement. For example, some liberal-egalitarian philosophers prefer to say that they are committed to a very broadly defined conception of the good life, while being neutral between its countless specific versions. The simple characterization proposed is open to such amendments but will suffice for present purposes.

4. The theory offered in Van Parijs (1995) is still the one I am prepared to defend today, with two major qualifications. First, I am inclined to drop the constraint of undominated diversity (for reasons explained in Van Parijs 2009). Secondly, to accommodate some convictions that took shape and gained strength as I was working towards the present book, I gradually realized that an acceptable conception of justice must make room for a dimension of respect or dignity that is irreducible to real freedom for all. This dimension will be introduced and its implications for linguistic matters discussed in Chapters 4 and 5.

5. See Alan Patten's (2009 and forthcoming) useful discussion of the interpretation of linguistic rights as 'rights of toleration' and its limits.

6. As emphasized by many, from Karl Renner (1902: 63: 'The multilingual state is forced to regulate the language use of its citizens, and above all in which language its own organs interact with the citizen and with one another') to Will Kymlicka (1995: 111) or Alan Patten (2001: 693; 2003a: 371).

7. See Patten (2003a and fothcoming) for the most systematic argument along these lines.

8. This *accommodating linguistic regime* will be discussed thoroughly in §§5.1–5.5 below.

9. Asserting the importance of this difference does not amount to denying that positive externalities can arise for the current members of a religious community—like for those of linguistic community—as a result of one more person joining (the benefit from expanding the circle of interaction, trust, and solidarity is likely to offset the nuisance from overcrowding in the church—or in the paradise). It excludes even less the possibility that religion may be a public good for reasons unaffected or hardly affected by the sizes of the communities it forms, for example by fostering mutual care or by facilitating law enforcement.

10. At any rate to the extent consistent with other freedoms recognized as fundamental. In the choice of one's spouse, for example, religious and

linguistic discrimination is presumably not more (nor less) illegitimate than gender discrimination. It may even be argued that letting religious, linguistic, or gender considerations play a role in this choice does not qualify as 'discrimination' as defined. What about requiring a Catholic bishop to be Catholic, or a teacher in a Catholic school, or a pupil in a Catholic school? And what about requiring a Catholic bishop to be a man? The conflict between fundamental formal freedoms and the equalization of opportunities is—fortunately for my present purposes—less tricky in the case of 'linguistic discrimination' than in the case of 'religious discrimination'.

11. The maxi-min language use described earlier (§1.4) is central in creating this advantage. Here is how. If the extent of use of the various languages in a multilingual environment—and hence the demand for jobs requiring proficiency in those languages—were not governed by the maxi-min rule, but simply proportional to the number of native speakers of each of them ('fair division'), no bias would emerge in favour of the native speakers of the languages more widely spread. If use and hence demand were proportional to average competence in each of the languages, the demand for skills in the dominant language would increase relative to others, but precisely in line with the supply. Under the maxi-min rule, by contrast, a mediocre level of proficiency in some language widely spread is sufficient to trigger its exclusive use for all sorts of purposes. Hence a steep leap in the demand for the services of those mastering that language, as illustrated by the four trends described below.

12. Three examples. First, an American colleague explained to me how in his youth he earned a good salary teaching English to Japanese executives and Thai supervisors, so that they could talk to each other in a factory that the Japanese multinational was in the process of setting up in Thailand. Secondly, France's former education minister Claude Allègre argues (*L'Express*, 14 March 2005) that 'this is the time to use Europe and make sure there are a few permanent English native teachers in each [French] secondary school.' Finally: 'The common perception that many Korean instructors of English have poor skills in spoken English has also resulted in a premium in the tutoring fees charged by instructors who are perceived to be native speakers of English, i.e. Americans, Canadians and Australians.' (Stevens et al. 2006: 172).

13. According to a British Council estimate (Phillipson 2007: 6), the contribution of the English-language business to the British economy comes close to €2 billion per year. See Grin (2005a) for more estimates.

14. For example, if you want to work for the EU in Moscow, mastering English is apparently more crucial than mastering Russian: 'Delegation of the European Commission in Russia. Press and Information Section seeks: A Stagiaire. The candidate must have excellent drafting skills in English (preferably of English mother tongue)' (European Commission website, 30 March 2003). The Esperanto website www.lingvo.org has been particularly active in documenting discrimination in favour of English native speakers in and around the EU's institutions by collecting hundreds of job offers such as the following: 'The Union of Independent Retail Traders in Europe is currently in search of a Jurist. You are English native speaker and fluent in French. Knowledge of the German language is an asset.' (*The Bulletin*, Brussels, 8 March 2001).

15. In several national contexts, various studies have tried to estimate the rent associated to having the dominant language as one's mother tongue on the basis of the associated unemployment rates and wage differentials. See e.g. Grin and Vaillancourt (1997), Grin (1999), Dustmann and Fabbri (2003), and several chapters in Chiswick and Miller (2007).

16. This general claim holds in the short term with some qualifications about the advantage, in some contexts, of knowing (global) English as a second language rather than as an (apparently) native tongue (see §1.11 above), but may not hold in the longer term (see §3.9 below).

17. See Melitz (1999) for some fragmentary yet edifying data.

18. Not only is it the case that books initially published in some language A are often discovered by potential publishers in some other language B only if and when they are first translated from A into English. Sometimes, for lack of suitably qualified translators from A into B, the B version of the book is even translated, not straight from the original A version, but from its English translation.

19. This is what I am doing at this very moment.

20. The issue of ideological hegemony, causally linked but normatively very different, was addressed in §1.11. Only the direct impact of this asymmetric audience on distributive issues is our present concern.

21. See Chiswick and Miller (2007: ch. 15).

22. Another variant of this tinkering strategy, with a straightforward rationale in terms of linguistic justice, would consist in imposing an artificial language as the official language instead of both the dominant and the local language. Part 2 of the Appendix to Chapter 1 explains why this strategy is unpromising. However, the option for Bahasa in Indonesia or for ex-colonial languages elsewhere is to some extent analogous.

23. See Chiswick and Miller (2007: 454).

24. An altogether different—and far stronger—case for protective language legislation will be presented and discussed in Chapter 4.
25. For an in-depth discussion of alternative interpretations of the difference principle and a justification of the one adopted here, see Van Parijs (2002b).
26. And hence not a distinction—more consistent with some of Dworkin's (e.g. 2000: 81–3; 2004: 339–50) own formulations—which moves from the (insurable) luck side to the (uninsurable) choice side those unchosen features with which people identify: their ancestral religion, for example, or their gender or indeed their mother tongue (as opposed, say, to their flat feet or poor memory).
27. For example, if informed that French has lost much of its communicative value relative to English, you may henceforth insure yourself better against the possibility that you may emerge from behind Dworkin's veil of ignorance talking nothing but French, and agree to contribute to the corresponding transfer in case it turned out that you emerged from the veil with English flowing effortlessly from your lips.
28. See especially Dworkin (1981: 325–6; 2000: 335–8, 345; 2006: 115–16). For a discussion of Dworkin's successive formulations of his conception of distributive justice and a defence of the interpretation adopted here, see Van Parijs (2009: §2).
29. 'After studying [the theory of exploitation] for some time, I came to believe that it is not in itself a fundamental theory of (in)justice.... I think that some egalitarian theory, of the Rawls–Sen–Dworkin–Arneson–Cohen variety, is needed to justify the Marxian accusation that workers are unjustly treated under capitalism' (Roemer 1996: 9). Roemer's (1982) conception of exploitation as asset-based inequality is also flexible enough to allow for job-based, citizenship-based exploitation or indeed language-based exploitation (see Van Parijs 1993: chs 6–7).
30. Roemer's proposal is to partition each type into centiles in terms of the degree of effort they make—for example, in the context of educational achievement, how many hours they spend studying. A factor or combination of factors is deemed neutralized, and hence opportunities equalized along the dimension under consideration, when each centile of effort in each type can expect the same level of achievement. Because there is generally no policy that can satisfy this very demanding objective, Roemer proposes a maximin policy, i.e. a transfer scheme across types that maximizes (with an exogenously given budget) the average achievement of the type with the lowest level of achievement, bearing in mind the effects of the transfer scheme on levels of effort and hence on levels of achievement. Modelling these effects is no straightforward matter. Moreover, the definition and the operationalization of

a meaningful concept of effort, while tricky enough by reference to specific achievements (such as education), become prohibitively problematic when it is opportunity for welfare generally that needs to be equalized. Last and not least embarrassing, Roemer himself shows that the maxi-min policy can lead to making low-effort members of the worst-off type worse off than they would be under the status quo.

31. See also, in the same spirit, Ackerman and Alstott's (1999) proposal to impose a lump-sum tax on people with highly educated parents.

32. See Van Parijs (1995, 2009). Like Rawls's difference principle, this maximin-gift principle refers to income and may therefore look like an outcome-egalitarian principle but is definitely opportunity-egalitarian in the sense of §3.1.

33. See, most explicitly, Rawls (2001: §50).

34. This also holds for liberal-egalitarian theories not discussed in §3.4. Take, for example, Bruce Ackerman's (1980: 116) criterion of undominated diversity—a weak egalitarian criterion that could be developed into a general principle for the just distribution of endowments (Van Parijs 1995: ch. 3). Its satisfaction could be pursued through lump-sum transfers from (some of) those endowed 'from birth' with the more valuable language to (some) of those endowed with an economically useless language, but also through the efficient acquisition of competence in the more valuable language. Adding such competence to the endowment of the native speakers of the less valuable language may well be a safer and cheaper way of achieving a situation in which none of these will be unanimously regarded as less well endowed, all things considered, than some native speaker of the more valuable language. This possibility is even more obvious in the case of Amartya Sen's (1985, 2009a) approach to justice in terms of basic capabilities, as the enjoyment of some of these may require competence in the dominant language for reasons irreducible to access to an income.

35. Including by sending children on language courses abroad. Stevens et al. (2006: 172) mention that the financial burden of English learning can consume up to one-third of a middle class Korean family's income.

36. Consider, for example, the proportion of people who declare they know English well or very well (EU 15, Eurobarometer 2001, Table 1). To no one's surprise, the five Germanic countries (the UK and Ireland not included) score better in terms of self-assessed knowledge of English (with an unweighted average of 65%) than the four Latin countries (with an unweighted average of 38%). This seems to provide strong support for the common wisdom that this sizeable inequality is rooted in the fact that English is an (admittedly quite latinized) Germanic language, and hence intrinsically easier to learn for the average

citizen of the former set of countries than for the average citizen of the latter. However, confidence in this common wisdom is shattered by the observation that 61% of the Finns and 47% of the Greeks declare they know English well or very well. Even worse, for the under-40s, we find 87% for Finland, 79.5% for the average Germanic country, 71% for Greece and 61.5% for the average Latin country, not exactly a smooth monotonic decrease with linguistic distance (Ginsburgh and Weber 2003). It is not difficult to find a better predictor. Let us simply classify our eleven countries into four groups according to the number of native speakers of their official language worldwide: competence then decreases gently as we move from languages with less than 10 million speakers (72%), to between 10 and 50 million (58.5%), between 50 and 100 million (45%) and over 100 million (35.5%). For the under 40s, this becomes 88%, 75.5%, 66.5%, and 60%, respectively. Why this should be so is explained in the text.

37. The average cost of one hour of dubbing is estimated to be about fifteen times the cost of one hour of subtitling (see e.g. Luyken et al. 1991). Dubbing is to be distinguished from so-called voice-over, an off voice which does not try to imitate the tone—sometimes not even the gender—of the actors and leaves the original sound track weakly audible in the background. This technique, systematically used, for example, in Poland, Latvia, and Lithuania (but not Estonia) is much cheaper than dubbing and hence economically viable for small audiences, while not being any less damaging than dubbing for learning purposes.

38. In the Netherlands, for example, it has been estimated that children spend about half their TV time watching programmes with English-language sound (Koolstra and Beentjes 1999: 16) and that Dutch viewers generally spend about 5 to 6 hours per week reading subtitles (Koolstra et al. 2002: 325).

39. See, especially, van de Poel and d'Ydewalle (1996) and Koolstra and Beentjes (1999) for some experimental evidence on learning English through watching subtitled programmes. Along the same line, Chaudenson (2001: 145, 155–6) refers to the competence in Italian acquired by Tunisian and Albanian children with no exposure to it other than the watching of Italian TV channels.

40. More specific evidence about the difference made by dubbing versus subtitling can be found by comparing linguistic competence in Belgium's Dutch-language and French-language communities. Their school systems are quite similar, but the French-speaking population watches the bulk of English-medium films in dubbed form, while the Dutch-speaking population watches them all in subtitled form. First,

despite similar volumes of English lessons at school, self-assessed competence in English is far higher on average among Dutch speakers than among French speakers (52% versus 20% report good or very good knowledge in Eurobarometer 2006). Secondly, average knowledge increases sharply from the oldest cohort (65+) to the youngest (15–24) cohort among both Dutch and French speakers, with one exception: the youngest cohort of French speakers (Van Parys and Wauters 2006: Figure 3). This strongly suggests that the learning of English is far from completed in their case (as it has to rely mainly on the education system), whereas it is essentially completed at the same age for Dutch speakers. Thirdly, detailed data about competence in French and in English of Dutch-speaking pupils at the end of secondary school show that, despite French teaching starting two years earlier and exceeding on average by 35% the number of hours of English teaching, competence scores in written and, above all, in spoken English, are higher than in French (which, unlike English, is hardly present on Dutch-language TV). They also show that the variation in average competence from school to school is significantly narrower for English than for French. This latter fact suggests, as the authors of the report put it, that there is a 'far greater extra-curricular contribution' in the case of English (Housen et al. 2003: 34–47, 54).

41. See Koolstra et al. (1997) for experimental evidence in support of this claim. This might even go some way towards explaining why Finland, apart from doing remarkably well in terms of competence in English despite an exceptionally great linguistic distance, comes top of the league as regards both average and equality in mother tongue competence too, as revealed by Pisa surveys (see GERESE 2005).

42. See Koolstra et al. (2002: 331).

43. In Catalonia, over 90% of film watching in cinemas is in Spanish, and over 70% of TV watching (see Vila I Moreno and Vila Mendiburu (2010) for data about secondary school pupils in 2006–7).

44. To realize how unpromising this strategy is, it may suffice to refer to the strong resistance mounted by the film industry against the Catalan government's very toned down proposal that required only half the copies of some foreign films shown in Catalan cinemas to be dubbed in Catalan with the cost of dubbing entirely borne by the Catalan government. See 'La Generalitat reabre la eterna batalla del doblaje en catalán', *El Pais*, 5 March 2009.

45. Thus, a deputy from Belgium's green party Ecolo declares in Parliament: 'I shall content myself with one proposal, simple but far more important than one might think at first sight: abolishing the dubbing of spoken texts on the radio, on TV and in cinemas' (Henry 2003: §2).

46. Thus, according to a document issued by the DG Education and Culture (European Commission 2002: 16), 'In some member states, TV programmes and films in foreign languages seldom get onto our screens, or if they do they are often dubbed rather than subtitled because the local market prefers dubbing; yet research shows that films and TV can encourage and facilitate language learning if they are made available in their original language, with subtitles instead of dubbing; subtitling provides an economical and effective way of making our environment more language-friendly.' Along the same lines, a general-public brochure on language policy recommends that steps be taken 'to provide more sub-titling on television and in the cinema' (European Commission 2004: 16).

47. Thus, on 8 July 2003, the Committee on Culture, Youth, Education, the Media and Sport of the European Parliament approved a motion calling on the Commission, the Member States and the Regions, 'to promote the showing and broadcasting of movies in their original version' and 'to prefer subtitling in one or more languages above dubbing, if translation is required' (European Parliament 2002, item 17).

48. In response to the item 'I prefer to watch foreign films and programmes with subtitles, rather than dubbed', 90–94% of the respondents 'tend to agree' in subtitling countries Sweden, Finland, Denmark, and the Netherlands, compared to 19–31% in dubbing countries Germany, Austria, Spain, Italy, and France (Eurobarometer 2006: Table 11.8). This contrast had already been pointed out on the basis of a different dataset by Koolstra and Beentjes (1999).

49. In the Indian context, Amartya Sen (2009b) makes a parallel plea for the democratization of competence in English as an option far superior to the proposal made by Uttar Pradesh leader Mulayam Singh Yadav to ban English in his state: 'There is an elite which is much more familiar with English, which is not the case with many other people.... That's an argument why others who are excluded from it ought to have the opportunity to [learn English].... So rather than being an egalitarian force, the exclusion—if it is carried out—will have exactly the opposite effect: that is to keep the stratification as it is.'

Chapter 4

1. Van Parijs (1995). With its more specific concern for the 'social bases of self-respect', Rawls's (1971: 178–9, 2001: 59–60) interpretation of liberal-egalitarian justice offers a more explicit anchor for an integration of this dimension.

2. First reported, it seems, in the Francophone Belgian newspaper *La Dernière Heure*, this story was subsequently commented on at some length in the French press (see e.g. 'Stéphane Bern se voit reprocher de ne pas parler flamand à Bruges', website Agence France Press, 2 September 2008) and in the Flemish press (see e.g. 'Vlaanderen Vlaams!', *De Morgen*, 31 October 2008).

3. This simple definition will suffice for present purposes. See Parekh (2009), Sen (2009c), and Qizilbash (2009) for a recent discussion of this confusing notion.

4. The choice of this label is inspired by Chapter 1, section 6 of South Africa's 1996 Constitution: 'All official languages must enjoy parity of esteem and must be treated equitably.'

5. Under a variety of labels, this dimension and the associated notions of recognition, collective identity, dignity, etc. have been highlighted and critically discussed by many authors (Honneth 1990; Taylor 1992; Kymlicka 1995; Fraser 1998; Appiah 2005; Patten forthcoming, etc.). An in-depth discussion of these approaches and of how they relate to the normative framework on which I shall be relying to articulate my third interpretation of linguistic injustice is beyond the scope of this chapter and this book. In the process of spelling out the implications of this framework for institutions and policies relevant to language issues, I shall point out a number of similarities and differences and, in some cases, defend explicitly the choices I am making.

6. This feature is the third difference between language and religion mentioned earlier (§3.2). It can be viewed as a generalization of 'undisestablishability': it is not only the state and its institutions that are unable to bracket language out. Any interaction between human beings is forced to make a linguistic choice in a way in which it is not forced to make a religious choice. This is the fundamental reason why linguistic justice, in the sense to be developed below, has no equivalent in terms of religious justice. It is by no means being assumed that people's collective identity is universally linked with their native language, and even less that it is more often or more strongly linked with their native language than with their religion or anything else.

7. In Brussels, as in many other officially bilingual places, great care is taken to make sure that signs appear in both languages, however small the contribution to efficient communication. How useful is it to be told, for example, that you are entering the municipality of 'Auderghem/ Oudergem' or receiving a letter from the municipal administration of 'Schaerbeek/Schaarbeek'? Yet, deliberately dropping one of the two designations would be interpreted as provocation.

8. See Smejkalova (2007: 39–40) for an instructive account of this small replay of the (locally) notorious *Ortstafelsturm* of the 1970s.

9. In national contexts, when an obvious (usually quantitative) rationale is available, some languages are given an official recognition that is far less extensive, though still, on cheap occasions, more than proportional: think of Romansch in Switzerland or German in Belgium, in each case with native speakers accounting for less than 1% of the population. Similarly, at EU level, Gaelic has been added to the official languages, but is being given a smaller place for reasons that can be understood and accepted by all without too much difficulty. This does not mean that the issue of which languages should have some recognition, or how much, is unproblematically settled. What about Catalan? And then also Basque and Galician? But then what about Romani? And Luxemburgish? In each case, the challenge is to articulate and publicize a simple criterion of selection that does not lend itself to any disparaging interpretation.

10. Publicly accessible at http://eur-lex.europa.eu.

11. In its search for a neutral language, perhaps the Consilium would be well advised to switch from Latin to Esperanto—notwithstanding all that can be said against the latter's prospects as a lingua franca (see part 2 of the Appendix to Chapter 1). True, Esperanto is not exactly a 'neutral' language but it has a far stronger claim to equidistance from the EU's twenty-three official languages than Latin has, and one that would be most welcome in order to correct somewhat, after the 2004 enlargement, the Western bias of the symbolic trio of working languages (French–German–English), to which I return below (§4.4). Moreover, the Esperanto movement's ideal of universal peace and trans-national understanding is one with which the EU may wish to be associated more closely than with the religious flavour of the sacred language of the Catholic Church, let alone with the Roman imperialism that spread Latin across Europe.

12. In addition to the Council, the Parliament, and the Commission, both consultative committees also have their headquarters in Brussels, side by side. On their huge common glass front, the Committee of the Regions first wrote its name in English then switched to Dutch and French, while the Economic and Social Committee first opted for English and French, and next for English only.

13. As mentioned before (§1.6) they provide an important category of systematic exceptions to the maxi-min rule.

14. The adoption of the English language as a medium of expression should, however, be kept firmly distinct from the adoption of the conceptual apparatus of the British or American legal tradition. The

obligation to make every EU rule translatable and intelligible in other languages arguably operates as an automatic check against the blurring of this distinction, as does the primacy given to French in the proceedings of the Luxemburg Court of Justice (see Aziz and Van Parijs 2002). If this obligation is dropped, vigilance may need to be scaled up. But there are bound to be ways of effectively exercising such vigilance that are immensely cheaper than systematic translation into over twenty languages, as well as less alienating than having the European court operate in a language known to a stagnating small minority of the EU population.

15. Thus, over 500 significant mistakes were detected in the officially published version of the Latvian translation of the EU draft constitution which the Latvian Parliament was asked to ratify (Ina Druviete, Latvian Minister of Education, at the IVth Nitobe Symposium, Vilnius, 30 July 2005).

16. According to David Graddol (2005), the maritime industry spent millions of euros getting clarity from the courts about the (only authoritative) English version of international maritime law. Just try to imagine what this cost would be like if all versions were meant to be authoritative.

17. This practice was generalized in response to the 2004 enlargement. With at least one interpreter for each combination of languages, there would have been a need for more interpreters than members of the European Parliament, and no hemicycle could have been big enough to fit the interpreter booths.

18. See Mamadouh (1995) and Mamadouh and Hofman (2001): among the older members of the 1992 European Parliament, 48% were able to communicate in French, and 51% in English. Among the younger members of the 2000 European Parliament, 54% could communicate in French, and 89% in English.

19. It is sometimes argued that Euro MPs should not be expected to be plurilingual: they should be selected on the basis of the trust their electorates can have in them, not in the light of their linguistic skills. This is nonsense. It is obviously in the interest of any electorate that its representatives should do a good job at linking up effectively with colleagues and other actors from other countries. Elected to the European Parliament, they will perform far better if they master languages other than their native one, especially those most widely known among their colleagues, among the staff of the European Parliament, of other EU institutions and of all the trans-national organizations with which it is important that Euro MPs should communicate. Linguistic skills of the right sort are therefore an exceedingly meaningful

criterion of selection and self-selection for political positions at EU level. For those who lack these skills and are not determined to acquire them quickly, there are plenty of linguistically cosier levels of government at which they can pursue their political careers.

20. The citizens' individual right to communicate with EU officials in all official languages could provide a further illustration. How far one has already needed to move away from it is illustrated by EPSO (European Personnel Selection Office), the agency in charge of recruiting the EU's personnel: its homepage gently warns applicants from all member states in twenty-three languages: 'For operational reasons ['practical reasons' in Danish, French, Swedish, Spanish; 'organizational reasons' in Dutch, German, Greek], EPSO is only able to respond to questions submitted in English, French and German.' (http://europa.eu/epso, 22 July 2010).

21. See Grin (2004) for some estimates. We should not let ourselves be reassured too easily by the observation that this only amounts to the trivial cost of two cups of coffee per year and per person. First, the tax burden is very unequally shared by the 500 million Europeans, and the well-to-do EU citizens to whom the reassuring message is addressed are actually contributing the equivalent of many cups of coffee. Secondly and more fundamentally, one can just as legitimately ask how many thousands of African children could be saved from starvation each year if that money were optimally used instead by the European Commission's DG Development: the total cost of the EU's language services—about 1% of the EU total budget, itself about 1% of the EU's GDP (GRASPE 2010: 48)—amounts to nearly half the GDP of a country like Burundi. As long as the fair running of the EU polity requires this huge expense on language services, we may be able to face without shame an answer to this question. Probably not if nothing is left to justify the expense but (some) member states' linguistic vanity.

22. A proposal of this sort that attracted some publicity was made in 2003 by the Swedish Prime Minister Göran Persson. Instead of having all countries paying jointly (roughly according to their wealth) for the translation of every official document into every official EU language, he proposed that the cost of language services should be covered by the countries requesting them or—in an attempt to (over-)correct for the pro-British bias inherent in the proposal—that it should be shared equally between the countries from whose language and into whose language the translation is being made. As a growing majority of texts is being produced in English and as Swedes are so competent in English that they need no translation for most documents, the proposed rule, if

adopted, would eventually have exempted Sweden from any contribution to the funding of the EU's language services.

23. See Fidrmuc and Ginsburgh's (2007) instructive estimates of the per capita marginal cost of 'linguistically enfranchising' (i.e. enabling to communicate with EU institutions) native speakers of the various official languages of the EU, i.e. the cost, under present arrangements, of adding their native language to the official languages once all official languages with a higher potential for enfranchisement have been added, divided by the number of people enfranchised as a result of adding this language.

24. Especially since the 2004 enlargement, European institutions have tried to minimize the occurrence of such extreme cases in various ways: by introducing the practice of using a relay language, by widening the spectrum of languages from which each interpreter is expected to be able to translate, and by trying to identify more finely the real interpretation and translation needs. However, the savings made in this way are partly offset by increased organizational and training costs. And of course, the remaining cost is still huge compared to a monolingual regime.

25. I shall return below (§5.14) at greater length to this question of who should pay for linguistic justice as parity of esteem, in connection with what I shall argue is a far more important way of pursuing justice so conceived under contemporary conditions.

26. This can often be combined with a conflict of material interests. For example, in his attempt to break the deadlock on EU patents, Commissioner Michel Barnier pointed out that the average cost of protecting a patent in the US was €1865, whereas in the EU the translation costs alone amounted to €14000. The proposal to reduce the number of languages to three (English, German, and French) did not only hurt the Spaniards' and Italians' pride, but also their interests: Italian or Spanish inventions will be handicapped as a consequence of having to be filed in one of the three privileged languages (www.euractiv.com, 2 July 2010).

27. On the inefficiency of any plural lingua franca regime, see part 3 of the Appendix to Chapter 1. That even such a more modest trilingual formula is under siege is illustrated by a widely reported incident that happened on 23 March 2006 at a meeting between the Council of the European Union and the European 'social partners': as the French chairman of the European employers association UNICE, Ernest-Antoine Seillière, started his intervention in English, President Jacques Chirac and his two Ministers left the room. At the press conference that followed the meeting, Chirac explained why he had

been 'profoundly shocked to hear a Frenchman express himself in English at the Council table': 'We are not going to found tomorrow's world on a single language, and therefore a single culture.' Seillère, nonetheless, persisted and finished his speech in English ('Seillière parle anglais. Chirac part faché', www.lefigaro.fr, 23/3/2006).

28. There is plenty of all that in the European institutions' many declarations on Europe's wonderful linguistic diversity and in the very creation of a commissioner job in charge of multilingualism (in 2004, the Slovak Jan Figel, as an appendix to education; in 2007, the Rumanian Leonard Orban, as his sole competence; since 2009, the Cypriot Androulla Vassiliou, again as an appendix to education). From the member states' standpoint, this rhetorical flourish involves a risk of overshooting that is better controlled in the official equal recognition strategy: if Europe's linguistic diversity is so great, why not honour and revive the many regional languages that often do not enjoy recognition, let alone equal recognition, in their respective national contexts?

29. Witness, for example, the recurrent debate about the respective places of English and of the second national language in the school curriculum of various Swiss cantons. In our Bruges anecdote, a crucial background fact is that, because of an inextricable combination of maxi-min dynamics and negative attitudes, the Francophone Belgian's competence in Dutch remains on average far poorer than the Flemings' competence in French.

Chapter 5

1. I owe this anecdote to Geoffrey Meade, former columnist for *The Bulletin* (Brussels, 25 January 2008).

2. This is the position best defended by Alan Patten, as briefly presented in §3.2 above.

3. To illustrate, here is Slovenia's version of a coercive linguistic regime, as laid down in its *Law on the Public Use of the Slovenian Language* (2004): 'The law states that Slovenian shall be used orally and in writing in public life. . . . It stipulates that the names of all state bodies, local administrations, public organizations, public companies, and political parties shall be in Slovenian. Public insignia as well as the names of private companies, premises and shops should be in the Slovenian language, too. All proceedings involving public and private companies should be carried out in the Slovenian language. Slovenian is also prescribed as the language of public notices, conferences, press releases, announcements, and product

labelling and instructions. Contracts with Slovenian companies must be written only in Slovenian and only this version may be considered as an original. In addition, all companies and individuals under private law must communicate with their customers in Slovenian and only people with appropriate knowledge of Slovenian can be employed in jobs that require communication skills.' (Kodelja and Krivic 2007: 9.)

4. The sort of coercive institution considered here is consistent with respect for the fundamental liberties protected by any liberal conception of justice (in the sense of §3.1). The coercion it involves does not apply to what people are allowed to do or say, but on the conditions under which they are entitled to certain benefits or services (including the use of wavelengths and open public spaces). One case that could be regarded as problematic is the linguistic constraint on private education. But presented as a condition to be satisfied if parents are to discharge the obligation to have their children properly educated, this is not more (nor less) problematic than this 'paternalistic' obligation itself. Another potentially problematic case is the internal life of private firms. Why is it legitimate to constrain language use within a firm whereas it is not within a household or a voluntary association? Perhaps for reasons analogous to what circumscribes the legitimate scope of anti-smoking and anti-discrimination legislation. The exact limit need not be specified here. All that is assumed is that plausible interpretations of 'fundamental liberties' are far from entailing the adoption of an accommodating linguistic regime and leave plenty of room for legitimate coercive linguistic regimes.

5. The Grand Duchy of Luxemburg can be interpreted as illustrating the conjunctive variant (with Luxemburgish, German, and French), the Region of Brussels-Capital as illustrating the disjunctive variant.

6. What rules are effective is highly dependent on the context. Consider the following subtle example. Basque parents can freely choose to send their children to Spanish-medium, Basque-medium, or bilingual schools. Spanish-medium schools used to form the overwhelming majority in the Basque country, but they have been quickly losing ground. Why? The rule is that public administration at each level, municipal, provincial, and regional, must have a proportion of employees fluent in Basque equal to the (currently much higher) proportion of 'Bascophones' in the relevant administrative unit, where 'Bascophones' are defined as people who declare on census forms that they can speak or read at least some Basque. Bearing in mind that most Basques speak Spanish at home, it follows that the bulk of new public sector hirings in the foreseeable future will be of people who became fluent in Basque by attending a Basque or bilingual school. Even abstracting from the possibility that Basque schools were made more attractive to many

parents because of lower proportions of immigrant children, it is not surprising that the proportion of children attending Basque schools has kept growing, thereby increasing the recorded proportion of 'Basco-phones' in the population and hence further increasing the demand for proficient Basque speakers in the public sector. (This is a stylized account of an aspect of the Basque country's linguistic legislation, as described by Urko Aiartza at the workshop 'The public discourse of Law and Politics in Multilingual Societies', Oñati, June 2002. See Arzoz 2006 for a more comprehensive overview.)

7. Note that some countries that are on the surface perfectly accommo-dating—their legal system does not impose any overt restriction on language use or the medium of education—can be said to be coercive at a deeper level. This is the case for political systems that would swiftly bring in coercive rules if migration flows and the resulting pattern of linguistic preferences were such that convergence to a single language would no longer be spontaneous. In the case of some nation states, the probability of such a reaction may be (perceived as) so high that the demand for services in languages other than the dominant one never takes shape. Despite the absence of any formal restriction, we may want to characterize such states as possessing an implicit coercive regime.

8. Standard uses of the distinction frequently (though not always clearly) made between a 'linguistic territoriality principle' and a 'linguistic per-sonality principle' correspond closely to the distinction made here between a territorially differentiated coercive regime and an accommo-dating regime (*not* to the distinction between territorially and categori-cally or personally differentiated coercive regimes). See e.g. Réaume 2003; Patten 2003b; Francard and Hambye 2003; De Schutter 2008.

9. When a territorial regime is being put into place, it does not matter as such, therefore, for how long the linguistic community has been living on the territory concerned. It only matters indirectly as it is likely to be strongly correlated with the degree of geographical concentration of the population and may significantly affect the community's willing-ness to pay the cost of implementing the linguistic territoriality regime (see §5.9 below).

10. This important distinction was emphasized by Kymlicka (1995: ch. 2) and has played a major role in the debate on multiculturalism. The parity-of-esteem-based justification of territorial regimes constitutes one way of grounding its normative importance in language matters. Giving it any importance is obviously in tension with a principled presumption in favour of an accommodating regime.

11. The English-Only movement in the USA, for example, takes for granted that a tacit territorial linguistic regime was in place, and legitimately so, before Hispanics arrived *en masse*, yet that it was absent when the first Anglophones settled in Los Angeles or Nuevo Mexico. Needless to say, no 'right of the soil' could be appealed to in support of protecting either English or Spanish.

12. De Schutter's (2008) searching critique of the 'linguistic territoriality principle' takes the complex case of pre-existing linguistic diversity (to which I turn in §5.12) as the standard case, and explicitly abstracts from immigration (2008: 106). By doing so, he runs the risk of missing the central point of territorial regimes.

13. For forceful statements from Switzerland and Canada, see e.g. Papaux (1997: 133): 'it is absolutely necessary to determine the territorial domains of each language and to protect autochthonous linguistic communities, whether or not they are threatened, in their traditional spreading areas. For the persistence of national languages cannot conceivably be guaranteed without ascribing to each an exclusive territory'; and Laponce (2005: 2): 'The cardinal rule that should guide a minority language is the territorial imperative: territorialize and keep territorializing.'

14. See especially Ernest Gellner's (1983) and Rogers Brubaker's (1992) insightful analyses.

15. The phrasing is mine, but the process at work is perceptively described by the French political scientist and University of British Columbia professor Jean Laponce (1984, 1993a, 1996).

16. See, for example, the statistics on the language prevailing in mixed (French/English) couples in Canada (Laponce 1993b: 34–5).

17. Quite often, the top-down and bottom-up mechanisms operate side by side and reinforce each other. But sometimes the Laponce-type mechanism is observable in a fairly pure form, for example in Quebec until 1975, in Flanders between 1898 and 1932, or in Brussels up to the present day. In these areas and periods, officially affirmed bilingualism is supposed to have switched off the Gellner-type mechanism as regards the two recognized languages, while the dominant language (English in Canada, French in Belgium) keeps spreading at the expense of the weaker one through differential conversion rates of both native and immigrant families. It is the realization of the steady progress of English in Montreal (despite the inflow and higher birth rate of Catholic Francophones) and of the steady progress of French in Brussels and all major Flemish cities that gave the key impulse to the demands for a coercive territorial regime as a more serious way of implementing equal respect for the two languages than the sheer formal affirmation

of equality against the background of an accommodating regime. See Levine (1990) on Montreal and Robberechts and van der Straeten (1969: 194–5) or Nelde and Darquennes (2001: 94–6) on Belgium.

18. See Laitin (1993) for an insightful analysis of the collective action problem involved.

19. In a comment on a case relating to discrimination against French-language pupils living in the Flemish periphery of Brussels, the European Court of Human Rights (23 July 1968) stated that there was nothing arbitrary in the 'defence of the region's linguistic homogeneity', as it is inspired by 'the public interest of making sure that all state schools in a monolingual region should provide their teaching in the primary language of that region'. In connection with another case relating to the political representation in the Flemish Parliament of francophone citizens living in Flanders, the Court also condoned 'the necessity for linguistic minorities of voting for people able and prepared to use the language of their region', on the ground that an obligation of this kind 'is found in many other states' and 'as experience demonstrates, need not threaten the interests of the minorities' (Alen and Ergec 1998: 786–8). It is most unlikely that the Court would also have found a categorically differentiated coercive regime equally unobjectionable.

20. I am not sure anyone believes in such rights, although some formulations are ambiguous. For example, when Rubio-Marín (2003: 56) speaks of 'a linguistic group's fair chance of cultural reproduction', this may plausibly be interpreted along the lines of my parity-of-esteem-based argument. But what about Skutnabb-Kangas (2003: §1) wanting 'all the world's languages to have a fair chance of being maintained and developed'?

21. See Kymlicka (1989) for the initial formulation of this interesting argument, and Patten (2009) for a persuasive critique.

22. This third link between parity of esteem and linguistic territoriality runs parallel to the link that is sometimes established between demand for respect and nationalism, understood as the attempt to obtain statehood for a nation, often linguistically circumscribed. Thus, according to Isaiah Berlin (1979: 346), nationalism 'is in the first place a response to a patronising or disparaging attitude towards the traditional values of a society, the result of wounded pride and a sense of humiliation in its most socially conscious members, which in due course produce anger and self-assertion'.

23. As a social-democrat, Otto Bauer (1907: 363–6) was bothered by this objection, which his scheme quickly triggered from the left (see also Deutsch 1975: 14–15). Himself an assimilated Jew, Bauer devoted a

whole section (§23 *Nationale Autonomie der Juden?*, oddly in small print in the original edition) to explaining why the Empire's Jewish population, though significantly more numerous than some of the eight recognized 'nations', should not be made a ninth nation. A key argument was that segregated schools, by preventing integration into the locally dominant group, would impair the equalization of opportunities (Bauer 1907: 377–80)

24. The Austro-Hungarian Empire fell apart before Renner and Bauer came to power and could try to implement the personal federalism they advocated. Some form of non-territorial federalism was tried elsewhere, for example in Estonia in 1925, in Cyprus in 1960, and in South Africa in 1984, yet never with great success. The only—limited but still recognizable—example that subsists is Belgium's federalism of Communities. Next to its three territorially defined Regions (Flanders, Wallonia, and Brussels), Belgium has three linguistically defined Communities (Dutch-, French-, and German-speaking). Two of them overlap on 0.5% of the country's territory (the Region of Brussels-Capital), where they both exercise competences in matters of education, culture, and some aspects of social policy for Dutch speakers and French speakers, respectively: this is a genuine, though modest, version of Renner and Bauer's scheme, but arguably one whose demise is both probable and desirable (see Van Parijs 2011: chs 7–8).

25. If full independence is considered, it may be wise to impose as a condition that those thereby claiming full queen status for their language should not reduce the degree of solidarity (if any) with the populations of the territories from which they secede (see Drèze 1993). Separatism is justified when driven by a demand for parity of esteem, not by collective selfishness.

26. See Renner's (1902: §18) and Bauer's (1907: §21) arguments against territorial federalism in the Austrian Empire.

27. See, for example, the discussion of the relevance of frequent country-wide referendums (Stojanovic et al. 2009) and of a country-wide electoral district (Deschouwer and Van Parijs 2009) for the healthy operation of the Swiss and Belgian plurilingual federal *demoi*. Obviously, the challenge of multilingualism comes on top of the standard challenge of reconciling trans-regional solidarity and regional responsibility when policy competences are largely decentralized. See Roland et al. (1999), Decoster (2009), Decoster and Van Parijs (2010).

28. How can respect then be expressed to a language with a population too small to have a protected territory? The limit, however, may be very low. Thus Romansch, with about 35,000 speakers, obtained in 2006 the protection of a territorial regime that should help halt its decline

(Stojanovic 2010). So did Belgium's German-language Community with about 70,000 speakers, with a separate government gradually gaining more power. But what about traditionally nomadic peoples like the Roma? Even for them, a territorial solution is no longer sheer utopia. The municipality of Shutka (or Šuto Orizari), a suburb of Skopje (Macedonia), has a population of over 20,000 inhabitants, most of them Roma, and has Romani as its co-official language. With a surface area of 7.5 km^2, this is no doubt significantly less comfortable than the other two cases mentioned (with a chunk of about 1,500 km^2 of the canton of Graubünden or of 850 km^2 of the Walloon Region), but is it fundamentally different?

29. Analogous incentives to linguistic subdivision are intrinsic to the equal-net-community-benefit criterion of cooperative justice briefly discussed and dismissed in note 17 of chapter 2.

30. When discussing the possibility of addressing distributive injustice by tinkering with the language regime (in §3.4), we saw that the introduction of a territorial linguistic regime improved the economic prospects of Francophones in Québec, but worsened those of people with neither English nor French as their native language.

31. This is not incompatible with valuing immigrant languages and encouraging their preservation, even though some trade-off is unavoidable: the more effectively the coercive rules work to spread the local language in the whole population, the less secure, *ceteris paribus*, the local persistence of the immigrant languages (see §6.7 below).

32. Aside from accelerating linguistic integration, a territorial regime presumably also depresses the total volume of immigration (relative to an accommodating regime) and induces a linguistic self-selection of immigrants, which further contributes to reducing the negative externality under discussion.

33. This pacification-based argument for a territorial regime takes for granted that cheap and efficient access to the local language is available to all newcomers. Unavoidably, however, the universalization of proficiency takes time, especially if the flow of immigrants is rapid, concentrated, and linguistically homogenous. Even in the transitional period, it might be argued (somewhat perversely) that a territorial coercive regime has a pacifying effect, relative to an accommodating one. For during this possibly long period, it gives vulnerable insiders an edge over outsiders in access to at least some jobs, housing possibilities and social services made less accessible to newcomers by the regime's linguistic rigidity. It thereby reduces the insider's hostility—as expressed, at the limit, in anti-immigrant riots—against a population

with which contact is poor and difficult and which is perceived as a threat on the labour and housing markets even more than in the streets. This putative mechanism is more likely to concern the case of immigrants with weaker languages. Needless to say, it is also unconnected to the parity-of-esteem-based argument.

34. Moreover, Laitin's own 'sons of the soil' hypothesis mentioned above makes it necessary to distinguish, when linguistic concessions are made, between territorial and other regimes, as only the former can be expected to contribute to pacification in the light of that hypothesis, whereas accommodation should rather be expected to have the opposite effect.

35. True, as long as this language does not cover the whole world, the regime would still be 'territorially differentiated' when looked at on some higher scale (see §5.1). Still, territorial differentiation would not be the strategy adopted for dealing with the linguistic heterogeneity concerned.

36. From Karl Renner (1902: §18) and Otto Bauer (1907: §21) to Francard and Hambye (2003) or De Schutter (2007, 2008), the lack of realism of this 'Westphalian' assumption of homogeneity (*cuius regio, eius lingua*) is often invoked as the main reason for rejecting the territorial approach. As documented by Rustow (1975: 48–50) with some instructive statistics, the fairly neat correspondence between linguistic and political borders is largely a European phenomenon. But even in Europe, linguistic heterogeneity is now more and more the rule rather than the exception.

37. I am leaving for the next chapter a detailed discussion of alternative concepts of linguistic diversity, heterogeneity, fragmentation, etc. (§§ 6.1–6.2). An intuitive understanding will suffice for present purposes.

38. One may wish to add, as a separate category, the cost of functioning as a separate political entity. Though not a defining feature, this is a natural corollary of a territorial regime if part of its point is to make the local language a 'queen' or at least a 'princess' (§5.5). However, how much this represents will greatly depend on the extensiveness of the powers devolved to the relevant political entity that would not have been devolved otherwise. This will not amount to much for the Romansch municipalities of Graubünden, for example. Even for the EU's 'sovereign' member states, the related linguistic cost will be shrinking fast if EU-level proceedings and legislation are increasingly in English (§4.3). In any case, this queen-status-related cost of a territorial regime is bound to be small, compared to the other two potential dimensions of cost discussed here.

39. On the linguistic situation in the Democratic Republic of the Congo, see the (very fragmentary) findings of the *Observatoire des langues nationales* summarized by Mukash Kalel (2003). On the power structure that preserves the primacy of the colonial language, see de Swaan (2001: ch. 6). Shifting to the national languages in education may make it possible for provincial administration and politics to shift in the same way. The accountability of politicians and public officials to the population they govern can reasonably be expected to be enhanced if they have to operate in a language understood by the majority of the citizens instead of just a small elite that has every interest in preserving the economic and political privileges its knowledge confers. If significant, this effect would further contribute to making the cost of introducing a national-language-based territorial regime negative (abstracting from the argument of the next section).

40. The cost increase may not only take the form of greater teaching resources, but also of policies aimed at mixing immigrants and locals, or immigrants from different origins, in school, work, recreational, and residential contexts.

41. In Western Europe and in other countries in which a significant part of the immigrant population and their offspring can live on welfare benefits, the weaker grip of language learning through work contact amplifies the challenge created by linguistic heterogeneity (I return to this factor in §6.7 in connection with the tension between local linguistic diversity and sustainable solidarity).

42. See especially Docquier and Marfouk (2005). It is only recently that it has become possible to document with some statistical accuracy the existence of such an asymmetric flow. In its 1998 Migration Report, the OECD focused on this phenomenon for the first time, by devoting an entire chapter to the migration of high-skilled workers (SOPEMI 1998). Subsequent reports for the OECD and the World Bank confirmed, expanded, and refined these observations.

43. See e.g. Stevens et al. (2006: 175): 'Korean adults, particularly those in the prime child-raising years, are much more likely to take their children along with them when visiting English-dominated countries than when visiting countries dominated by other languages.'

44. Truc (2006: 6) notes that only 3,500 Poles and Balts moved to Sweden as a result of prospective and actual EU enlargement, whereas 360,000 moved to the UK and 120,000 to Ireland. Why such a huge difference? 'Above all because they massively took to learning English since independence', according to Latvia's Institute for Social and Political Research.

45. Docquier and Marfouk (2005: 23) observe that 'immigrants are particularly educated in Canada, Australia, New Zealand, the United States and the United Kingdom', i.e. in the world's five main Anglophone countries. And Beine et al (2009: §5.1) show that linguistic proximity is a more powerful predictor of the destination of migration for the highly skilled than for other workers. According to the OECD (SOPEMI 2004: 121), the percentage of foreign-born Ph.D. holders who work in the USA is 25%. It is 45% in Australia and 54% in Canada.

46. Indeed, asymmetry in the net flow of students is at least as pronounced as in the net flow of graduates. In 2008–09, more than 670,000 foreign students studied in the USA, 70% among them with funding from their home country (opendoors.iienetwork.org). Even more spectacularly, as first documented by Eurostat (1998–99), the flow of students from the continental part of the EU to the UK exceeds the flow in the other direction by a ratio of about ten to one, despite higher fee levels.

47. In a way, this is simply a global blow-up of a familiar phenomenon on a national scale. See Calmfors et al. (2003: 128–9): 'In a global world, most intellectual talent may end up being located in the United States, just as [within national economies] it deserted rural and provincial areas to go to political centres and big cities one hundred years ago. This situation may be a self-sustaining equilibrium.'

48. Arthur Schlesinger (1998: 127) neatly sums it up in the case of the USA: 'We have shifted the basis of admission three times this century—from national origins in 1924 to family reunification in 1965 to needed skills in 1990.'

49. In addition to the creaming-off effect on economic dynamism, there is some evidence—admittedly inconclusive as regards the direction of causation—in support of the view that the cultural diversity generated by the immigration of skilled workers is strongly correlated with innovation (Ottaviano and Peri 2003). On the other hand, the constant replenishment of local heterogeneity may make trust and collaboration more problematic and thereby impair the efficient production of public goods (see Alesina and La Ferrara 2000).

50. See e.g. Kapur and McHale (2003). To remittances *stricto sensu* one should add the accumulated assets repatriated by temporary migrant workers and long-term migrants who decide to retire in their home country.

51. See OECD (2002) and Docquier and Rapoport (2010) for various instructive country case studies.

52. This further accentuates the asymmetric free riding on Anglophone intellectual production that stems from the spreading of the lingua franca and can be interpreted as partial compensation for the free

riding of native speakers of the lingua franca on the learning of their language by others (see §2.12).

53. This may sound far-fetched but may go some way towards explaining the fact, noted and deplored by Samuel Huntington (2004: 325), that America's leaders increasingly 'pass laws and implement policies contrary to the views of the American people'. For example, 'in seven polls from 1974 to 1998, no more than 53 percent of the public and no less than 86 percent of the leaders supported giving economic aid to other nations' (ibid.: 328). Along with 'seizing the megaphone' (§1.11), influential infiltration of this sort may be part of what is needed in order to neutralize the negative effect on the prospects for global justice of Anglophone ideological domination.

54. On the gradual and very unequal spreading of English as the medium of higher education beyond the ground floor, see Ammon (2001a), Maiworm and Wächter (2002), Wächter and Maiworm (2008).

55. In the case of the gradual expansion of the place of English in Flanders' higher education, see e.g. the reactions by Salverda (2001) and Willems (2002) and, after a further step, by Sanders and Van Dijck (2010) and De Vreese (2010).

56. If, as one might expect, the areas picked as linguistically free zones are small urban areas, one can anticipate spill over pressures of the 'American in Waterloo' type (§5.3) in their suburban hinterland. Containment of such 'colonial' outgrowth is inherent in the strategy.

57. One might be tempted to argue that the net cost (if any) is much lower because of the pacification effect that can be expected from the coercive protection of weaker languages (§5.7). One must beware, however, of making the argument viciously circular. If the pacification effect ascribed to a territorial regime derives from the local population feeling respected, then there is no pacification gain forgone if it is the population itself which decides, in the light of expected costs of a different nature, to waive its right to protect its language on a particular territory. It would therefore be wrong to deduct from these expected costs of protection the likely cost of the conflict that would arise in the absence of protection.

58. Here is some evidence that can be interpreted as supporting this paradoxical claim. The inflow of both capital and human capital into the USA, while boosting its GDP and lowering that of the rest of the world (relative to what it would otherwise have been), has been going hand in hand with a fall in the average real income of the pre-existing population of the USA that can be attributed, at least in part, to competition with newcomers. See Davis and Weinstein (2002, 2005).

59. In addition, being a speaker of a less widespread language and having to learn at least one other language as a result may systematically enable those who have to make that effort to escape the insensitivity to cultural differences that comes too easily to those who have never had to undergo that humbling process and are invariably in the comfortable position of being able to use their mother tongue. Without noticing, such insensitivity can trigger rancour, resentment, even hatred. Besides their greater aptitude to bilingualism, this greater cultural sensitivity may contribute to giving a long-term advantage to non-Anglophones in the sort of world we now live in.

60. The Basque regime is at first sight a disjunctive regime since parents have the choice to send their children to Spanish-only, Basque-only, and bilingual schools. But if the indirect pressure to opt for a Basque school is effective (see the stylized description in note 6 above), it will end up being as much of a conjunctive regime as the Catalan one.

61. Predictably, the native speakers of the stronger language will be those most opposed to this conjunctive regime, as the maxi-min dynamics made them and will keep them less bilingual. Even when they form a minority of the territory's population, their opposition is likely to be decisive. 'Cette théorie est imbécile', was how Belgium's Francophone leader Jules Destrée (1923: 127) summarized his assessment of the plea for such a regime when it was contemplated in the 1920s. This harsh judgement was no doubt in part motivated by the expectation that the enforcement of symmetric bilingualism (e.g. by requiring it in the civil service throughout the country) would give a systematic advantage to Flemings over Francophones, given the massive pre-existing asymmetric bilingualism (far more Flemings knew French than Walloons knew Dutch). But it can also be justified by the prohibitive cost of motivating and teaching pupils (and teachers) for the learning of a language which pupils feel little point in learning since the other linguistic group is anyway learning theirs.

62. In his 'non-Westphalian' critique of the linguistic territoriality principle, De Schutter (2008: 111–12) assumes that the territoriality principle and the coercive protection of a single language are coextensive. Once the contrast is clearly made between a territorial regime (as a territorially differentiated coercive linguistic regime) and an accommodating regime, this is not so by definition (§5.1). But for the reasons just mentioned, this may well be close to being so for all practical purposes.

63. In the Grand Duchy of Luxemburg, French functioned since independence (1839) as the official language, with German as a second compulsory medium of education, but in 1984 Luxemburgish was promoted to the status of official language and made an additional compulsory

medium at the initial stage in all schools (see Pou 1993, Ziegler 2010). That this demanding conjunctive regime is very costly is strongly suggested, though hardly established, by the following fact: with one of the very highest GDPs per capita in the world, Luxemburg is near the bottom of the OECD league and well below the average in the PISA assessment of pupils' educational achievement (in the language of their choice) at age 15 (see http://pisacountry.acer.edu.au).

64. In the officially bilingual Region of Brussels-Capital, over 95% of adult residents say they speak French well or very well, compared to 29% for Dutch (Janssens 2007: ch. 3). While the proportion of Dutch native speakers keeps falling, the percentage of Brussels residents who know Dutch well or very well because they learned it as a second or third language keeps growing. The reason for this is less the linguistic regime in Brussels itself than the fact that it is completely surrounded by a now prosperous Region—Flanders—in which Dutch enjoys the protection of a coercive territorial regime. But we are obviously very far from a conjunctive regime. The latter would arguably require, analogously to Catalonia and Luxemburg, that Dutch should be used as the medium of teaching at the first stage in all Brussels schools.

65. Just as a coercive linguistic regime can have a powerful impact on the language people speak in private conversations without transgressing the fundamental freedom of language choice in private contexts, similarly it can have a powerful impact on the place where people choose to live without transgressing the (plausibly) fundamental freedom to stay living in the area where one was born.

66. Consider the forced transfer of my home institution (the Université catholique de Louvain) to the other side of Belgium's language border, as decided by Belgium's government under strong Flemish pressure in 1968. This decision certainly led to making Flanders linguistically more homogeneous than it would otherwise have been. It can therefore be regarded as a form of linguistic cleansing, though a mild one fully consistent with fundamental liberties. Forcing a large organization to move is different from forcing individual native speakers of a particular language to move, even if the only reason for forcing the organization to move is that it will induce some people to move.

67. The 'linguistic facilities' introduced in Belgium in 1962–63 for residents caught on the wrong side of the linguistic border that was then fixed were not phrased in this way: any newcomer or newborn was entitled to claim the same linguistic rights. Those who understood these facilities as 'temporary' expected that newcomers would no longer need to claim them after some time. Insight into the maxi-min dynamics should have made them realize how unrealistic this expectation was, and hence why

'temporary' facilities understood in this way were a recipe for never-ending disputes.

68. As emphasized, for example by Laitin and Reich (2003) or Francard and Hambye (2003: 53–4).

69. By way of food for thought on this issue, see the interesting 'dynamic territoriality principle' applied in the Romansch-language area of Switzerland (Stojanovic 2010).

70. In Belgium, the peak of the linguistic tension was reached in the early 1960s. A large number of Flemish mayors then decided to boycott the linguistic part of the decennial census and two massive Flemish marches on Brussels called for the end of the 'oil stain' around the bilingual capital (see e.g. Witte and Van Velthoven 1999: 177–85). Up until then (and since the introduction of a territorial regime in 1932), an officially monolingual municipality was automatically converted into a bilingual one when the census showed that a threshold of presence of self-declared speakers of the other language was reached. This was perceived as condoning a steady expansion, all around Brussels, of the area in which a disjunctively bilingual (and hence de facto accommodating) regime allowed French to drive out Dutch, whether through 'colonial' settlement or through 'conversion'.

71. See Kymlicka (1989), as briefly discussed above (§5.4)

72. A higher cost to be borne by virtue of a feature one possesses might be regarded as unfit for compensation because one chose to possess it; or because, even though one did not choose to possess it, one could choose to give it up; or because one would not choose to give it up even if one could. Arguably, only the third ground for non-compensation applies to a religion into which one is born, whereas the second ground too is available in our linguistic case. Consequently, for the sake of the present argument, there is no need to choose between something like choice and something like identification to define the demarcation line between personal responsibility and fair compensation, as discussed, for example, by Dworkin (2000, 2004) and Cohen (2010: chs I–V).

73. Consequently, one dimension of this expense for which each linguistic community can be held responsible is the need to learn the lingua franca as a second language. This has crucial implications for the proper way of framing the question of cooperative justice (§2.2). The 'commuting cost' (i.e. the cost of learning the lingua franca generation after generation) is higher than the 'one-off conversion cost' of switching to the lingua franca as the native language of later generations. If the cost of the territorial protection of each language could legitimately be imputed to all, we would have a straightforward argument for

requiring the whole of the recurrent commuting cost (rather than just the one-off conversion cost) to be shared by all cooperating communities. If instead, as argued here, this cost needs to be borne by the community that requests territorial protection, only the conversion cost should be shared on grounds of cooperative justice, and the rest of the commuting cost is part of the cost to be borne by those 'peripheral' communities that choose not to 'convert'. For the whole of the commuting cost to be cooperatively shared by the beneficiaries of the lingua franca, a different argument is needed. It was offered in §2.2.

74. Only if this is the way the communities decide (through processes of the sort explored in §5.13) to use the real freedom gained as a result of greater distributive justice. Just as in the case of the symbolic assertion of equality among languages (§4.4), it would be inappropriate to allocate *a priori* to this specific purpose any leeway there may be for redistribution to the less wealthy communities, rather than let them define their own priorities. Nothing compels them to sacrifice other things they care about, such as the average income of their members or the quality of the environment in which they live, to the protection of their language.

Chapter 6

1. 'Diversity' is sometimes distinguished from sheer 'variety' precisely on the ground that the former, unlike the latter, is regarded as intrinsically valuable (see e.g. Heyd 2005). In the sequel, however, I shall adopt a normatively neutral definition of diversity: diversity may be good, but not by definition.

2. This index, first proposed by Simpson (1949), is equivalent to the simplest (A) among the indices of linguistic diversity independently proposed by Greenberg (1956). Its negative term (the sum of the squares of the shares) is also known in the industrial organization literature, as the Herfindahl–Hirschman index of industrial concentration (first proposed in Hirschman 1945, ch. 7), with s_i now interpreted as a firm's share in the total sales on a specific market. The Simpson index can be shown to correspond to a particular value (1) of a parameter in a more general index of diversity combining richness and evenness, with richness corresponding to the other extreme value of that parameter (–1) and the Shannon–Weaver index of entropy corresponding to an intermediate value. For discussions of the formal relationships between diversity

indices and their respective advantages, see Harmon and Loh (2004: Appendix), Ottaviano and Pinelli (2005) and Bossert et al. (2008).

3. The probability for some member of type i to meet a non-member of i, assuming an equal probability of meeting any particular member of the population (including herself), is given by $(N - n_i)/N = 1 - s_i$. The weighted average of this probability over all types i is given by Σs_i. $(1 - s_i) = 1 - \Sigma s_i^2$, which is precisely the Simpson index.

4. See, for example, Weitzman (1992).

5. This is exactly what is proposed by Bossert et al. (2008) with their illuminating axiomatic derivation of a generalized index of dissimilarity. The Simpson index of fractionalization corresponds to the special case in which distance is posited to be 1 for two individuals belonging to different types, and 0 for two individuals belonging to the same type.

6. See Lee and Bean (2004) and Hochschild et al. (2005) for insightful empirical studies of the distinct effects of (continuous) colour and (discrete) race.

7. One odd consequence is that the Dyen index makes French lexically closer to German than to English, despite the massive import of French words into English. This index is used, among others, by Desmet et al. (2005) and by Fidrmuc and Ginsburgh (2007).

8. The US Department of State organizes intensive language courses for its diplomats sent to countries whose languages they know hardly or not at all beforehand. It has records of the standards of competence measured at different intervals. For the small number of language combinations involved, some assessment of distance can be extracted from these records and has been used to design an index of linguistic distance by Chiswick and Miller (2007: ch. 20).

9. Desmet et al. (2005) show that the degree of redistribution, interpreted as the share of social spending in GDP is more strongly correlated with linguistic diversity when linguistic distance is taken into account (a correlation to which I shall return in §6.6). The underlying mechanism that is being suggested does not involve a causal impact of linguistic distance as such. But an index of linguistic proximity is nonetheless useful as a proxy for how close and recent contact has been between the populations concerned.

10. Inspired by the same intuition, Greenberg (1956: 111–12) suggests indices (his variants C to H) that look at repertoires rather than languages. He notes, however, that what he ends up with (his variant H, the probability of two members of a population taken at random lacking a common language) makes more sense as an index of non-communication than as an index of diversity. Unlike this variant of

Greenberg's index, the more general notion of (degree of) lack of overlap between repertoires presented here can make a claim to capturing linguistic diversity. To see this, imagine a situation in which the members of a population with a number of distinct native languages all speak perfectly some common lingua franca. In this situation, Greenberg's index H is zero, but there is still a significant lack of overlap between repertoires and hence a degree of diversity (in the definition I propose here) far higher than if all had the lingua franca as their native tongue and spoke nothing else.

11. See Strubell (2007) for a comprehensive overview of the declarations by the Commission, the Council and the Parliament.

12. As described in §§1.3–1.5 and discussed as a serious obstacle to the European Commission's 'Mother tongue plus two' objective in §4.6.

13. The existence of some tension between the EU's ritual encouragement of trans-national contact and mobility and hence multilingualism on the one hand, and, on the other hand, the EU's emphasis on the preservation (if not the promotion) of linguistic diversity has been noted by several commentators (e.g. Phillipson 2003: 193–8) and indeed by the European Commission itself: 'While recognising the emergence of English as the most widely-spoken language in Europe, the Union also wants to make sure that this does not become, over time, a factor limiting linguistic diversity within its frontiers' (European Commission 2004: 22).

14. See McWhorter (2001: ch. 3) for many illustrations.

15. At the limit (with universal asymmetric bilingualism and random pairing of speech partners), the proportion of conversations held in any language i other than the lingua franca f shrinks from n_i/N to $(n_i/N)^2$ (with n_i the number of natives of language i and N the total population), while the proportion of conversations held in the lingua franca rises from n_f/N to $1 - \Sigma(n_i/N)^2$. Take, for example, the case of five languages, each with 20% of the native speakers. If the members of each linguistic community speak only among themselves, 20% of the conversations are conducted in each of the five languages. If one of the languages becomes a lingua franca and conversation partners are picked randomly, 84% of all two-by-two conversations happen in the lingua franca and 4% in each of the other four languages.

16. When the European Commission settled in the brand new Berlaymont building in the late 1960s, there were only four official native languages among its personnel. French was the language most used in conversations between people not sharing the same mother tongue, but the distribution of language use in office meetings and coffee breaks was fairly even, as the probability of a German addressing an audience

consisting only of Germans (or of Luxemburgers and Dutch people with a good command of German), or of an Italian addressing an audience consisting only of Italians was still large. Forty years later, when the twenty-seven Commissioners from the twenty-seven member states took possession of the same building after its ten-year-long renovation, the number of official languages had jumped from four to twenty-two, and the number of native languages even more markedly. Yet, precisely because the probability of audiences being linguistically mixed rose sharply as a result, the distribution of the languages adopted in casual conversations involving more than a couple of people has become, I am told, incomparably more concentrated. Diversity fell as regards performances precisely because it rose as regards competences.

17. As Antoine Meillet (1918: 117), among many others, puts it: 'The local idiom is useless the day the whole population, knowing the common language, is bilingual. The young then no longer feel the need to know the local idiom: even if they practiced it in their childhood, they forget it as they grow older.' See also Crystal (2000: ch. 3) on this unstable 'stage 2' of language shift, and the various formal models that show bilingualism to be a transient unstable state on the way to extinction (e.g. Choi 2002, Castello et al. 2006).

18. The former definition ($\beta = \gamma/(\Sigma_i/K)$) was proposed by Whittaker (1972) and the latter ($\beta = \gamma - \Sigma_i/K$) by Lande (1996), with $_i$ the number of species in habitat i, γ the number of species in the landscape as a whole, and K the number of habitats in the landscape. When the habitats are undifferentiated, i.e. when all species are present in each habitat, Whittaker's index is equal to 1 and Lande's to 0. When the habitats are as specialized as the sizes of the species allow, Whittaker's index is equal to the number K of habitats or the number γ of species in the landscape, whichever is smaller, while Lande's is then given by $\gamma - \gamma/K$. Lande's measure has the advantage of enabling the richness of the landscape (γ) to be intuitively formulated as the sum of how rich the habitats are on average (Σ_i/K) and how much they differ from each other (β).

19. In addition to the index of segregation mentioned below, the so-called dissimilarity index can also be used to operationalize this notion of inter-local diversity (see Massey and Denton 1988), and so can the 'country Gini coefficient' developed by economists to express how specialized a country is, i.e. to what extent the distribution of its output between industrial sectors diverges from the distribution of the output of a larger entity (say, the European Union or the world) of which it is a part. When averaged over all local units (here, countries), this index can be used to measure the degree of inter-local diversity, i.e. in this

case the degree of sectoral differentiation of countries (see Maignan et al. 2003).

20. Lieberson's (1964) generalization of variant A of Greenberg's (1956) index of linguistic diversity may look like a simpler alternative way of measuring inter-local diversity: the probability of meeting someone belonging to a different type from oneself (i.e. speaking a different language) in random encounters with someone from a different local unit. However, a high score on this index is consistent with the lack of any differentiation between local units: all may be characterized by the same high level of heterogeneneity.

21. The probability of meeting at random someone from the other group in one's own region is $(1/10) \times (9/10) + (9/10) \times (1/10) = 18/100$ under the uneven 90/10 distribution, whereas it is $(1/2)^2 + (1/2)^2 = 50/100$ under the uniform distribution.

22. Just as the richness of a population can be made equal to the sum of average richness of its local units and of the β-diversity of its population (using Lande's index of biodiversity: see note 18 above), the Simpson index of a population is equal to the sum of the average Simpson index of its local units and the index of inter-local differentiation as defined here.

23. This trade-off is self-evident under the simple interpretation of inter-local diversity that only takes richness (the number of languages) into account. But it also holds under interpretations that incorporate evenness (the relative spread of languages), such as the one inspired by the segregation literature used above by way of illustration. To see why this is the case, let us start from a situation of zero inter-local diversity (same distribution of languages in all local units). It is then possible to increase inter-local diversity while also increasing local diversity in some of the local units (through swaps that make the distributions more even in each of these units than in the whole entity), but this can only be done at the cost of sharpening concentration (and hence reducing local diversity) in other local units.

24. For an extreme example, see Feld (1998).

25. See Gellner (1983) for the classic formulation, and Pagano (2004) for a subtle variant of this argument to be discussed below (§6.8).

26. Not quite as explicit on the linguistic dimension but very much on the same line is Mill's (1861: 294–5) famous sentence: 'Nobody can suppose that it is not more beneficial to a Breton, or a Basque of French Navarre, to be brought into the current of the ideas and feelings of a highly civilised and cultivated people ... than to sulk on his own rocks, the half-savage relic of past times, revolving in his own little mental

orbit, without participation or interest in the general movement of the world.'

27. What is so great, for example, about endeavouring to accentuate the divergences between variants of the same language (Serb and Croat, for example, or Macedonian and Bulgarian, or Hindi and Urdu) up to the point where they would not just be called by different names, but would have become mutually unintelligible?

28. For an interesting yet unpersuasive unconventional interpretation of the Babel failure as a blessing that saved mankind from uniformity and totalitarianism, see Wenin (2003) and Ost (2009: ch. 1). Troy provides a somewhat less mythical parable for the curse of linguistic diversity. Why did the Acheans win the war? Not because of the cunning of the wooden horse but because their *koine*, their shared language, enabled them to coordinate effectively, whereas the cacophony that prevailed between Trojans and their allies turned out to be a decisive handicap (see Ross 2005). Both Trojans and Babelians (after Yahweh's intervention) can be regarded as the neatly paradigmatic victims of a very general tension between ethno-linguistic diversity and the efficient production of public goods (see Alesina and La Ferrara 2000).

29. For a comprehensive and lucid survey of the most common arguments, see Crystal (2000: ch. 2).

30. See, for example, Skutnabb-Kangas (2003: §3) and the website www. terralingua.org.

31. One version of this claim was discussed and rejected above in connection with the 'ideological hegemony' objection to the adoption of English as a global lingua franca (§1.11).

32. Suppose the citizens of today's France were speaking a dozen quite diverse Gaelic and Germanic languages rather than the variety of vulgar Latin to which their predecessors gradually converged or converted. Assuming linguistic differences impact the 'world views' of native speakers, what reason is there to believe that we would have gained knowledge in this scenario, relative to what has been made possible by the sharing of the French language by a large population? The (putatively single) 'world view' associated with the latter is no doubt different from what the 'world views' of the dozen or so separate linguistic communities would have been, had they been allowed to develop. But could one not presume this single 'world view' to be better or richer, by virtue of more people having been given the chance to contribute to it?

33. See UNDP (2004) for a forceful plea for cultural diversity largely along these lines. Note that, if the point of cultural diversity is 'cultural freedom', i.e. the possibility to choose between quite different cultures

besides one's own, there is a paradox involved. A culture is not just any set of thoughts and practices, but one that is linked to distinctive multi-generational communities. Hence, the more people make use of their cultural freedom and opt for a culture different from the one they inherited from their parents, the weaker the trans-generational continuity, and therefore the less *cultural* diversity (as distinct from diversity *tout court*, which may be increasing). Cultural diversity makes cultural freedom possible, but the exercise of cultural freedom erodes cultural diversity. This paradox is related to, but distinct from, the one pointed out in §6.3: linguistic diversity makes multilingualism possible, but multilingualism erodes linguistic diversity.

34. The measurement of economic solidarity so defined is quite tricky. Simple indicators like the average rate of income tax or the share of social transfers in GDP are only very imperfect proxies. For example, a reform that increases the tax burden on the poor and boosts pensions for the rich would increase economic solidarity if it were so measured. A more appealing measure is the difference between the Gini indices of inequality before and after taxes and transfers, but it needs to be handled with care. One reason is that much of the measured difference simply reflects income shifts along the life cycles of the same people, most massively in the form of earnings-related old age pensions. Another reason is that opting for this difference as an appropriate index can make solidarity look comparatively generous in a country not because it possesses a strongly redistributive tax and transfer system but because the primary income distribution on which the latter operates is particularly unequal as a result, for example, of a very inegalitarian education system. Hence, an increase in the level of 'solidarity' so measured may simply be the mechanical reflection of greater inequality in primary incomes. For all these reasons, the statistical findings referred to in this section, however robust, need to be interpreted with great caution.

35. See Alesina et al. (2003), especially Table 13e. This result is even strengthened when the linguistic diversity index is refined to incorporate linguistic distance (Desmet et al. 2005: §5.2).

36. One striking counter-example is offered by the comparison of South Africa and Brazil, up to the late 1990s, two recent federal democracies with a comparable level of development and a similarly high level of gross income inequality. Given the massive prevalence of Portuguese in Brazil, any reasonable measure of (evenness-sensitive) linguistic diversity should uncontroversially rank South Africa above Brazil. Yet South Africa displayed a far higher level of redistribution than Brazil, mainly because of the expansion of a non-contributory pension

scheme at the end of the apartheid regime (Seekings 2004). However, the dramatic development of cash transfers under the Cardoso and Lula governments got rid of what, in the light of the econometric findings, was a spectacular anomaly.

37. Generous solidarity is arguably more a matter of conquest than of generous sentiments. See, for example, Stephens (1979) on the negative correlation between ethnic diversity and the strength of the labour movement. La Ferrara's (2004) findings about the negative impact of ethnic heterogeneity on participation in the production of a public good are also relevant.

38. On the basis of a large US survey, Putnam (2007) shows that there is a robust negative correlation between the degree of ethnic diversity (using a Simpson index and the five US Census categories: White/ Black/Asian/Hispanic/Native American) and the level of trust (in members of one's own category as well as of the other categories). This global correlation may hide a more subtle and differentiated dynamics, but it may suffice here, combined with more anecdotal evidence, to make the existence of such an identification mechanism empirically plausible.

39. Miller (2004) argues, on the basis of international comparisons of people's revealed sense of justice, that there is little inter-ethnic variation as regards conceptions of distributive justice. However, the finer structure of legitimate solidarity ('What counts as an illness?', 'To what extent and how should it be cared for collectively?' etc.) may vary significantly in culturally diverse communities, possibly also, as suggested by Anne Phillips (2004), for reasons that owe more to differences in their recent histories and present conditions than to differences in their remote cultural roots.

40. See, along these lines, Soroka et al.'s (2004) emphasis on the importance of an inclusive, non-ethnic identity in the Canadian context.

41. Against the claim, made by Brian Barry (2001) and others, that multiculturalism policies undermine economic solidarity, Banting and Kymlicka (2004) documented empirically that this cannot be said to have been the case so far, as there appears to be a positive correlation between levels (or rates of increase) of economic solidarity and multiculturalism policies. Critics of the latter, such as Dominique Schnapper (2002, 2004), need not be unsettled by such findings. For both multiculturalism policies and welfare policies stem, they argue, from the same 'providential' dynamics of the contemporary democratic state, which drives the latter to accommodate an ever expanding set of factional demands. This is consistent with multiculturalism policies slowly undermining the welfare state, if only by hindering a rapid

reduction of the linguistic and cultural diversity that keeps being amplified by immigration. Because of the time required for these sociological processes to work themselves out and the randomness involved in their being politically exploited, this effect is most unlikely to show up immediately, even though the weakening of the fellow-feeling between all citizens and the decreasing ability of the worse-off to join forces in a common struggle make the 'providential' set-up increasingly vulnerable. The point I want to make here is that the impact of multiculturalism policies cannot be assessed by treating them as a homogeneous lump. The fine grain is crucial.

42. Forcing the autochthonous pupils of a school to attend immigrant language classes when offered would no doubt be even more counter-productive than introducing it as an optional subject. On the contrary, managing to convince some of them (and their parents) of the interest they may have in learning languages such as Arabic, Turkish, Hindi, or Spanish would be a welcome achievement, providing it is not so successful that it reduces significantly the opportunity and incentive for immigrant children to learn the local language.

43. This presumption may need to be qualified in various ways. For example, Soroka et al. (2004) note, in the light of some Canadian data, that 'the high level of geographic concentration of immigrant minorities in certain regions and especially certain urban areas' may be better for interpersonal trust, which itself clearly has a positive effect on support for the welfare state.

44. Fostering economic participation through employment is not equiva-lent to implementing a repressive workfare state. Distributive justice, as interpreted above (§3.1) is a matter of possibilities, of real freedom, not only of income levels, and workfare is, fortunately, not the only version of an 'active social state', i.e. one that boosts the prospects of low-income households without trapping them in unemployment. Alternatives include wage subsidies, earned income tax credit schemes and (my preferred variant) the provision of a non-means-tested income floor, conceivably coupled with language courses, compulsory or not, for those who do not master the local official language. See Van Parijs et al. (2000) and Vanderborght and Van Parijs (2005: ch. 2) for pre-sentations of the various versions of this non-repressive 'active welfare state' and discussions of their respective advantages.

45. Economic participation is particularly significant in this positive feed-back mechanism. Whether or not tacit discrimination plays a role in addition to poor language skills, the exclusion from employment of non-native speakers of the official language tends to be self-perpetuating, as the scarcity of work contacts, joined with the typically intra-community

nature of family, neighbourhood, and religious ties, prevents them from acquiring the language skills which would enable them to get into the mainstream. This in turn prevents geographical de-segregation through social mobility, and hence fosters a growing homogeneity of neighbourhoods and schools (constantly reinforced by the selective flows of information, structured by language borders, about housing and/or schooling options), which carries over the poverty of local language skills into the next generation.

46. As the point is sometimes put (e.g. Salas 2003: ch. 1), the more intercultural interaction there is, the less multicultural society becomes.

47. See D'Antoni and Pagano (2002) and Pagano (2004) on the welfare state aspect.

48. See Baldwin (1990).

49. Instead of lamenting all this (as the tone adopted rightly suggests I do), should one not rejoice at the constraints to which the national Leviathans are thereby subjected? The disciplining of rulers by a mobile tax base may sometimes provide a powerful and salutary lever for instilling respect for the rule of law, or for fostering the efficiency of the public sector, or for promoting a better match between the public goods supplied by a government and those the populations really want. But we live in a world in which globalization, privatization, and trade union decline make incomes ever more unequal. We also live in a world in which secularization, marital instability, and geographical mobility keep eroding the once powerful income-sharing function of the family. For these two sets of reasons, the redistributive role of the tax system is more crucial than ever to the achievement of anything remotely resembling distributive justice. If it turns out that, in the wake of financial and industrial capital, human capital has to be immunized from redistributive taxation, it will be impossible for anyone who cares about distributive justice not to be deeply concerned.

50. This pressure of market competition on decentralized polities helps account for the negative correlation between federalism (vs. unitarism) and economic solidarity as documented, e.g,. by Banting and Kymlicka (2004). See also Peterson (1995) for an analysis of the lack of interindividual redistribution at decentralized levels.

51. This need not be because of any intrinsic feature of the language (see §6.5), but simply because of the way in which our current preferences and beliefs have been shaped by a long history of influences that are shared by virtue of belonging to the same trans-generational linguistic community. See Patten (2008: esp. §4) for an interesting interpretation along these lines of Herder's claim that democratic states must be (linguistically circumscribed) nation states.

52. See Mill (1861: ch. 16). The two lines of reasoning could again be contrasted in terms of democracy functioning best with a common ethnos versus a common demos (see §1.10 and §6.7).

53. See Van Parijs (2004b), Decoster (2009), and De Grauwe and Dewatripont (2010) for in-depth discussions of this issue and ways to address it in the Belgian case.

54. At least providing one rules out—as I argued one must (§5.5)—non-territorial political decentralization à la Renner–Bauer, i.e. the assignment of subsets of the same local population to the authority of different governments.

55. Invoking the cost of linguistic conflict would have been viciously circular when discussing the cost to be taken into account when a linguistic community has to *decide whether to make use* of its right to linguistic protection (see note 57 in chapter 5). It is not when discussing the cost of *denying* this right to a linguistic community.

56. See the discussion of the 'diaspora buffers' in §5.11 and the 'compensatory poaching' in §2.12.

57. The sizes of the positive and negative transfers to and from the various countries and hence the linguistic communities that live in it will be affected by exogenous circumstances, but also unavoidably by collective choices they make. Their net contribution to the system will be smaller or their net benefit from it higher, for example, if they forgo exploiting some of their natural resources, encourage part-time work or indeed implement a costly territorial protection of their language. How relevant such self-inflicted 'handicaps' are to the optimal design of a just world will depend to some extent on the way each of the lax opportunity-egalitarian theories of distributive justice (such as those considered in §3.5) handles the distinction between opportunities and achievement. For reasons whose weights may vary from one theory to another, however, all of them are likely to end up not penalizing those countries that are poor by virtue of a costly linguistic choice as opposed to some exogenous factor. First, if the cost is mainly related to the ground floor effect, the transfer will simply be partial compensation (along with the other buffering mechanisms discussed in §5.11) for the relocation of wealth creation to some other part of the world. Secondly and more generally, as the sustainable maximin typically recommended in a lax-egalitarian perspective is likely to diverge significantly from strict equality, the material burden of costly choices will tend to be borne far more than proportionally by the communities that make them. Finally, distributive justice, whether domestic or global, is between individuals. And collective choices, which cannot be interpreted as lucky or unlucky circumstances at the level of

collectives, must be so considered at the level of individuals, who may or may not have subscribed to the collective decision.

58. In a situation of universal diglossia, David Crystal (2000: 81) notes, the weaker local language is there 'to express the identity of the speakers as members of their community.... The dominant language cannot do this,' but a point may come 'where people have completely lost their sense of identification with their ethnic origins', and then the new language can 'offer an alternative and comfortable linguistic home'.

BIBLIOGRAPHY

Abrams, Daniel M. and Steven H. Strogatz. 2003. 'Modelling the Dynamics of Language Death', *Nature* 424, 900.

Ackerman, Bruce. 1980. *Social Justice in the Liberal State*. New Haven and London: Yale University Press.

Ackerman, Bruce and Anne Alstott. 1999. *The Stakeholder Society*. New Haven and London: Yale University Press.

Adams, Douglas. 1979. *The Hitchhiker's Guide to the Galaxy*. London: Heinemann.

Alen, André and Rusen Ergec. 1998. 'Le principe de territorialité dans la jurisprudence belge et européenne. Essai de synthèse', *Journal des Tribunaux* 5904, 785–90.

Alesina, Alberto and Eliana La Ferrara. 2000. 'Participation in Heterogeneous Communities', *Quarterly Journal of Economics* 115(3), 847–904.

Alesina, Alberto, Arnaud Devleeschauwer, William Easterly, Sergio Kurlat, and Romain Wacziarg. 2003. 'Fractionalization', *Journal of Economic Growth* 8, 155–94.

Ammon, Ulrich. 2001a. *The Dominance of English as a Language of Science. Effects on Other Languages and Language Communities*, Berlin and New York: de Gruyter.

Ammon, Ulrich. 2001b. 'Die Stellung der deutschen Sprache in Europa und in der Welt', in R. Chaudenson (ed.), *L'Europe parlera-t-elle anglais demain?* Paris: L'Harmattan, 57–74.

Ammon, Ulrich. 2006. 'Language Conflicts in the European Union. On Finding a Politically Acceptable and Practicable Solution for EU institutions that Satisfies Diverging Interests', *International Journal of Applied Linguistics* 16(3), 319–38.

Anderson, Benedict. 1993. 'Nationalism', in J. Krieger (ed.), *The Oxford Companion to the Politics of the World*, Oxford: Oxford University Press, 614–19.

Appiah, Kwame Anthony. 2005. *The Ethics of Identity*. Princeton: Princeton University Press.

Arneson, Richard. 1989. 'Equality and Equal Opportunity for Welfare', *Philosophical Studies* 56, 77–93.

Arnsperger, Christian and Philippe Van Parijs. 2000. *Ethique économique et sociale*. Paris: La Découverte.

Arzoz, Xabier. 2006. 'Die geschichtlichen Autonomien der Basker, Galizier und Katalanen als Beispiel eines multinationalen "Quasi-Föderalismus" im Einheitstaat', in P. Pernthaler (ed.), *Die Entstehung des modernen Nationalitäten- und Minderheitenschutzes in Europa*, Wien: Wilhelm Braumüller, 363–88.

Aziz, Miriam and Philippe Van Parijs. 2002. 'Language Legislation for XXIst century Europe', Université catholique de Louvain: Chaire Hoover, DOCH 87, www.uclouvain.be/8680.

Baldwin, Peter. 1990. *The Politics of Social Solidarity: Class Bases of the European Welfare State*. Cambridge: Cambridge University Press.

Banting, Keith and Will Kymlicka. 2004. 'Do Multiculturalism Policies Erode the Welfare State?' in P. Van Parijs (ed.), *Cultural Diversity versus Economic Solidarity*, Brussels: De Boeck Université, 227–84, www.uclouvain.be/en-12569.

Barbier, Jean-Claude. 2008. *La longue marche vers l'Europe sociale*. Paris: P.U.F.

Barry, Brian. 2001. *Culture and Equality: An Egalitarian Critique of Multiculturalism*. Cambridge: Polity Press.

Bauer, Otto. 1907. *Die Nationalitätenfrage und die Sozialdemokratie*, Wien: Ignaz Brand; 2nd edn Wien: Verlag der Wiener Volksbuchhandlung, 1924. (English translation: *The Question of Nationalities and Social Democracy*, Minneapolis: University of Minnesota Press, 2000.)

Beine, Michel, Frédéric Docquier, and Caglar Özen. 2009. 'Diasporas', Université catholique de Louvain: IRES Discussion Paper 2009-02.

Benda, Julien. 1933. *Discours à la Nation européenne*. Paris: Gallimard, 1979.

Berlin, Isaiah. 1979. 'Nationalism: Past Neglect and Present Power', in I. Berlin, *Against the Current*, London: Hogarth Press, 333–55.

Bossert, Walter, Conchita D'Ambrosio, and Eliana La Ferrara. 2008. 'A Generalized Index of Fractionalization'. Université de Montréal: Département de sciences économiques.

Brubaker, Rogers. 1992. *Citizenship and Nationhood in France and Germany*. Cambridge, MA: Harvard University Press.

Calmfors, Lars, Giancarlo Corsetti, John Flemming, Seppo Honkapohja, John Kay, Willi Leibfritz, Gilles Saint-Paul, Hans-Werner Sinn, and Xavier Vives. 2003. *Report on the European Economy*. Ludwig-Maximilian Universität München: Centre for Economic Studies (European Economic Advisory Group).

Castellino, Claudio, Santo Fortunato, and Vittorio Loreto. 2009. 'Statistical Physics of Social Dynamics', *Reviews of Modern Physics* 81, 591–646.

Castelló, Xavier, Victor Eguíluz, and Maxi San Miguel. 2006. 'Ordering Dynamics with two Non-Excluding Options: Bilingualism in Language Competition', *New Journal of Physics* 8, 308–22.

Castelló, Xavier, Victor Eguíluz, and Maxi San Miguel. 2008. 'Modelling Language Competition: Bilingualism and Complex Social Networks', in A. B. Smith, K. Smith, and R. Ferrer y Cancho (eds), *The Evolution of Language*, Singapore: World Scientific Publishing Company, 59–66.

Chaudenson, Robert. 2001. 'Rapport de synthèse', in R. Chaudenson (ed.), *L'Europe parlera-t-elle anglais demain?* Paris: L'Harmattan, 139–57.

Chiswick, Barry R. and Paul W. Miller. 2007. *The Economics of Language. International analyses.* London and New York: Routledge.

Choi, E. Kwam. 2002. 'Trade and the Adoption of a Universal Language', *International Review of Economics and Finance* 11, 265–75.

Church, Jeffrey and Ian King. 1993. 'Bilingualism and Network Externalities', *Canadian Journal of Economics* 26, 337–45.

Cohen, G. A. 1989. 'On the Currency of Egalitarian Justice', *Ethics* 99(4), 906–44; reprinted in Cohen (2010), 3–43.

Cohen, G. A. 1992. 'Incentives, Inequality and Community', *The Tanner Lectures on Human Values*, Salt Lake City: University of Utah Press: 261–329.

Cohen, G. A. 2000. *If You're an Egalitarian, How Come You're So Rich?* Cambridge, MA: Harvard University Press.

Cohen, G. A. 2010. *On the Currency of Egalitarian Justice and Other Essays in Political Philosophy.* Princeton and Oxford: Princeton University Press.

COURRIEL. 2010. 'Appel internationaliste et progressiste à la résistance linguistique et culturelle', July, www.courriel-languefrancaise.org.

Crystal, David. 1997. *English as a Global Language.* Cambridge: Cambridge University Press.

Crystal, David. 2000. *Language Death.* Cambridge: Cambridge University Press.

Dakhlia, Jocelyne. 2008. *Lingua Franca. Histoire d'une langue métisse en Méditerrannée.* Arles: Actes Sud.

D'Antoni Massimo and Ugo Pagano. 2002. 'National cultures and social protection as alternative insurance devices', *Structural Change and Economic Dynamics* 13, 367–86.

Davis Donald R. and David E. Weinstein. 2002. 'Technological superiority and the losses from migration', Washington DC: NBER Working Paper 8971.

Davis Donald R. and David E. Weinstein. 2005. *United States Technological Superiority and the Losses from Migration.* Washington DC: Center for Immigration Studies.

de Briey, Laurent and Philippe Van Parijs. 2002. 'La justice linguistique comme justice coopérative', *Revue de philosophie économique* 5, 5–37.

de Candolle, Alphonse. 1885. 'Avantage pour les sciences d'une langue dominante et laquelle des langues modernes sera nécessairement dominante au XXe siècle', reprinted in *Histoire des sciences et des savants depuis deux siècles*, Paris: Odile Jacob, 1987.

De Grauwe, Paul and Mathias Dewatripont (eds). 2010. *Towards a More Efficient and Fair Funding of Belgium's Regions?* Brussels: Re-Bel e-book no. 5, www.rethinkingbelgium.eu.

De Schutter, Helder. 2007. 'Language Policy and Political Philosophy: On the Emerging Linguistic Justice Debate', *Language Problems and Language Planning* 31(1), 1–23.

De Schutter, Helder. 2008. 'The Linguistic Territoriality Principle—A Critique', *Journal of Applied Philosophy* 25(2), 105–20.

de Swaan, Abram. 1993. 'The Evolving European Language System: A Theory of Communication Potential and Language Competition', *International Political Science Review* 14(3), 241–55.

de Swaan, Abram. 2001. *Words of the World*. Cambridge: Polity Press.

De Vreese, Jozef. 2010. 'Ban het Nederlands niet uit de master-opleidingen', *De Tijd*, 28 August.

Decoster, André (ed.). 2009. *On the Interaction between Subsidiarity and Interpersonal Solidarity*. Brussels: Re-Bel e-book no. 1, www.rethinkingbelgium.eu.

Decoster, André and Philippe Van Parijs. 2010. 'Towards more responsible regions', in P. De Grauwe and M. Dewatripont (eds), *Towards a More Efficient and Fair Funding of Belgium's Regions?* Brussels: Re-Bel e-book no. 5, 38–44, www.rethinkingbelgium.eu

Deproost, Paul-Augustin. 2003. 'La latinité médiévale. Une langue sans peuple et sans frontière', in P. A. Deproost and B. Coulie (eds), *Les Langues pour parler en Europe*, Paris: L'Harmattan, 71–90.

Deschouwer, Kris and Philippe Van Parijs. 2009. *Electoral Engineering for a Stalled Federation. A Federal Electoral District for the Belgian Parliament* (with comments by L. de Briey, D. Horowitz, B. Maddens, and B. O'Leary). Brussels: Re-Bel e-book 4, www.rethinkingbelgium.eu.

Desmet, Klaus, Ignacio Ortuño-Ortín, and Shlomo Weber. 2005. 'Peripheral diversity and redistribution', Paper presented at the conference 'Capitalism, Socialism and Democracy' in honour of John E. Roemer, Amherst, MA, May.

Destrée, Jules. 1923. *Wallons et Flamands. La Querelle linguistique en Belgique*. Paris: Plon.

Deutsch, Karl W. 1975. 'The Political Significance of Linguistic Conflicts', in J. G. Savard and R. Vigneault (eds), *Multilingual Political Systems: Problems and Solutions*, Québec: Presses universitaires de Laval, 7–28.

Dieckhoff, Alain. 2002. 'L'Invention de l'hébreu, langue du quotidien national', in D. Lacorne and T. Judt (eds), *La Politique de Babel. Du monolinguisme d'Etat au plurilinguisme des peuples*, Paris: Karthala, 261–76.

Docquier, Frédéric and Abdeslam Marfouk. 2005. *International Migration by Educational Attainment (1990–2000)*. Washington DC: World Bank, March.

Docquier, Frédéric and Hillel Rapoport. 2009. 'Documenting the Brain Drain of "la crème de la crème": Three case studies on international migration at the upper tail of the education distribution', *Journal of Economics and Statistics* 229, 679–705.

Doerr, Nicole. 2008. 'Deliberative Discussion, Language, and Efficiency in the World Social Forum Process', *Mobilization* 13(4), 395–410.

Drèze, Jacques H. 1993. 'Regions of Europe: A feasible status, to be discussed', *Economic Policy* 17, 266–307.

Durand, Charles. 2001. *La Mise en place des monopoles du savoir*. Paris: L'Harmattan.

Dustmann, Christian and Francesca Fabbri. 2003. 'Language Proficiency and Labour Market Performance of Immigrants in the UK', *The Economic Journal* 113, 695–717.

Dworkin, Ronald. 1981. 'What is Equality? Part II: Equality of Resources', *Philosophy and Public Affairs* 10(4), 283–345.

Dworkin, Ronald. 2000. *Sovereign Virtue: The Theory and Practice of Equality*. Cambridge, MA: Harvard University Press.

Dworkin, Ronald. 2004. 'Ronald Dworkin Replies', in J. Burley (ed.), *Dworkin and his Critics*, Oxford: Blackwell, 339–95.

Dyen, Isidore, Joseph B. Kruskal, and Paul Black. 1992. 'An Indo-European classification: A lexicostatistical experiment', *Transactions of the American Philosophical Society* 82(5).

Dworkin, Ronald. 2006. *Is Democracy Possible Now?* Princeton: Princeton University Press.

Edwards, John. 1995. *Multilingualism*. London: Penguin Books.

Edwards, John. 2010. *Challenges in the Social Life of Language*. London: Palgrave Macmillan.

Eurobarometer. 2001. *Europeans and their Languages*. Eurobarometer 54, Luxemburg: European Commission.

Eurobarometer. 2006. *Europeans and their Languages*. Eurobarometer 64.3, Luxemburg: European Commission.

European Commission. 2002. *Promoting Language Learning and Linguistic Diversity: Consultation.* DG Education and Culture, Staff Working paper SEC 1234, 13 November.

European Commission. 2004. *Many Tongues, One Family. Languages in the European Union.* Luxemburg: European Commission, July.

European Parliament. 2002. *Resolution on Cultural Industries.* Brussels: European Parliament, document 2002/2127.

Fearon, James D. 2003. 'Ethnic and Cultural Diversity by Country', *Journal of Economic Growth* 8(2), 195–222.

Fearon, James D. and David D. Laitin. 2011. 'Sons of the Soil, Migrants, and Civil War', *World Development* 39(2), 199–211.

Feld, Stacy Amity. 1998. 'Language and the Globalization of the Economic Market: the Regulation of Language as a Barrier to Free Trade', *Vanderbilt Journal of Transnational Law* 31, 153–202.

Fichte, Johann Gottlied. 1808. *Reden an die deutsche Nation.* Hamburg: Felix Meiner, 1978. (English translation: *Addresses to the German Nation.* New York: Harper Torch Books, 1968.)

Fidrmuc, Jan and Victor Ginsburgh. 2007. 'Languages in the European Union: The Quest for Equality and its Cost', *European Economic Review* 51(6), 1351–69.

Fidrmuc, Jan, Victor Ginsburgh, and Shlomo Weber. 2005. 'Le Français, deuxième langue de l'Union européenne?', *Economie publique* 15, 43–63.

Francard, Michel and Philippe Hambye. 2003. 'Des langues minoritaires et des hommes. Aspects linguistiques, identitaires et politiques', in P. A. Deproost and B. Coulie (eds), *Les Langues pour parler en Europe*, Paris: L'Harmattan, 29–58.

Fraser, Nancy. 1998. 'Social Justice in the Age of Identity Politics: Redistribution, Recognition, and Participation', in N. Fraser et al., *The Tanner Lectures on Human Values* 19, Salt Lake City: University of Utah Press, 1–67.

Gauthier, David. 1986. *Morals by Agreement.* Oxford: Oxford University Press.

Gellner, Ernest. 1983. *Nations and Nationalism.* Oxford: Blackwell.

GERESE 2005. *L'équité des systèmes éducatifs européens. Un ensemble d'indicateurs.* Université de Liège: Service de pédagogie théorique et expérimentale.

Ginsburgh, Victor and Shlomo Weber. 2003. 'Language Disenfranchisement in the European Union', Université libre de Bruxelles: ECARE and Université catholique de Louvain: CORE, June.

Graddol, David. 2005. 'Language Trends and Scenarios: Views from Western Europe', intervention at the conference 'Language Policy Aspects of the Expansion of the European Union', Vilnius (Lithuania), 31 July.

Graddol, David. 2006. *English Next.* London: The British Council.

GRASPE. 2010. 'Multilinguisme et interculturalité au Coeur de l'Europe. La traduction à la Commission européenne 1958–2010', *Cahier du Groupe de Réflexion sur l'avenir du Service Public Européen* 16, 45–49.

Greenberg, Joseph H. 1956. 'The Measurement of Linguistic Diversity', *Language* 32, 109–15.

Grégoire, Henri-Baptiste. 1794. 'Rapport sur la nécessité et les moyens d'anéantir les patois et d'universaliser l'usage de la langue française', reprinted in M. de Certeau, D. Julia, and J. Revel (eds), *Une politique de la langue*, Paris: Gallimard, 2002, 300–17.

Grewal, David Singh. 2008. *Network Power. The Social Dynamics of Globalization*. New Haven: Yale University Press.

Grimm, Dieter. 1995. 'Does Europe Need a Constitution?', *European Law Journal* 1(3), 282–302.

Grin, François. 1999. *Compétences et récompenses. La valeur des langues en Suisse*. Fribourg: Editions universitaires.

Grin, François. 2004. 'On the Costs of Cultural Diversity', in P. Van Parijs (ed.), *Cultural Diversity versus Economic Solidarity*, Brussels: De Boeck Université, 193–206 (www.uclouvain.be/en-12569).

Grin, François. 2005a. *L'Enseignement des langues étrangères comme politique publique*. Paris: Haut Conseil de l'Evaluation de l'Ecole, Rapport no. 19 (www.ladocumentationfrancaise.fr).

Grin, François. 2005b. 'L'Anglais comme lingua franca: questions de coût et d'équité', in *Economie publique* 15, 33–42.

Grin, François and François Vaillancourt. 1997. 'The Economics of Multilingualism', *Annual Review of Applied Linguistics* 17, 43–65.

Habermas, Jürgen. 1995. 'Remarks on Dieter Grimm's "Does Europe Need a Constitution?"', *European Law Journal* 1(3), 303–7.

Habermas, Jürgen. 2001. 'Warum braucht Europa eine Verfassung?', *Die Zeit*, 29 Juni.

Harmon, David and Jonathan Loh. 2004. *Index of Biocultural Diversity*. Terralingua, www.terralingua.org.

Henry, Philippe. 2003. 'L'apprentissage des langues étrangères dans le système scolaire', intervention at the Parlement de la Communauté française de Belgique, Bruxelles, 8 janvier.

Herbillon, Michel. 2003. *Les Langues dans l'Union élargie: pour une Europe en V.O.* Délégation de l'Assemblée nationale pour l'Union européenne, juin.

Heyd, David. 2005. 'Cultural Diversity and Biodiversity: A Tempting Analogy', paper presented at the conference 'Democracy, Equality and Justice', London: British Academy.

Hirschman, Albert O. 1945. *National Power and the Structure of Foreign Trade*. Berkeley: University of California Press.

Hochschild, Jennifer, Traci Burch, and Vesla Weaver. 2005. 'Effects of Skin Color Bias in SES on Political Activities and Attitudes', paper presented at the Wiener Center's Inequality and Social Policy Seminar, Harvard University.

Homans, George C. 1961. *Social Behaviour. Its Elementary Forms.* London: Routledge & Kegan Paul, 1973.

Honneth, Axel. 1990. *Kampf um Anerkennung.* Frankfurt: Suhrkamp. (English translation: *The Struggle for Recognition.* Cambridge: Polity Press, 1996.)

Housen, Alex, Sonja Janssens, and Michel Pierrard. 2003. *Le Français face à l'anglais dans les écoles secondaires en Flandre.* Gembloux: Duculot.

Huntington, Samuel P. 2004. *Who are we? The Challenges to America's National Identity.* New York: Simon & Schuster.

Janssens, Rudi. 2007. *Van Brussel gesproken. Taalgebruik, taalverschuivingen en taalidentiteit in het Brussels hoofdstedelijk gewest.* Brussels: VUB Press.

Kantner, Cathleen. 2004. *Kein modernes Babel. Kommunikative Voraussetzungen europäischer Öffentlichkeit.* Wiesbaden: VS Verlag.

Kapur, Devesh and John McHale. 2003. 'Migration's New Payoff', in *Foreign Policy* 139, 49–57.

Kjaer, Anne Lise and Silvia Adamo (eds). 2011. *Linguistic Diversity and European Democracy.* Farnham: Ashgate.

Kodelja, Zdenko and Matevz Krivic. 2007. 'Language Rights in Education in Slovenia', in *Education, Law and Language Rights*, Antwerp: European Association for Education, Law and Policy, 1–17.

Koolstra, Cees M. and Johannes W. J. Beentjes. 1999. 'Children's Vocabulary Acquisition in a Foreign Language through Watching Subtitled TV Programmes at Home', *Educational Technology Research and Development* 47(1), 51–60.

Koolstra, Cees M., T. H. A. van der Voort, and L. J. T. van der Kamp. 1997. 'Television's Impact on Children's Reading Comprehension and Decoding Skills: A Three-Year Panel Study', *Reading Research Quarterly* 32, 128–52.

Koolstra, Cees M., Allerd L. Peeters, and Herman Spinhof. 2002. 'The Pros and Cons of Dubbing and Subtitling', *European Journal of Communication* 17(3), 25–54.

Kraus, Peter A. 2008. *A Union of Diversity. Language, Identity and Polity-Building in Europe.* Cambridge: Cambridge University Press.

Kymlicka, Will. 1989. *Liberalism, Community and Culture.* Oxford: Clarendon Press.

Kymlicka Will. 1995. *Multicultural Citizenship.* Oxford: Oxford University Press.

Kymlicka, Will. 1999. 'Citizenship in an Era of Globalization: Comment on Held', in I. Shapiro and C. Hacker-Cordón (eds), *Democracy's Edges*, Cambridge: Cambridge University Press, 112–126; reprinted in W. Kymlicka, *Politics in the Vernacular*, Oxford: Oxford University Press, 2001, 317–26.

La Ferrara, Eliana. 2004. 'Solidarity in Heterogeneous Communities', in P. Van Parijs (ed.), *Cultural Diversity versus Economic Solidarity*, Brussels: De Boeck, 2004, 69–80 (www.uclouvain.be/en-12569).

Laitin, David D. 1988. 'Language Games', *Comparative Politics* 20, 289–302.

Laitin, David D. 1993. 'The Game Theory of Language Regimes', *International Political Science Review* 14(3), 227–39.

Laitin, David D. 2000. 'What is a Language Community?', *American Journal of Political Science* 44(1), 142–55.

Laitin, David D. 2004. 'Language Policy and Civil War', in P. Van Parijs (ed.), *Cultural Diversity versus Economic Solidarity*, Brussels: De Boeck, 171–88 (www.uclouvain.be/en-12569).

Laitin, David D. and Rob Reich. 2003. 'A Liberal Democratic Approach to Language Justice', in W. Kymlicka and A. Patten (eds), *Language Rights and Political Theory*, Oxford: Oxford University Press, 80–104.

Lande, Russell. 1996. 'Statistics and Partitioning of Species Diversity, and Similarity among Multiple Communities', *Oikos* 76, 5–13.

Laponce, Jean. 1984. *Langue et territoire*. Québec: Presses universitaires de Laval. (English translation: *Languages and their Territories*. Toronto: University of Toronto Press, 1987.)

Laponce, Jean. 1993a. 'Do Languages Behave Like Animals?', *International Journal for the Sociology of Language* 103, 19–30.

Laponce, Jean. 1993b. 'The Case for Ethnic Federalism in Multilingual Societies: Canada's Regional Imperative', *Regional Politics and Policy* 3(1), 23–43.

Laponce, Jean. 1996. 'Minority Languages in Canada: Their Fate and Survival Strategies', in A. Lapierre, P. Smart, and P. Savard (eds), *Language, Culture and Values in Canada at the Dawn of the 21st Century*, Ottawa: Carleton University Press, 75–89.

Laponce, Jean. 2004. 'Comments on Laitin and Grin', in P. Van Parijs (ed.), *Cultural Diversity versus Economic Solidarity*, Brussels: De Boeck, 203–10 (www.uclouvain.be/en-12569).

Laponce, Jean. 2005. 'The Governance of Minority Languages: Principles and Exceptions', paper presented at the conference 'Debating Language Policies in Canada and Europe', University of Ottawa.

Lee, Jennifer and Frank D. Bean. 2004. 'America's Changing Color Lines: Immigration, Race/Ethnicity and Multiracial Identification', *Annual Review of Sociology* 30, 221–42.

Lehman-Wilzig, Sam. 2000. 'The Tower of Babel vs the power of babble. Future political, economic and cultural consequences of synchronous automated translation systems', *New Media & Society* 2(4), 467–94.

Leparmentier, Arnaud. 'L'Elargissement renforce la domination de l'anglais au sein de l'Union', *Le Monde*, 17 April 2004.

Levine, Marc V. 1990. *The Reconquest of Montreal. Language Policy and Social Change in a Bilingual City.* Philadelphia: Temple University Press.

Lieberson, Stanley. 1964. An Extension of Greenberg's Linguistic Diversity Measures, *Language 40*, 526–31.

Luyken, G., Herbst, T., Langham-Brown, J., Reid, H., and Spinhof, H. 1991. *Overcoming Language Barriers in Television: Dubbing and subtitling for the European audience.* Manchester: European Institute for the Media.

Maalouf, Amin et al. 2008. *A Rewarding Challenge. How the Multiplicity of Languages Could Strengthen Europe.* Brussels: European Commission, http://ec.europa.eu/education/policies/lang/doc/maalouf/report_en.pdf.

McWhorter, John. 2001. *The Power of Babel. A Natural History of Language.* New York: Times Books.

Maignan, Carol, Gianmarco Ottaviano, Dino Pinelli, and Francesco Rullani. 2003. *Bio-Ecological Diversity vs Socio-Economic Diversity: A comparison of existing measures.* Fondazione Eni Enrico Mattei, January.

Maiworm, Friedhelm and Bernd Wächter. 2002. *English-Language-Taught Degree Programmes in European Higher Education. Trends and Success Factors,* Bonn: Lemmens.

Mamadouh, Virginie. 1995. *De Talen in het Europees Parlement.* Universiteit van Amsterdam: Instituut voor sociale geografie.

Mamadouh, Virginie and Kaj Hofman. 2001. *The Language Constellation in the European Parliament.* Amsterdam: Report for the European Cultural Foundation.

Martinet, André. 1960. *Eléments de linguistique générale.* Paris: Armand Colin.

Massey, Douglas S. and Nancy A. Denton. 1988. 'The Dimensions of Residential Segregation', *Social Forces* 67, 281–315.

Maurais, Jacques. 2003. 'Towards a New Global Linguistic Order?', in J. Maurais and M. A. Morris (eds), *Languages in a Globalising World,* Cambridge: Cambridge University Press, 13–36.

Meillet, Antoine. 1918. *Les Langues dans l'Europe nouvelle.* Paris: Payot, 2nd edn, 1928.

Melitz, Jacques. 1999. *English-Language Dominance, Literature and Welfare.* London: Centre for Economic Policy Research, Discussion Paper 2055.

Milanovic Branko. 2005. *Worlds Apart: Measuring International and Global Inequality.* Princeton: Princeton University Press.

Mill, John Stuart. 1861. *Considerations on Representative Governement*, in *On Liberty and Other Essays* (ed. J. Gray), Oxford: Oxford University Press, 1991, 203–467.

Miller, David. 2004. 'Social Justice in Multicultural Societies', in P. Van Parijs (ed.), *Cultural Diversity versus Economic Solidarity*, Brussels: De Boeck Université 2004, 13–32 (www.uclouvain.be/en-12569).

Miller, David. 2007. *National Responsibility and Global Justice*. Oxford: Oxford University Press.

Minett, James W. and William S.-Y. Wang. 2008. 'Modelling Endangered Languages: The Effects of Bilingualism and Social Structure', *Lingua* 118(1), 19–45.

Ministère des affaires étrangères. 2002. 'La politique européenne de la France. Le français dans les institutions européennes'. Préface de Lionel Jospin, mars.

Mira, José and Angel Paredes. 'Interlinguistic Similarity and Language Death Dynamics', *Europhysics Letters* 69(6), 1031–34.

Mukash Kalel, Timothée. 2003. 'Situation linguistique et dynamique des langues en République Démocratique du Congo contemporaine'. Kinshasa: Observatoire des langues nationals, unpublished mimeo.

Nagel, Thomas. 2005. 'The Problem of Global Justice', *Philosophy and Public Affairs* 33(2), 113–47.

Nelde, Peter and Jeroen Darquennes. 2001. 'Sprachwechsel in der Großstadt—eine Brüsseler Perspektive', in J. Born (ed.), *Mehrsprachigkeit in der Romania*, Wien: Praesens, 91–104.

Nick, Christoph. 2006. 'Response to Robert Graham's "A European public opinion is just an EU pipe dream"', *Europe's World* 2, Spring, 13–14 (www.europesworld.org).

Nowikov, Jacques. 1911. *Le Français, langue internationale de l'Europe*. Paris: Grasset.

Nunberg, Geoffrey. 2002. 'Langues et communautés linguistiques à l'époque du discours électronique', in D. Lacorne and T. Judt (eds), *La Politique de Babel. Du monolinguisme d'état au plurilinguisme des peuples*, Paris: Karthala, 321–43.

OECD. 2002. *International Mobility of the Highly Skilled*. Paris: Organisation for Economic Co-operation and Development.

Okrent, Arika. 2006. 'A Visit to Esperantoland', *The American Scholar* 75 (1), 93–108.

Ost, François. 2009. *Traduire. Défense et illustration du multilinguisme*, Paris: Fayard.

Ottaviano, Gianmarco and Giovanni Peri. 2003. *The Economic Value of Cultural Diversity: Evidence from US Cities*, London: Centre for Economic Policy Research.

Ottaviano, Gianmarco and Dino Pinelli. 2005. 'Bio-Ecological Diversity versus Socio-Economic Diversity: A Comparison of Existing Measures', paper presented at the Euro-Div conference, Eni Enrico Mattei Foundation.

Pagano, Ugo. 2004. 'Cultural Diversity, European Integration and the Welfare State', in P. Van Parijs (ed.), *Cultural Diversity versus Economic Solidarity*, Brussels: De Boeck Université, 315–30 (www.uclouvain.be/en-12569).

Papaux, Alexandre. 1997. 'Droit des langues en Suisse: Etat des lieux', *Revue suisse de science politique* 3(2), 131–4.

Parekh, Bhikhu. 2009. 'Logic of Identity', *Politics, Philosophy and Economics* 8(3), 267–84.

Patten, Alan. 2001. 'Political Theory and Language Policy', *Political Theory* 29(5), 683–707.

Patten, Alan. 2003a. 'Liberal Neutrality and Language Policy', *Philosophy and Public Affairs* 31(4), 356–86.

Patten, Alan. 2003b. 'What Kind of Bilingualism?', in W. Kymlicka and A. Patten (eds), *Language Rights and Political Theory*, Oxford: Oxford University Press, 296–321.

Patten, Alan. 2008. '"The most natural state": Herder on Nationalism', Princeton University, Department of Political Science.

Patten, Alan. 2009. 'Survey Article: The Justification of Minority Language Rights', *Journal of Political Philosophy* 17(1), 102–28.

Patten, Alan. Forthcoming. *Equal Recognition: the Moral Foundations of Minority Cultural Rights*.

Peterson, Paul E. 1995. *The Price of Federalism*. Washington, DC: Brookings.

Phillips, Anne. 2004. 'Comments on Miller and Soroka, Johnston and Banting', in P. Van Parijs (ed.), *Cultural Diversity versus Economic Solidarity*, Brussels: De Boeck Université, 59–64 (www.uclouvain.be/en-12569).

Phillipson, Robert. 2003. *English-Only Europe? Challenging Language Policy*. London: Routledge.

Phillipson, Robert. 2007. 'Why More Action on Language Policy is Urgently Needed—in the unfree European linguistic market', Copenhagen Business School.

Piron, Claude. 2001. 'L'Européen trilingue: un espoir réaliste?', in R. Chaudenson (ed.), *L'Europe parlera-t-elle anglais demain?* Paris: L'Harmattan, 93–102.

Pool, Jonathan. 1991. 'The Official Language Problem', *American Political Science Review* 85(2), 495–514.

Pou, Jame Corbera. 1993. 'Le trilinguisme au Luxembourg', *Language Problems and Language Planning* 17(1), 55–61.

Putnam, Robert. 2007. '*E Pluribus Unum*: Diversity and Community in the Twenty-first Century', *Scandinavian Political Studies* 30(2), 137–74.

Qizilbash, Mozaffar. 2009. 'Identity, Community and Justice. Locating Amartya Sen's Work on Identity', *Politics, Philosophy and Economics* 8(3), 251–66.

Rawls, John. 1971. *A Theory of Justice*. Cambridge, MA: Harvard University Press.

Rawls, John. 1999. *The Law of Peoples*. Cambridge, MA: Harvard University Press.

Rawls, John. 2001. *Justice as Fairness. A Restatement*. Cambridge, MA: Harvard University Press.

Rawls, John and Philippe Van Parijs. 2003. 'Three Letters on The Law of Peoples and the European Union', in *Autour de Rawls*, special issue of *Revue de philosophie économique* 8, 7–20.

Réaume, Denise. 2003. 'Beyond *Personality*: The Territorial and Personal Principles of Language Policy Reconsidered', in W. Kymlicka and A. Patten (eds), *Language Rights and Political Theory*, Oxford: Oxford University Press, 271–95.

Renner, Karl. 1902. *Der Kampf der österreichischen Nationen um den Staat*. Leipzig and Wien: Franz Deuticke, revised as *Das Selbstbestimmungsrecht der Nationen, in besonderer Anwendung auf Oesterreich.* Leipzig and Wien: Franz Deuticke, 1918.

Robberechts, Fons and Jan van der Straeten. 1969. *De Kwestie. Geillustreerde generiek van de Vlaamse Beweging*. Hasselt: Heideland.

Roemer, John E. 1982. *A General Theory of Exploitation and Class*. Cambridge, MA: Harvard University Press.

Roemer, John E. 1996. *Theories of Distributive Justice*. Cambridge, MA: Harvard University Press.

Roemer, John E. 1998. *Equality of Opportunity*. Cambridge, MA: Harvard University Press.

Roland, Gérard, Toon Vandevelde, and Philippe Van Parijs. 1999. 'Repenser la solidarité entre les régions et entre les nations', in F. Docquier (ed.), *La solidarité entre les régions*, Brussels: De Boeck, 99–115.

Ross, Shawn A. 2005. '*Barbarophonos*: Language and panhellenism in the *Iliad*', *Classical Philology* 100(4), 299–316.

Rubio-Marín, Ruth. 2003. 'Language Rights: Exploring the Competing Rationales', in W. Kymlicka and A. Patten (eds), *Language Rights and Political Theory*, Oxford: Oxford University Press, 52–79.

Rustow, Dankwart A. 1975. 'Language, Nations and Democracy', in J. G. Savard and R. Vigneault (eds), *Multilingual Political Systems: Problems and Solutions*, Québec: Presses universitaires de Laval, 43–60.

Salas Astrain, Ricardo. 2003. *Etica Intercultural. (Re)lecturas del Pensamiento Latinoamericano*. Santiago de Chile: UCSH.

Salverda, Reinier. 2001. 'De lokroep van het Engels. Taalbeleid op z'n Nederlands', *Ons Erfdeel* 44(1), 3–10.

Sanders, Ted and Leen Van Dijck. 2010. 'Engelse Master mag geen alibi zijn voor verwaarlozing Nederlands', *De Standaard*, 22 July.

Schlesinger, Arthur M. 1998. *The Disuniting of America. Reflections on a Multicultural Society*. New York: W.W. Norton.

Schmitt, Carl. 1926. *Die geistesgeschichtiche Lage des heutigen Parlamentarismus*. Berlin: Duncker & Humblot, 1963.

Schnapper, Dominique. 2002. *La Démocratie providentielle. Essai sur l'égalité contemporaine*. Paris: Gallimard.

Schnapper, Dominique. 2004. 'Linguistic Pluralism as a Serious Challenge to Democratic Life', in P. Van Parijs (ed.), *Cultural Diversity versus Economic Solidarity*, Brussels: De Boeck, 213–26 (www.uclouvain.be/en-12569).

Schwartz, Ros. 2005. 'Global English, mythe ou réalité? Quelles sont les implications pour le métier de traducteur?', in *Traduire* 205, 73–9.

Seekings, Jeremy. 2004. 'Institutional Design, Cultural Diversity and Economic Solidarity. A Comparison of South Africa, Brazil and Nigeria', in P. Van Parijs (ed.), *Cultural Diversity versus Economic Solidarity*, Brussels: De Boeck, 101–38 (www.uclouvain.be/en-12569).

Selten, Reinhard and Jonathan Pool. 1991. 'The Distribution of Foreign Language Skills as a Game Equilibrium', in R. Selten (ed.), *Game Equilibrium Models* Vol. 4, Berlin: Springer, 64–87.

Sen, Amartya. 1985. *Commodities and Capabilities*, Amsterdam: North-Holland.

Sen, Amartya. 2009a. *The Idea of Justice*. London: Penguin.

Sen, Amartya. 2009b. 'Mind your language, Amartya Sen tells Mulayam Singh Yadav', *The Economic Times*, 20 April.

Sen, Amartya. 2009c. 'The Fog of Identity', *Politics, Philosophy and Economics* 8(3), 285–8.

Shorto, Russell. 2004. *The Island at the Center of the World. The Epic Story of Dutch Manhattan and the Forgotten Colony that Shaped America*. New York: Random House.

Simpson, Edward H. 1949. 'Measurement of Diversity', *Nature* 163, 688.

Skutnabb-Kangas, Tove. 2003. '(Why) Should Diversities Be Maintained? Language Diversity, Biological Diversity and Linguistic Human Rights', Glendon Distinguished Lecture, York University, Toronto.

Smejkalova, Tereza. 2007. 'Slovenian Minority in Austria', *The Annual of Language and Politics* 1, 35–42.

SOPEMI. 1998. *Trends in International Migration*. Paris: OECD.

SOPEMI. 2004. *Trends in International Migration*. Paris: OECD.

Soroka, Stuart N., Richard Johnston, and Keith Banting. 2004. 'Ethnicity, Trust, and the Welfare State', in P. Van Parijs (ed.), *Cultural Diversity versus Economic Solidarity*, Brussels: De Boeck, 33–58 (www.uclouvain.be/en-12569).

Stephens, John. 1979. *The Transition from Capitalism to Socialism*. Urbana: University of Illinois Press.

Stevens, Gillian, Jin Kinam, and Song Hyun Jong. 2006. 'Short-term Migration and the Acquisition of a World Language', *International Migration* 44(1), 167–79.

Stojanovic, Nenad. 2010. 'Une conception dynamique du principe de territorialité linguistique. La loi sur les langues du canton des Grisons', *Politique et Sociétés* 29(1), 231–59.

Stojanovic, Nenad et al. 2009. *Can a Democracy Work Without a United Public Opinion?* Brussels: Re-Bel e-book no. 3 (www.rethinkingbelgium.eu).

Strubell, Miquel. 2007. 'The Political Discourse on Multilingualism in the European Union', in D. Castiglione and C. Longman (eds), *The Language Question in Europe and Diverse Societies*, Oxford: Hart, 149–84.

Taylor, Charles. 1992. 'The Politics of Recognition', in A. Gutmann (ed.), *Multiculturalism and the 'Politics of Recognition'*, Princeton: Princeton University Press, 25–73.

Tonkin, Humphrey. 2003. 'Why Learn Foreign Languages?', in H. Tonkin and T. Reagan (eds), *Language in the 21st Century*, Amsterdam and Philadelphia: John Benjamins, 145–55.

Truc, Olivier. 2006. 'Les travailleurs de l'Est ont boudé la Suède', *Le Monde*, 11 mars.

UNDP. 2004. *Cultural Liberty in Today's Diverse World. The Human Development Report 2004*. New York: United Nations Development Program.

van de Poel, Marijke and Géry d'Ydewalle. 1999. 'Incidental Foreign-Language Acquisition by Children Watching Subtitled Television Programmes', *Journal of Psycholinguistic Research* 28, 227–44.

van de Steeg, Marianne. 2002. 'Rethinking the Conditions for a Public Sphere in the European Union', in *European Journal of Social Theory* 5(4), 499–519.

van Heerikhuizen, Annemarie. 2004. 'Woorden van Europa: een vroeg sociologisch pleidooi voor een gemeenschappelijke taal', in A. van

Heerikhuizen et al. (eds), *Het Babylonische Europa*, Amsterdam: Amsterdam University Press, 263–76.

Van Parijs, Philippe. 1993. *Marxism Recycled*. Cambridge: Cambridge University Press.

Van Parijs, Philippe. 1995. *Real Freedom for All. What (if Anything) is Wrong with Capitalism?* Oxford: Oxford University Press.

Van Parijs, Philippe. 1996. 'Free Riding versus Rent Sharing', in F. Farina, F. Hahn, and S. Vanucci (eds), *Ethics, Rationality and Economic Behaviour*, Oxford: Oxford University Press, 159–81.

Van Parijs, Philippe. 2000. 'Power-Sharing versus Border-Crossing in Severely Divided Societies', in Steven Macedo and Ian Shapiro (eds), *Designing Democratic Institutions*, New York: NYU Press, 296–320; reprinted in Van Parijs (2011: ch. 6).

Van Parijs, Philippe. 2002a. 'Linguistic Justice', in *Politics, Philosophy and Economics* 1, 2002, 59–74; reprinted in W. Kymlicka and A. Patten (eds), *Language Rights and Political Theory*, Oxford: Oxford University Press, 2003, 153–68.

Van Parijs, Philippe. 2002b. 'Difference Principles', in S. Freeman (ed.), *The Cambridge Companion to John Rawls*, Cambridge, Cambridge University Press, 200–40.

Van Parijs, Philippe. 2004a. 'Europe's Linguistic Challenge', *Archives européennes de sociologie* 45(1), 111–52; reprinted in D. Castiglione and C. Longman (eds), *The Language Question in Europe and Diverse Societies*, Oxford: Hart, 2007, 217–53.

Van Parijs, Philippe. 2004b. 'Just Health Care in a Pluri-National Country', in S. Anand, F. Peter, and A. Sen (eds), *Public Health, Ethics and Equity*, Oxford: Oxford University Press, 163–80.

Van Parijs, Philippe. 2007. 'International Distributive Justice', in R. Goodin, P. Pettit, and T. Pogge (eds), *The Blackwell's Companion to Contemporary Political Philosophy*, Oxford: Blackwell, Vol. II, 638–52.

Van Parijs, Philippe. 2009. 'Egalitarian Justice, Left Libertarianism and the Market', in S. de Wijze, M. H. Kramer, and I. Carter (eds), *Hillel Steiner and the Anatomy of Justice*, London: Routledge, 145–63.

Van Parijs, Philippe. 2011. *Just Democracy. The Rawls–Machiavelli Programme*. Colchester: ECPR Press.

Van Parijs, Philippe and Jonathan Van Parys. 2010. 'Brussels as the Capital of the European Union: A Sustainable Choice?', *Brussels Studies* 38.

Van Parijs, Philippe, Laurence Jacquet, and Claudio Salinas. 2000. 'Basic Income and its Cognates', in L. Groot and R. J. van der Veen (eds), *Basic Income on the Agenda*, Amsterdam: Amsterdam University Press, 53–84.

Van Parys, Jonathan and Sven Wauters. 2006. 'Les connaissances linguistiques en Belgique', Bruxelles: Facultés universitaires Saint Louis.

Vanderborght, Yannick and Philippe Van Parijs. 2005. *L'allocation universelle*, Paris: La Découverte.

Vila I Moreno, Xavier and Nacho Vila Mendiburu. 2010. 'Language(s) and Education in Barcelona', presentation at the Aula Magna workshop 'Effective education in multilingual cities', Brussels: King Baudouin Foundation, 28 May, www.aula-magna.eu.

Wächter, Bernd and Friedhelm Maiworm. 2008. *English-Taught Programmes in European Higher Education*. Bonn: Lemmens.

Walzer, Michael. 1995. 'Response', in D. Miller and M. Walzer (eds), *Pluralism, Justice and Equality*, Oxford: Oxford University Press, 281–307.

Wedgwood, Cicely Veronica. 1944. *William the Silent*. London: Jonathan Cape.

Weinstock, Daniel. 2003.'The Antinomy of Language Policy', in W. Kymlicka and A. Patten (eds), *Language Rights and Political Theory*, Oxford: Oxford University Press, 250–70.

Weitzmann, Martin. 1992. 'On Diversity', *Quarterly Journal of Economics* 107, 363–405.

Wenin, André. 2003. 'La Dispersion des langues à Babel: malédiction ou bénédiction?', in P. A. Deproost and B. Coulie (eds), *Les Langues pour parler en Europe*, Paris: L'harmattan, 13–28.

Whittaker, Robert H. 1972. 'Evolution and Measurement of Species Diversity', *Taxon* 21, 213–51.

Willems, Jacques. 2002. 'De euro in de brieventas, een Engelstalig diploma in de boekentas?' *Deus ex Machina* 100, 24–8.

Wilmet, Marc. 2003. 'Unification linguistique ou uniformisation de la pensée', paper presented at the 2nd Forum of the University Foundation, 'Go English? Which language for Higher Education in 21st Century Europe?', Brussels, 16 October, www.universityfoundation.be.

Witte, Els and Harry Van Velthoven. 1999. *Language and Politics. The Situation in Belgium in a Historical Perspective*. Brussels: VUB Press.

Ziegler, Gudrun. 2010. 'Linguistic Aspects of Education', presentation at the Aula Magna workshop 'Effective education in multilingual cities', Brussels: King Baudouin Foundation, 28 May, www.aula-magna.eu.

INDEX